MORE PRAISE FOR
BLOOD AND OIL

"*Blood and Oil* is the fascinating and highly entertaining tale of Mohammed bin Salman's rise to power. With fly-on-the-wall reporting and palace intrigue worthy of Machiavelli, it will keep you turning the pages at a fast clip until its tragic denouement. And more importantly, it will leave you with a deep and nuanced understanding of the crown prince's thinking and its implications for Saudi Arabia and the entire Middle East."
— **John Carreyrou, author of *Bad Blood***

"This is as close to the truth, to the real story of the corruption, vulgarities, horrors, and lies of the kingdom and its current despot as we are likely to get. It also can be read as a Shakespearean story of utter greed."
— **Seymour Hersh, author of *Chain of Command***

"*Blood and Oil* is the best book I've read about the Middle East. It gets deep into the most opaque place on earth without a false note anywhere. Not to mention the book is a wonderfully readable page-turner, and indispensable if you want a glimpse of the future of Saudi Arabia and the world."
— **Robert Baer, author of *See No Evil* and** *Sleeping with the Devil*

"Bradley Hope and Justin Scheck story of MBS's rise in the deep, n experienced *Wall Street Journal*

reads like a novel, but it also plays the critically important role of illuminating a real person who is going to shape our world in ways we would all be better for understanding."

—Bethany McLean, author of *Saudi America* and coauthor of *The Smartest Guys in the Room*

"Hope and Scheck confront us with the conundrum of a young man who is doing good by his kingdom, brilliantly describing how the enigmatic crown prince is bringing progress to Arabia as we would see it in the West while operating with ruthlessness and absolutism that make the stomach curl. *Blood and Oil* is compelling reading. We are challenged and enthralled on every page."

—Robert Lacey, bestselling author of *The Crown* and *Inside the Kingdom*

"*Blood and Oil* is a revelatory book that resonates with a stranger-than-fiction quality as the authors' analysis of the crown prince's brutishness, outlandishness, and reformer's mentality is as riveting as it is profound."

—Bryan Burrough, author of *Public Enemies* and coauthor of *Barbarians at the Gate*

"[*Blood and Oil* is] lively and well written, and it draws a sharp portrait of the man at its heart....Hope and Scheck have done a great deal of digging and have unearthed some eye-popping tales." **—*The New York Times Book Review***

"A crisp page-turner of a book teeming with telling detail...*Blood and Oil* is particularly good on the link-up between the Saudi sovereign wealth fund and Masayoshi Son of SoftBank....There is plenty more in Hope and Scheck's splendid book."

—*Financial Times*

"An engrossing new book. . . . Bradley Hope and Justin Scheck. . . deliver a vivid portrait of treachery and power grabs in the Saudi royal court, and attempt to uncover what drives some of the young royal's often reckless decision-making." **—NPR.org**

"A thorough delineation of the rapacious, ambitious new economic plan for Saudi Arabia by the heir apparent to the throne, Mohammed bin Salman. . . . *Wall Street Journal* reporters Hope and Scheck diligently chart the rapid rise-and recent faltering-of MBS. . . . [A] meticulous, highly relevant narrative . . . an excellent work of impressive research on a dangerous world leader." **—*Kirkus Reviews* (starred)**

"Scheck and Hope follow the money, emphasizing the crucial role that billion-dollar development projects, investment funds, and public stock offerings played in securing MBS's legitimacy among international elites and the chaotic and highly transactional Trump administration. The authors also caution that MBS, just turning 35, remains a work in progress." **—*Booklist* (starred)**

"A masterful biography . . . This fast-paced, well-researched book is an excellent primer on current U.S.-Saudi relations and Middle Eastern dynamics, and will also draw in those interested in palace intrigue." **—*Library Journal* (starred)**

"For once, the publisher's hype is true. *Blood and Oil* really is a riveting page-turner, a descent into a nest of vipers, a chilling profile of Saudi crown prince Mohammed bin Salman." **—*The Irish Times***

"*Game of Thrones* has nothing on Mohammed bin Salman's grab for power in Saudi Arabia, the cunning, lies, threats, and murderous ambition with which an also-ran of a prince in his early thirties carved his way to the top of the royal heap documented here in chilling detail." **—Daily Mail**

"*Blood and Oil* hits the ground running at a frenetic pace with the 2017 arrests. The action and drama underpinning the desert kingdom and its denizens proves completely engrossing. The authors have done admirable work in their profile of Mohammed Bin Salman and his Machiavellian ways. A gripping biography and geopolitical narrative." **—San Francisco Book Review**

"Hope and Scheck take a comprehensive and alarming look at Saudi crown prince Mohammed bin Salman.... [They] marshal their research into a page-turning narrative that persuasively casts MBS as a grave danger to the region. This detailed exposé rings true." **—Publishers Weekly**

BLOOD
AND OIL

BLOOD
AND OIL

MOHAMMED BIN SALMAN'S RUTHLESS
QUEST FOR GLOBAL POWER

BRADLEY HOPE AND
JUSTIN SCHECK

hachette
BOOKS
NEW YORK

Hachette Books
Hachette Book Group
1290 Avenue of the Americas
New York, NY 10104
HachetteBooks.com
Twitter.com/HachetteBooks
Instagram.com/HachetteBooks

First Trade Paperback Edition: September 2021

Published by Hachette Books, an imprint of Perseus Books, LLC, a subsidiary of Hachette Book Group, Inc. The Hachette Books name and logo is a trademark of the Hachette Book Group.

The Hachette Speakers Bureau provides a wide range of authors for speaking events.

To find out more, go to www.hachettespeakersbureau.com or call (866) 376-6591.

The publisher is not responsible for websites (or their content) that are not owned by the publisher.

Print book interior design by Sean Ford.

Library of Congress Control Number: 2020015477

ISBNs: 978-0-306-84666-3 (hardcover), 978-0-306-84663-2 (trade paperback), 978-0-306-92381-4 (international trade paperback), 978-0-306-84665-6 (ebook)

Printed in the United States of America

LSC-C

Printing 2, 2021

To Wayne Hope and William LaRue—BH
To Chelsea, Owen, and Henry—JS

CONTENTS

AUTHORS' NOTE

We started this project because Mohammed bin Salman is one of the world's most important new political and business figures, but he remains a mystery to those affected by the huge decisions he's making every few months. Whether it's Middle Eastern countries adjusting to his brusque use of power, technology companies growing thanks to billions of dollars he has invested, families of dissidents and regime critics whose lives have been upended, or people affected by his decision to start using oil as an economic weapon in early 2020, no one really has a clue what's driving his decision making or how he was able to rise so rapidly.

We are investigative reporters who focus on money—how it's spent, where it flows, and what it's used for—so we entered into this project believing we needed to unlearn everything we thought we knew about Saudi Arabia and Mohammed, start from scratch, and follow the money. The further along we got in our reporting, the more thankful we were for having done that at the outset. So many things we thought we knew about him were caricatures of the truth and often spun in a way to exaggerate aspects of his personality to make him seem deranged, heroic, or out of control.

Of course, this comes with the territory of writing about a new ruler imposing rapid transformation on a country that hadn't changed much in decades, but what's lost is deeper knowledge of the person at the center of the storm. Without getting a better understanding of his personality, his family, his motivations, his stratagems, and the details of the battles he fought to get where he is, everyday observers won't have the information needed to help them come to a conclusion.

That's not to justify, apologize for, or laud decisions and actions Mohammed has taken over the past five years. This is the best account we could muster of his rise to power based on our reporting, beginning with our work at the *Wall Street Journal* in 2017, when we were both covering aspects of his economic reform plans from London and taking reporting trips to the kingdom.

Researching Mohammed bin Salman is a tricky task. It sounds counterintuitive, but being based in London and New York has been one of the greatest advantages in finding the revelations we were seeking. Few powerful figures based in the Persian Gulf countries would feel comfortable speaking openly about the crown prince at home, for fear of being electronically surveilled (a likely possibility) or simply observed having meetings with suspicious people like us. Those same people on trips to London, Paris, or Manhattan feel a huge weight lifted from their shoulders, and the facts slide out a little easier.

The other reason being based in these two world capitals is useful is that the story of Mohammed bin Salman from his earliest days in the Royal Court is entangled with business and finance. Few world leaders are so entranced by and involved with issues of global business as Mohammed. The Al Saud family rule Saudi Arabia absolutely, so there's an element of everyday governance akin to running a family investment office, but from an early age Mohammed was transfixed by stories of entrepreneurs and tycoons, as well as famous strongman political figures from history. To understand him, it's imperative to know that he's not just the day-to-day leader of the kingdom—he's also the CEO of Al Saud Inc.

This book is the product of years of reporting, but especially that done in 2019, when we dedicated ourselves to interviewing everyone we could find who interacted with Mohammed over the years as we traveled from country to country, unearthing old financial filings and confidential government records that document his growing personal and political empires, and read everything we could dig up that had been written about Mohammed and Saudi Arabia.

Most of our sources spoke to us "on background," a kind of anonymity that protects them from being identified by name. That required us to be especially diligent about finding multiple people with experiences of the same events to feel certain of their veracity. Every anecdote is based on the recollection of multiple sources and, as often as possible, backed up by emails, legal documents, photographs, videos, and other records. The quotes and conversations rendered here were reconstructed from participant notes, recollections, recordings, and other supporting material. We also mined public databases, many of which held clues to Mohammed's personal business networks in plain sight.

We hope this book brings a new understanding of one of the world's most ambitious young leaders, one who could be in charge for decades to come.

CAST OF CHARACTERS

THE AL SAUD

King Salman bin Abdulaziz Al Saud, son of the kingdom's founder and father of Mohammed bin Salman

Crown Prince Mohammed bin Salman Al Saud

Prince Khalid bin Salman Al Saud, Mohammed's younger brother and former ambassador to the United States

Sultana bint Turki Al Sudairi, King Salman's first wife

Fahdah bint Falah al-Hithlain, King Salman's third wife and mother of Mohammed bin Salman

Crown Prince Muqrin bin Abdulaziz Al Saud, King Salman's half brother and briefly heir apparent

Crown Prince Mohammed bin Nayef Al Saud, King Salman's nephew and a longtime antiterrorism official close to the US government

King Abdullah bin Abdulaziz Al Saud, King Salman's half brother and predecessor

Prince Miteb bin Abdullah Al Saud, King Abdullah's son and former chief of the Saudi Arabia National Guard

Prince Turki bin Abdullah Al Saud, the seventh son of King Abdullah

Prince Badr bin Farhan Al Saud, a prince from a distant branch of the family, minister of culture, and a longtime friend of Mohammed bin Salman

Prince Abdullah bin Bandar Al Saud, another prince and longtime friend of Mohammed bin Salman and head of the National Guard

Prince Sultan bin Turki Al Saud, the son of one of King Salman's brothers, and an outspoken prince whose criticisms got him into trouble with more powerful members of the family

THE PALACE

Khalid al-Tuwaijri, the head of King Abdullah's Royal Court

Mohammed al-Tobaishi, King Abdullah's chief of protocol

Rakan bin Mohammed al-Tobaishi, Mohammed bin Salman's protocol chief and the son of Mohammed al-Tobaishi

THE MBS ENTOURAGE

Bader al-Asaker, a longtime associate of Mohammed who runs his private foundation

Saud al-Qahtani, an advisor to Mohammed who specializes in quashing dissent

Turki Al Sheikh, a longtime companion of Mohammed who has brought foreign sports and entertainment events to Saudi Arabia

THE REGION

Mohammed bin Zayed Al Nahyan, crown prince of Abu Dhabi

Tahnoon bin Zayed, Abu Dhabi national security advisor

Tamim bin Hamad Al Thani, emir of Qatar

Hamad bin Khalifa Al Thani, former emir of Qatar

Abdel Fattah el-Sisi, president of Egypt
Saad Hariri, prime minister of Lebanon
Recep Tayyip Erdoğan, president of Turkey

RESIDENTS OF THE RITZ

Prince Alwaleed bin Talal Al Saud, a cousin of Mohammed and Saudi Arabia's most prominent international businessman
Adel Fakeih, a Saudi businessman who became minister of economy and planning
Hani Khoja, a Saudi management consultant
Mohammed Hussein Al Amoudi, a Saudi businessman with holdings in Ethiopia
Ali al-Qahtani, a general
Bakr bin Laden, scion of the bin Laden construction family

THE CRITICS

Jamal Khashoggi, newspaper columnist with a long history of working for and sometimes criticizing the Saudi government
Omar Abdulaziz, Canada-based dissident who criticizes Saudi leadership in online videos
Loujain al-Hathloul, women's rights activist arrested several times by Saudi Arabian authorities

THE US GOVERNMENT

President Donald Trump
Jared Kushner, Ivanka Trump's husband and an advisor to the president

Steve Bannon, former Trump advisor

Rex Tillerson, ex-CEO of ExxonMobil, later US secretary of state

THE BUSINESSMEN

Jeff Bezos, founder and CEO of Amazon.com

David Pecker, CEO of American Media, which publishes the *National Enquirer*

Ari Emanuel, Hollywood agent and cofounder of Endeavor talent agency

Masayoshi Son, CEO of Japanese tech investor SoftBank

Rajeev Misra, head of SoftBank's Vision Fund

Nizar al-Bassam, Saudi deal maker and a former international banker

Kacy Grine, independent banker and confidant of Alwaleed bin Talal

A note on naming: In the Saudi convention, a man is identified through a patrilineal naming system. Mohammed bin Salman means Mohammed, son of Salman. His father is Salman bin Abdulaziz, since his father is Abdulaziz bin Saud (known as Ibn Saud), the founder of the current Al Saud dynasty. "Al Saud" denotes the family name.

THE AL SAUD DYNASTY

A SELECTED FAMILY TREE

The Al Saud is one of the world's biggest royal families, with thousands of members descending from the founder of the current dynasty, Abdulaziz, who had dozens of sons and daughters. Every king of Saudi Arabia since his death in 1953 has come from that pool of sons, and many of those sons have in turn have had dozens of children of their own. Crown Prince Mohammed bin Salman is destined to become the first king of the country from the third generation. A note on naming: *bin* means "son of." Mohammed bin Salman is the son of King Salman. The king, in turn, is Salman bin Abdulaziz, since his father was King Abdulaziz.

Source: Gulf family researcher Michael Field and interviews.

KING ABDULAZIZ
Born circa 1876; died 1953
Reigned from 1932 to 1953
Founder of the third Al Saud dynasty
Known in the West as Ibn Saud

PRINCE NAYEF BIN ABDULAZIZ
Born 1934; died 2012
Crown prince from 2011 to 2012

KING ABDULLAH BIN ABDULAZIZ
Born 1923; died 2015
Reigned from 2005 to 2015
Had at least fourteen sons and
twenty daughters

MOHAMMED BIN NAYEF
Born 1959
Former minister of
interior; close with
American CIA and
security services; crown
prince from 2015 to
2017

TURKI BIN ABDULLAH
Born 1971
Georgetown University–
educated former fighter
pilot and governor of
Riyadh

MITEB BIN ABDULLAH
Born 1953
Horse-loving former
commander of the
National Guard

KING SALMAN
Born 1936
Former longtime governor of Riyadh,
Al Saud family disciplinarian
Reign from 2015 to present
Had thirteen children from two wives

PRINCE TALAL BIN ABDULAZIZ
Born 1931; died 2018
Leader of the so-called Free Princes
political reform movement in the
1960s

FIRST WIFE, SULTANA BINT TURKI AL SUDAIRI
Died 2011

Fahd bin Salman
Sultan bin Salman
Ahmed bin Salman
Abdulaziz bin Salman
Faisal bin Salman
Hassa bin Salman

ALWALEED BIN TALAL
Born 1955
World-famous business-
man, co-investor with
people including Bill Gates
in international companies
Mother is daughter of Lebanese prime minister Riad
Al Solh

THIRD WIFE, FAHDAH BINT FALAH AL-HITHLAIN

Mohammed bin Salman (MBS)
Born 1985
Crown prince from 2017

Saud bin Salman
Turki bin Salman

Khalid bin Salman
Born 1988
Former Saudi ambassador to the United
States; Deputy defense minister

Nayef bin Salman
Bandar bin Salman
Rakan bin Salman

No dynasty lasts beyond the lifespan of three generations.
—Ibn Khaldun, *The Muqaddimah*

Seize opportunities, for they pass like clouds.
—Ali ibn Abi Talib

BLOOD
AND OIL

PROLOGUE

The call just before 4 a.m. was urgent and unnerving. The king needed to see his nephew, Prince Alwaleed bin Talal Al Saud, as soon as possible. "Come right away," the caller from the Royal Court said.

For decades, Alwaleed had been the world's best-known Saudi businessman. He was the kind of person people wanted to be around, if only to glimpse life with a seemingly bottomless supply of money. With personal wealth estimated at $18 billion, he was, in the eyes of many Americans and Europeans, the ultimate Saudi: fabulously rich, debonair, and excessive to the extreme. He had a fleet of planes, including a 747 jet with a throne-like chair in the middle, and a $90 million yacht that comfortably slept twenty-two guests with thirty crew members to look after them. When he found something he liked, he'd buy ten or twenty of it—even if it was an expensive and bulky exercise machine. One for each home, pied-à-terre, desert camp, and yacht.

Alwaleed delighted in that image and in representations of his own image, showing visitors to his offices in Riyadh, Paris, and New York thick stacks of magazines with his face on the cover or long interviews about his business career. Some rooms in his homes contained more than a dozen photos or paintings of Alwaleed at different stages of his life. He liked drinking tea from a mug with his face on it.

The prince was a force in American business, buying stakes in Citibank, Apple, and Twitter. In a partnership with Bill Gates, Alwaleed's Kingdom Holding Company owned a chunk of the Four Seasons hotel chain, famed for its luxury accommodations. When he traveled, he brought along a two-dozen-person retinue, including cooks, cleaners, butlers, and business advisors.

Yet here he was on a cool November night in 2017, feeling a chill down his spine as he got dressed at his desert retreat for the meeting with the king. Saudi Arabia was seeing huge changes, some of them obvious, like the retreat of religious police from the streets and the sound of music in cafés after decades of prohibition on anything that could arouse the senses. The country had so long been a refuge of the ultraconservative interpretation of Islam referred to by critics as Wahhabism that Saudi citizens felt truly dizzied by the fast-paced reforms: movie theaters were going up, women were walking around with more freedoms than ever before, and there was talk of shifting the economy away from oil for good.

The country's richest and most powerful also perceived something else, a cracking sound. The very foundations of their ornate palaces seemed to be weakening. It didn't matter that Alwaleed called heads of states and the wealthiest people in the world his friends. His unassailability as a billionaire prince was disintegrating.

After more than two years of the reign of his uncle King Salman bin Abdulaziz Al Saud, Alwaleed had heard the stories about royals summoned in the night or tricked onto airplanes only to find themselves dragged home to Saudi Arabia and put in confinement. The man behind those renditions was King Salman's son, Alwaleed's young cousin Mohammed bin Salman Al Saud, who was only thirty-two but had already gained a reputation for his temper and for charging ahead with aggressive changes.

Mohammed was the opposite of his uncles before him, the former kings who derived power from a royal consensus and tended toward extreme conservatism for fear of imperiling the dynasty. They had been desiccated old men by the time they took power, without the courage or energy to make big changes. But Mohammed was young and vital. He was well over six feet tall, with a smile so huge it made him squint, a big nose, and a tactile approach to conversation that could be simultaneously affectionate and menacing. He had plenty of energy, sending questions and commands to underlings at all hours of the day and night. In a short time, Mohammed had declared war on Yemen, led a boycott on a neighboring country, and consolidated more power than any member of the royal family since the founding of the kingdom.

Alwaleed reassured himself. The detained princes were fringe members of the family and often political dissidents, stirring up trouble for the Al Saud from their homes in France or the United Kingdom. He had told a visitor just months before how impressed he was with Mohammed's agenda and how excited he was to see Saudi Arabia finally transition from an illiberal bastion of the most conservative strain of Islam to a modern Arab power with a diversifying economy and more equal rights for men and women. Mohammed had even adopted some of Alwaleed's most aggressive ideas for financial reform.

"This is the change I've been waiting for my whole life," Alwaleed told Robert Jordan, a former US ambassador to Saudi Arabia, in April 2017. CEOs, bankers, and political leaders from around the world had visited him at the retreat where he was staying, a desert site outside Riyadh full of large tents where his guests pretended to re-create an idealized version of the Bedouin lifestyle his ancestors lived up until the mid-twentieth century.

What's more, Alwaleed was so generous. His crowd sat around feasts fit for a small village, complete with roast lamb, mounds of rice, and an assortment of juices. Alwaleed, a health nut who kept doctors around full-time, partook of specially prepared vegan meals. After his guests made a modest dent in the food, Alwaleed would invite poorer Saudis from the surrounding region to finish off the platters.

Afterward, he'd bring his guests for walks on the dunes and stargazing as they sat around a roaring fire. It wasn't entirely rustic. When the prince and his party retired to the tents, there were flat-screen televisions and trailers with gleaming bathrooms and hot showers.

Not long after the call, Alwaleed left the desert camp in his own car for the trip back into Riyadh. Arriving at the Royal Court more than an hour later, an aide to the king came outside to explain that the meeting was actually nearby at the Ritz-Carlton hotel. He was guided to a new car, part of a large convoy. "My phone, my bag," Alwaleed said, growing concerned. "They're in the car."

"Yes, we'll bring them," came the reply. Cut off from the world, Alwaleed grew anxious. His guards, assistant, and driver were placed in separate cars. The drive only took a few minutes, culminating in a slow journey up the grand, quarter-mile driveway from the security gate to the hotel.

Entering the lobby surrounded by security personnel of the Royal Court, he told friends later, he was struck by an eerie feeling that the hotel was empty. The Royal Court men took him into an elevator and then a hotel suite to wait. Worried and a bit bored, he turned on the television. News was flashing that dozens of businessmen, royal family members, and officials were being arrested on suspicion of corruption. He was the first to arrive. The Ritz was no longer a hotel but a makeshift prison.

*   *   *

The renovations had been ordered only hours earlier. Late on Friday, November 3, 2017, a team of engineers at the Ritz-Carlton fanned out across the hotel's nine floors and began drilling out the locks on two hundred hotel-room doors. Curtains were removed and shower doors dismantled. Several large suites usually reserved for visiting CEOs or jet-setting princes were converted into interrogation rooms.

The Ritz-Carlton, originally designed as a state guest house for visiting dignitaries, has a palm-lined driveway that allows visiting prime ministers and presidents to take in its grand palatial facade as they roll up in motorcades. The grounds—all owned by the nearby Royal Court—comprise fifty-two acres of benign opulence, with manicured lawns and a shaded courtyard with six-hundred-year-old olive trees imported from Lebanon. Visiting its ornate lobby, full of marble, guests are greeted by a large flower display, dramatic sculptures of stallions, and the faint smell of oud incense smoldering at tables where some Saudi men perfume their head coverings, known as *shemaghs*. President Barack Obama stayed on the grounds in 2014, and President Donald Trump stayed nearby for two days during a glitzy visit shortly after assuming the US presidency.

Arriving that night, a team of intelligence officers and Royal Court staff walked briskly inside to take over the hotel. Guards dispersed to posts on each floor and manned the exits. Hotel staff were directed to eject anyone still inside the building and cancel upcoming reservations.

"Due to unforeseen booking by local authorities which requires an elevated level of security, we are unable to accommodate guests until normal operations are restored," a concierge said, reading from a script, to a businessman with a reservation days away.

Near dawn, the special guests began to arrive.

For the first few nights, many of the detainees were made to stay in a function room with periodic bathroom breaks, always accompanied by an armed escort. Some of the men still had backup cell phones hidden in the folds of their *thobes*, since their escorts stopped searching after confiscating one phone from each man. Surreptitious photos taken that night show resigned men lying on thin mattresses with cheap, colorful blankets. The images don't make clear, however, that these were some of the most powerful men in the Arab world: would-be heirs to the throne, billionaire tycoons, ministers, and a dozen princes. Some held secrets that needed prying open. Nearly all of them had unimaginable wealth, which the new powers that be in the Kingdom of Saudi Arabia claimed were the fruits of decades of corruption.

The list was nearly unfathomable, including even Miteb bin Abdullah Al Saud, son of the former king and powerful head of the Saudi National Guard—a special branch of the armed forces designed to protect the royal family from any threat, with 125,000 men stationed across the country. One of its roles is to prevent military coups, but here was its chief, once seen as a potential heir to the throne, held against his will.

In the first few days, more than fifty were arrested. The coming weeks would see more than three hundred others "checked into" the Ritz and other secure locations in Riyadh.

The arrests were the work of a hitherto secret anticorruption committee created by a decree from the king. The Saudi attorney general announced he was seeking the return of $100 billion derived from corruption and theft over decades.

Though conducted in the name of King Salman, the arrests of Saudi Arabia's richest and most powerful men had been engineered by the king's sixth son, Mohammed. Three years earlier, even close Saudi watchers had never heard of him. Now the new crown prince was taking Saudi Arabia and the world by storm.

An in-house tailor team churned out identical white robes for each prisoner. Prisoners could watch television and make weekly phone calls with supervision. Swimming in the large tiled pool, beneath an ornate dome painted with a blue sky and clouds, was permitted, but only for two detainees at a time. Speaking wasn't allowed.

Interrogations could begin at any time. At 2 a.m., prisoners were jarred awake and told it was time to talk. For many detainees, the misery was the isolation and humiliation of being questioned for hours by Royal Court officers.

Some of these men felt they'd played a role in building the kingdom. In addition to construction magnates, there was a travel company owner who'd helped thousands of Saudi students get educated in the United States and Europe and a government minister who'd helped modernize the country's health-care and finance systems. Sure, they may have gotten rich in the process, some perhaps violating the letter of Saudi law. But no one had ever before called them criminals. Indeed, many of the deals that Mohammed was now characterizing as misdeeds had been approved by the previous king's closest deputies or even by the previous king himself. Their deeds had been acceptable at the time, but now the rules had changed.

There were allegations of physical abuse and torture. Major General Ali al-Qahtani, chief of security for fellow prisoner Turki bin Abdullah Al Saud, former governor of Riyadh and son of the former king, spat on his interrogators, questioning their authority. Only a select few know what happened next, but he ended up dying in captivity. Saudi Arabia has maintained that allegations of abuse and torture of those investigated are absolutely untrue.

Mostly, however, the prisoners acquiesced. Stripped of money and power, they were merely humans facing physical threats they'd never imagined. To increase the pressure on Alwaleed,

Mohammed threw his younger brother, Khaled bin Talal, in jail. The corruption allegations weren't publicly aired or admitted to by the detainees; the settlements were all private.

The Ritz arrests were all the more jarring because, just days beforehand, the same hotel and a neighboring conference center had hosted the top names in global finance, politics, and business for a three-day event referred to by organizers as "Davos in the Desert." It was presented as an unveiling of the new Saudi Arabia, an overture from a formerly insular country to show it was joining the mainstream business world.

In the grand marble lobby on October 30, the world's biggest money manager, Blackstone founder Steve Schwarzman, held court in one corner, while Tony Blair stood in another expounding on Mohammed's plans to a crowd of bankers. Investor Tom Barrack, a key Middle East advisor to President Trump and founder of Colony Capital, sat with his entourage, exchanging business cards with a stream of visitors. Trump Treasury chief Steve Mnuchin dined with his wife at Hong, the Ritz-Carlton's high-end Chinese restaurant. Masayoshi Son, founder of Japan's SoftBank, occupied one of the suites used days later to detain a prince.

The startling juxtaposition between Davos in the Desert and the Ritz's transformation into a prison—and the reversal of so many extraordinarily wealthy men's fortunes—make the crackdown a singular event in recent world political and business history. Never have so many billionaires, titans of finance who could move heaven and earth with their immense wealth, been deprived of their liberty and treasure so abruptly.

Seen in hindsight from 2020, with nearly all the detainees released and tens of billions of dollars' worth of cash and assets collected by Mohammed's government, the events were clearly a coming-out ceremony for Mohammed bin Salman.

More than the reform agenda and economic transformation

plans he announced, the Ritz arrests showed what was then largely concealed from observers, diplomats, and much of his own family: his cunning nature, love of a grand gesture, taste for risk, and ruthless streak. Until then, Mohammed could still have been an incremental reformer in the tradition of the five kings before his father. Each had a distinct leadership style, but none would have even considered blowing up the establishment to alter the path of the country's future. The aggressive Ritz move, later called the "sheikhdown" by many in the West, was the moment when Mohammed placed a bundle of dynamite on the status quo and blasted it to smithereens.

By the time the detritus was swept away, he controlled all branches of the military, the police, the intelligence agencies, and all government ministries and held controlling stakes in many of the country's largest businesses through government holding companies. He wasn't the king, but he was one of the most powerful men on earth.

Chapter 1

THE KING IS DEAD

December 2014–January 2015

Everyone was waiting for the king to die. It was December 2014, and Abdullah bin Abdulaziz Al Saud, the sixth member of the third Al Saud dynasty to rule in Arabia, was fading away in a hospital bed in the desert outside Riyadh.

Abdullah had always loved the desert. He went there to think and, as he got older, to escape the capital's traffic, its lines of men asking for favors, and the endless disappointments of a broken government he just couldn't seem to drag into modernity. The moonless winter nights on the dunes evoked stories of his father, the kingdom's founder, Abdulaziz, fighting on camelback to conquer Arabia. Those were simpler times.

The nation of Saudi Arabia was itself just eighty-three years old—younger than the ninety-year-old Abdullah. For much of his early life, it was a sparsely inhabited kingdom with few connections to the outside world save for the pilgrims who came to visit the Islamic holy cities of Mecca and Medina. A quarter of the people on earth turn to face the Kaaba in the heart of Mecca to pray and aim to travel there at least once in their lives.

By the time Abdullah hit his forties, rapid change was underway in Saudi Arabia. The discovery of an ocean of oil under the desert provided money to turn mud-walled cities into modern metropolises with skyscrapers and shopping malls. Yet the austere strain of Islam born in the country, referred to as Wahhabism after its eighteenth-century founder, the cleric Muhammad ibn Abd al-Wahhab, remained at the center of daily life. Criminals were beheaded in town squares, and joyless officers from the Committee for the Promotion of Virtue and the Prevention of Vice, or *ha'ya*, policed the streets looking for infractions, such as failure by women to fully cover their hair and bodies. The country's infrastructure modernized over the ensuing decades, but socially and politically it remained so stubbornly conservative that many visitors felt they were going back in time.

At the same time, by the 2000s Saudis were some of the most internet-connected people in the world. With money to buy smartphones and few social outlets, the burgeoning youth population spent hours a day on Twitter and Facebook and YouTube. They knew the ins and outs of Western pop culture even though they couldn't participate at home. Saudi Arabia had long ago barred public concerts and movie theaters and the public gathering of unmarried men and women.

For Abdullah, who ascended the throne in 2005, ruling the kingdom was a heavy burden with daily schedules more reminiscent of medieval times. Saudi kings actually hold court, alternately receiving a river of commoners, ministers, and advisors and posing for photos with visiting presidents and prime ministers, seated on couches in their cavernous, gilded palaces. The king's aides, relatives, and ministers see petitioners suffering from health problems, struggling with disputes, or pleading for debt relief by the tens of thousands every year.

After a lifetime of smoking, lavish meals, back problems, diabetes, and heart disease, Abdullah could no longer spend evenings reclined on cushions in the desert tents his workers set up with electrical wiring and big-screen TVs. His health had been failing since a series of surgeries in 2010, and in November

2014, one of Abdullah's top deputies, his nephew Prince Mohammed bin Nayef Al Saud, asked a doctor friend in the United States for a medical opinion: "What's the prognosis for lung cancer?" The doctor asked how advanced the cancer was. No one had told Abdullah, the prince replied, but the cancer was stage four. "No more than three months," the doctor said.

Less than eight weeks later, Abdullah was propped up in a makeshift hospital atop the sand, hooked up to monitors and intravenous drips, while his courtiers and more than a dozen sons—many of them middle-aged men of varying degrees of venality—scrambled to figure out what to do next.

These men knew that the death of a Saudi king marks a huge transition of wealth and power. Each handover in the country's history had led to a shake-up for the competing bloodlines that all traced back to Abdulaziz Al Saud, known in the West as Ibn Saud. He was the first king of today's Saudi Arabia, and every subsequent king has been one of his sons.

During each reign, the king made his own sons nearly untouchable. They received huge incomes on top of other benefits that accrued into billions of dollars of wealth. Often they were given powerful roles overseeing branches of government or the military.

Abdullah, however, had cut his sons off from some of the customary flood of riches and, for much of their lives, political power. The king granted his children monthly allowances that added up to millions of dollars a year on top of private-jet privileges, but they didn't have access to the billions of dollars that some of their cousins did. Abdullah, feeling his extended family had begun to spin out of control, put a stop to the era of unbridled excess of the Al Saud, starting with his own children.

Abdullah's sons felt that their father was perpetually disappointed in them. In the years before his death, Abdullah considered trying to move one of them into the line of succession for the throne, but he reached his deathbed unsure if any was fit to rule. Miteb, whom Abdullah installed as head of the National Guard, seemed more interested in his racehorses than his work and left much of the National Guard management to deputies. When Turki bin Abdullah, a former air force pilot and then, briefly, governor of Riyadh, came to see his father in the hospital in his final days, Abdullah spoke loudly to the surrounding medical staff, all of them top doctors and nurses from the United States and Europe. "Look at my son, the F15 pilot," he said, pausing to take a breath. "Look how fat he is. Do you think he could fit in an F15?"

The sons worried that the shift of power from Abdullah to a new king could pose a threat to their ambitions. They hadn't even had the chance to get really rich yet, and if the wrong family member became king, they never would.

They knew that after a succession in Saudi Arabia, the flows of money shift to the family of the new king, and over time the sons of the last king—like the sons of kings before him—see their power diminished and their income cut. Abdullah's sons had seen this play out repeatedly. What of the bin Khalid, the children of King Khalid, who ruled from 1975 to 1982? You hardly heard about them anymore.

The jostle for power among brothers, nephews, and cousins was built into the governance system set up by the kingdom's founder. Ibn Saud's three dozen or so sons by a parade of wives and concubines reached adulthood over the course of decades, creating a natural line of succession that worked because the age gaps between them amounted to generations. The oldest was born around 1900 and the youngest around 1947.

Ibn Saud died of a heart attack in his sleep in 1953, passing the throne to his eldest surviving son, Saud. Eleven years later, his brothers forced the dissolute Saud to relinquish the throne to a younger brother. Since then the crown had passed from one brother to the next, with Ibn Saud's sons collectively deciding on an heir by selecting the oldest brother whom they could all agree was fit to rule. The brothers known as the Sudairi Seven, sons of Ibn Saud with his favored wife, Hussa Al Sudairi, were especially powerful, but for sixty years, each of Ibn Saud's sons was hopeful that one day he would have his turn as king. It was the kind of speculation a prince would get up to with his entourage as they spent hour upon hour hanging out in palaces or yachts.

By 2015, most of the sons were dead, and most of the handful who were still alive were in their seventies or older. The throne was finally on the cusp of transferring to the third generation. The problem was there was no mechanism for figuring out which of those hundreds of grandsons was fit to be king. Seniority was an easy way to rank the original sons, but it was an impractical system to select from the hundreds of princes of the next generation.

Abdullah tried to fix this: After assuming the throne, he created a council that included each living son of Ibn Saud and descendants of the dead ones. The so-called Allegiance Council was supposed to elect a crown prince who would assume the throne upon the king's death and name a deputy who would be second in line. This arrangement was intended to prevent abrupt shifts in power. But by the end of Abdullah's life, he and his sons saw another purpose for it: They wanted it to limit the power of Abdullah's successor, Crown Prince Salman.

Abdullah and his sons knew that Salman, the most powerful of the living Sudairi Seven and a wily palace operator, would want to install his ambitious millennial son, Mohammed, in the line of succession. And they knew Mohammed would be a disaster for the Abdullah clan. For years he had clashed with the brothers and their top deputies, once spitting in the face of a powerful intelligence official. At best, an empowered Mohammed would cut off the Abdullah clan's access to power and money. At worst, he could take their assets and their freedom.

To sideline Mohammed, Abdullah's sons would rely on Khalid al-Tuwaijri, the chief of Abdullah's Royal Court.

With a straight moustache, diamond ring, and rimless glasses, Tuwaijri was the most powerful nonroyal in Saudi Arabia, virtually born into the job. His father fought alongside Ibn Saud to conquer parts of Saudi Arabia and later helped Abdullah transform the kingdom's National Guard into a formidable force.

As King Abdullah aged, Tuwaijri's power grew. He signed new laws in Abdullah's name and insinuated himself as secretary-general of the Allegiance Council. He was the only nonprince allowed in its secret meetings and the keeper of the single record of the council's deliberations.

Tuwaijri's most important role was controlling access to Abdullah, which was aided by the fact that the king didn't like talking on the telephone. He could only speak comfortably in person. Even the ambassador to the United States would fly from Washington, DC, to Riyadh for a two-hour conversation. Whether you were a businessman or a government minister or even the king's brother, meeting Abdullah required going through Tuwaijri. Court hangers-on and observers called him "King Khalid."

This was unprecedented power for someone outside the royal family, and it infuriated Crown Prince Salman and his son Mohammed. Tuwaijri knew that he would meet the same fate as Abdullah's sons—or worse—if Salman's power wasn't checked. To Salman and Mohammed, Tuwaijri represented everything that was wrong with Saudi Arabia. The functionary bought mansions, boats, and some two hundred luxury cars. He'd take weeks-long trips with a twenty-five-person entourage to the Ritz-Carlton on Central Park South, piling up millions of dollars' worth of expenses and taking pictures with locals as if he were royalty. "I thought he was some kind of prince," says Rahul Bhasin, who still has a photo of Tuwaijri behind the counter at Parkview Electronics, his tiny camera and cell phone store around the corner from the Ritz, where Tuwaijri used to buy iPhones by the dozen. Few things upset Salman more than a nonroyal acting like a prince.

One of Tuwaijri's chief allies, Mohammed al-Tobaishi, was the head of protocol for Abdullah. Essentially a glorified personal secretary, Tobaishi lived in a ninety-room Riyadh ranch called Samarra when he wasn't in one of his other luxury homes around the world. The two men were billionaire power brokers hiding behind servile titles, men who took money in exchange for providing access to senior officials (they neither admitted any wrongdoing nor were convicted of any crime, though they later had assets seized by the state). In the eyes of Salman and his son, they were a risk to the dynasty and examples of runaway graft.

Mohammed bin Salman had his own firsthand experiences with Tuwaijri, who had pretended to take an avuncular role with him when Mohammed was first working in government jobs in his twenties. But Mohammed learned Tuwaijri was two-faced. While pretending to support him, Tuwaijri took steps to prevent Mohammed's rise within the family hierarchy. "He laid traps for me," Mohammed told friends, describing how at every juncture, Tuwaijri tried to drive him out of government or, failing that, to bribe him into complacency. Mohammed was also bitter since, a few years earlier, Tuwaijri had disciplined him on Abdullah's orders for belittling senior military officials.

With Abdullah nearing death, Muqrin bin Abdulaziz Al Saud, the youngest of Ibn Saud's living sons, was second in the line of succession to the throne. Tuwaijri and his Abdullah-clan allies saw Muqrin as a buffer against any attempts to elevate young Mohammed. If they couldn't push Salman out of the succession line, they figured, they had to at least keep Muqrin.

Seventy-nine years old and tall, with a dyed-black goatee, Salman had been the family enforcer—and the keeper of Al Saud secrets—for half a century. Younger members of the royal family whispered that Salman must have had cameras in the bedrooms of powerful Al Saud figures.

Three generations of princes and their hangers on told stories of being slapped across the face with Salman's gold-and-emerald pinky ring as punishment for drinking alcohol, driving too fast on the outskirts of the capital, or getting caught trying to pull off a brazen corruption scheme.

His temper was the subject of Royal Court lore. Salman was often quiet and thoughtful, prone to quoting Islamic poetry over his nightly card game. But he could erupt with fury at a perceived show of disrespect. Striding through the Jeddah palace of his brother, then-king Fahd, in the early 1990s, Salman was shocked when Fahd's longtime guard stood in his way. The king, the guard told him, was busy.

Salman slapped the man so hard that his ring flew across the room. "I'm the prince! Who are you?" Salman shouted, while young courtiers and servants crawled around the floor, searching for the ring. After Fahd chided his brother, Salman left an envelope for the guard with one hundred thousand riyals—more than $20,000. "Give the idiot this," Salman muttered on his way out. (A royal family member disputes this happened.)

Unlike other sons of Ibn Saud who built fortunes by using their power to extract payments from companies doing business in the kingdom, Salman was less aggressive about building wealth.

He spent his royal allowance on his palaces, his wives, and his children and spent his energy running Riyadh, the Al Saud's historic center of power.

As the governor of the province for forty-eight years, Salman controlled millions of acres of land that grew in value as the city of Riyadh transformed from a village at the start of his governorship into a modern city of more than five million people. Salman also supervised the relationship with the Wahhabist clerics whose alliance with the Al Saud stretched back to Wahhab himself—and whose support had helped the Al Saud gain and maintain power since the kingdom's founding.

Salman welcomed a diversity of viewpoints into his palace, encouraging debate in a way other princes wouldn't countenance. His Saudi Research and Marketing Group owned two of the biggest Arabic newspapers in the Middle East. They weren't mere government mouthpieces either, encouraging views from across the region about the biggest issues of the time, especially the Palestinian cause. On the other hand, they never dared question the monarchy or criticize Saudi foreign policy. Salman invited writers, academics, and foreign diplomats to weekly dinners. He told one American contact that he'd read every novel ever published by a Saudi writer.

Salman's relationship with his older sons was chilly. Distant and imperious as a young father (Salman was just nineteen when his oldest son was born), he was a rigid disciplinarian who focused on educating the young men. He wanted his sons to learn there was more to the world than Saudi Arabia's twin pillars of oil wealth and Wahhabism. Life was full of poetry and literature and ideas, and Salman, the son of a man who conquered Saudi Arabia on camelback, wanted his own sons to gain knowledge that would later benefit them as statesmen.

Regular vacations to Spain and France brought intellectuals and businessmen into Salman's tea room. Members of the

Syrian-Spanish Kayali merchant family were frequent visitors to his palaces, as were members of the Assad family, which continues to rule Syria. In Paris, Salman invited lawyers and political contacts for discussions and debates, often on the fractious politics of the Middle East.

These lessons seemed to mold the sons Salman had with his first wife, Sultana bint Turki Al Sudairi, beginning in the 1950s. They went abroad for schooling and learned multiple languages. Fahd and Ahmed became successful businessmen, running Saudi Research and Marketing, raising world-class racehorses, and operating a lucrative partnership with UPS. Sultan became the first Saudi citizen to go into outer space, on the US space shuttle *Discovery*; Abdulaziz was an oil expert who handled sensitive relationships for the government with other petroleum-producing countries; and Faisal was the academic, achieving a doctorate in political studies from the University of Oxford with a dissertation on relations between the Gulf states and Iran from 1968 to 1971. They had friends in the United States and London and met often with politicians from abroad. They were impressive, cosmopolitan, and Western in their sensibilities. To some, they didn't seem very Saudi. They even objected when Salman decided to take a new wife while still married to their mother, a long-standing tradition in Saudi culture.

It was 1983, and the princes' mother, Sultana Al Sudairi, was in a Pittsburgh hospital for a kidney transplant. Sultana was a revered figure within the royal family and practically worshipped by her five sons and daughter. The family brought an entourage of dozens of relatives and aides to Pittsburgh; each morning they would rush to the Presbyterian-University Hospital lobby to make sure they were waiting when Salman arrived. Then flanked by two security guards, Salman would pace around the hospital awaiting news from doctors.

Before the trip, Salman's three oldest sons, Fahd, Sultan, and

Ahmed, learned that their father was getting ready to marry a much younger woman. It wasn't unusual; after marrying her, Salman would still have just two wives in a country where a man may be married to four women at once. But his westernized sons viewed polygamy as outdated, insulting to their mother, and particularly insensitive when she was facing a life-threatening illness.

Salman brushed aside his sons' concerns, but in Pittsburgh, Fahd doubled down, storming out of the hospital to a nearby airport and hopping on a private plane, where he wrote a letter to his father that he gave to a messenger to bring back to Pittsburgh. Don't marry this woman, Fahd wrote. It's an insult to your wife.

Salman married her anyway. The young woman, Fahdah bint Falah al-Hithlain, was the daughter of a leader of the Ajman tribe, which had a long history as warriors fighting alongside, and sometimes against, the Al Saud. Two years later, Fahdah would give birth to her first son, Mohammed bin Salman. Five more would follow.

Those six boys had a very different upbringing than their much older brothers. In middle age, Salman lost the rigidity with which he'd raised his first brood. During a nighttime card game in the Jeddah home of King Fahd's son, one courtier recalls, five-year-old Mohammed ran in and started knocking off the men's headdresses. The boy kicked over a cup of tea and threw some cards on the floor before Salman called him over, laughing, and gave the pudgy child a hug. "Take Mohammed back," Salman told one of the boy's minders. Young Mohammed proceeded to kick the minder in the crotch.

Mohammed and his full brothers didn't absorb the passion for academia and living abroad instilled in Salman's first brood. While the older brothers were establishing their careers, adolescent Mohammed seemed aimless. He had a habit of daydreaming during family events, a tendency some mistook for absentmindedness. On vacations to Marbella or elsewhere, he and his younger brother Khalid would go off exploring or scuba diving. He'd spend hours playing video games, including the Age of Empires series where you build armies and conquer enemies, and indulging a love of fast food. Salman still brought professors and writers around and hosted weekly seminars, but his requests that Mohammed study or read books rather than play video games seemed more like nagging than the strict orders the prince used to issue to his older sons.

One afternoon, Salman got a call from a flustered staffer: the preteen Mohammed was at a local supermarket, dressed in a military outfit and making a scene. The police wanted to detain him, but the young prince told them they couldn't. He was the nephew of the king and the son of the governor of Riyadh. Salman handled the affair quietly, but it was clear the stern old-timer had a soft spot for Mohammed, who was more like a grandson because of the nearly fifty-year age gap between them.

During a family trip to Cannes in 2000, Salman invited over a Paris-based lawyer named Elie Hatem, who had known members of the Saudi royal family through his work in pro-monarchist political groups and frequently mixed with them during their trips to France. "Instead of playing games, go read," Salman told the fifteen-year-old Mohammed one day when Hatem came for lunch. The men lingered over a lavish Middle Eastern food spread while Mohammed sat eating McDonald's. The boy responded with a desultory "OK, Dad."

One afternoon, Salman asked Hatem to check in on Mohammed and make sure he was doing something productive. Encourage him to read anything, even a magazine or newspaper, and stop playing games, Salman told the lawyer. The boy just watched TV.

Soon after that visit to France, things changed for the teenage prince. He had a realization that would alter his understanding of money and power. While observers like Hatem saw an aimless young man struggling in the shadow of his accomplished brothers, they misunderstood what the prince was absorbing during his years on the sidelines. While his brothers may have learned refinement from the teachers their father brought in, Mohammed was watching Salman closely and learning about power.

By the time Abdullah was lying on his deathbed, Mohammed was almost thirty and a formidable adversary for Abdullah's sons and courtiers, more energetic, creative, and cutthroat than anyone expected. He was driven and absolutely certain he knew what the country needed not just to survive but to flourish. And by staying close to his father's side through his twenties, rather than leaving Saudi Arabia for his schooling, Mohammed had learned in great depth about the frailties of his rivals within the royal family.

Salman's role as family enforcer was becoming more taxing and thornier as the royal family grew. Each prince could have up to four wives at a time, and with each wife he might have three or four sons and a similar number of daughters. During Salman's forty-eight years as Riyadh's governor, the extended family blossomed into some seven thousand princes and at least as many princesses, all of them growing up with a sense of entitlement to a share of the country's oil profits. Many lived wealthy but relatively normal lives, and some became philanthropists or investors; others were deadbeats, gamblers, or drunks. And more than a few were greedy beyond belief, spending unimaginable sums on collections of Bugattis and Patek Philippe watches such that "Saudi" became a synonym for profligate consumerism in Western cities.

The lives of luxury created an issue when it came to ruling the country. Ibn Saud and his sons who served as king had each spent at least some of their childhood in the desert, close to the Bedouin fighters and conservative clerics who supported them. For them a brand-new Cadillac, falcon hunting, and a surfeit of food constituted a life of luxury. This new generation was schooled abroad, living for long stretches in the privileged bubbles of London's Mayfair or Paris's 16th arrondissement. Many had lost part of their Saudi culture and their understanding of the Islamic interests that were locked in a powerful embrace with the House of Saud.

By the 2000s, many of the Al Saud's best and brightest weren't Saudi enough to connect with the explosion of youth in the country. Saudi Arabia's growing population was becoming more connected to the rest of the world and more restless in their straightjacketed lives, thanks to smartphones and social media. But the young princes were oblivious to much of what was happening at home, busy vacationing or pursuing degrees.

Salman tried to serve as a bulwark against this loss of identity, disciplining princes for Western behavior unbecoming in conservative Saudi Arabia. To many he seemed like an eccentric, a member of the Al Saud who wielded power within the family and within the kingdom but would never ascend beyond the role of Riyadh's governor. For Salman, the math just wasn't right.

By 2010, five years into King Abdullah's reign, Salman was over seventy years old and had two equally accomplished older brothers standing between him and the throne. For most of the time Abdullah reigned, there was no reason for Tuwaijri, the Royal Court chief, to see Salman or his children as a threat. They were too far from the line of succession.

Then one of those older brothers died in 2011 and the other in 2012. In each case, Abdullah named a new crown prince himself rather than having the Allegiance Council, which he had formed for the purpose, debate to determine the succession. When the second brother died, Abdullah made Salman crown prince and appointed his youngest living brother, former intelligence chief Muqrin, as deputy crown prince.

As Abdullah grew frailer, Tuwaijri tried to create distance between the king and the crown prince. He still hoped Abdullah was open to casting Salman aside. Tuwaijri sometimes denied Salman and his sons the use of royal planes. When Salman would call to set up a meeting, the court chief would tell him that Abdullah was too busy. After months of this, Salman realized what was happening when he saw Abdullah at a family occasion. "Why don't you come to see me anymore?" the king asked. "You're one of my favorite brothers." Salman understood Tuwaijri was trying to sideline him.

Tuwaijri activated his whisper network to spread the notion that Salman was suffering from dementia, a bid to hasten succession plans. He sought buy-in from other influential royals to carry out what would be the progress-minded Abdullah's last great reform: passing the crown to the next generation. Perhaps one of Abdullah's sons, maybe Miteb or Turki, could be placed in the line of succession as deputy crown prince so that he would one day be king. Or perhaps giving Mohammed bin Nayef, the domestic security chief with deep ties to the CIA and US State Department, a place in the line of succession might help get US buy-in. Bin Nayef also controlled the powerful Saudi Interior Ministry. As Abdullah's sons controlled the Saudi National Guard, the traditionally Bedouin force that protected the royal family, a union between the two branches would have clear control of the military.

For his plan to work, Tuwaijri had to finalize arrangements among the family before Salman could intervene. The best way to do that was to make sure Abdullah died in the desert, without the rest of the family around. That would give Tuwaijri time, hours at least but possibly days, to line up support for the plan and make sure Salman didn't put one of his sons in a senior role. As Abdullah's breathing grew shallower in the desert tent, Tuwaijri issued an order: Don't tell Salman.

Abdullah's sons were nervous but supported the scheme. They believed they were fit to rule. Before Abdullah's final illness, his son Miteb told US ambassador Joe Westphal that he expected to be in the running for the crown.

The problem with his plot, Tuwaijri would soon learn, was that his team had a leak. Out of view from the Abdullah clan, Mohammed bin Salman had assembled a group of loyal and effective functionaries, men who could gather information within the royal family as well as outside. They alerted Mohammed about the king's condition, and he made sure other senior Al Saud knew.

The wider family was shocked at the king's deterioration. Even those who knew of his cancer diagnosis didn't realize how close he was to death. They pressured Tuwaijri to move Abdullah from his desert retreat to a Riyadh hospital run by the National Guard. The move was done under cover of night, and the hospital ejected anyone who might leak news of the king's imminent death. One astonished doctor told friends he climbed a fence and slipped in the back door to check on patients. Secrecy is important in a succession to give the population the false impression of a seamless, inevitable transition.

By then the Abdullah clan and Tuwaijri had all but given up on retaining the crown. The best they could hope for was to ensure that if Salman took over, the next in line for the throne was someone without animosity toward Abdullah's children. Perhaps more important than anything else was making sure Salman wouldn't put his son Mohammed in line for the throne. They spread stories about the young prince's lack of expertise, brutish way of getting things done, and personal greed.

The situation remained unsettled for days. The Royal Court put up a tent outside the hospital to host friends and relatives visiting the dying king. Several thousand Saudis, many of them poor, gathered around the hospital and prayed through the night. Officials in Riyadh's US embassy kept hearing that the council of princes was going to meet to determine Abdullah's successor, but they could never pin down exactly when.

Most visitors stopped at the tent to sit with Miteb or Turki or one of Abdullah's other sons. Only those close to the king were allowed inside, where Abdullah was resting in a room on the first floor. Visitors walked down a one-hundred-yard corridor, past other patients' rooms, to a seven-foot-tall glass window. Behind it was the room where the king lay dying.

Several days into Abdullah's hospital stay, Mohammed called to ask about his uncle. Don't worry, Tuwaijri responded. He's stable. It sounded unbelievable. Just a couple days earlier, one of the king's older daughters had arrived to see her father through the window with a green cloth over his forehead and no visible signs of breath. He looked so small; to her companion, he looked dead.

Soon after, Mohammed got a call that Abdullah had died. He hurried his father into a convoy of cars and sped to the National Guard hospital. They found Tuwaijri waiting in the hallway. Salman had had enough of the man. He hit the court chief across the face with a slap that rang through the hospital corridor loudly enough to be heard through the wall in the waiting room. Tuwaijri knew then that he'd wagered big on trying to marginalize Salman and lost it all. With a slap to the face, the new king and his young son beside him announced the beginning of a new reign unlike anything since the kingdom was a patchwork of fiefdoms raiding each other for camels and food and gold.

The news of King Abdullah's death took hours to travel, thanks in part to the deference of local journalists to the requests of the Royal Court. Away from view of the public, Salman immediately removed Tuwaijri from his position as Allegiance Council secretary and jettisoned him from the Royal Court, even while he kept many of the other officials in their jobs. As chief of his father's court, Mohammed insinuated himself deep in the deliberations and planning. When his father tired or needed a break, Mohammed powered through the night, holding meetings and making calls. There was no doubt that this was as much Mohammed's moment as his elderly father's.

When the announcement came, Salman appointed his half brother Muqrin as crown prince and his nephew Mohammed bin Nayef as deputy crown prince. These seemed measured choices intended to reassure the wider family and tribal leaders who held power over small dominions across the country that it was business as usual. During the ceremonies, Mohammed bin Salman, who had been named defense minister but remained outside the immediate line of succession, quietly deferred to his elder relatives out of respect, even as he was kicking a series of ambitious plans into gear.

More liberal family members worried that yet another Saudi Arabian era of morass was in the offing. The word diplomats reserved for the pace of change in the kingdom for half a century was "glacial." Little did they know that the country was about to embark on an upheaval.

Chapter 2

MBS

January 23–May 1, 2015

The generals sitting around the Saudi Defense Ministry's situation room table thought they had a pretty good idea of what was about to happen. They'd been running the Saudi armed forces for decades and believed their new defense minister would be pretty much like the last one. When facing adversity, Saudi Arabia followed the lead of the United States of America, its longtime protector. There would be grave deliberations and a decision to have more grave deliberations the following day and the following week until Washington, DC, decided what to do.

But when Mohammed bin Salman, twenty-nine years old and with less than eight weeks of experience running the Saudi military, sat down at the head of the V-shaped table and issued an unprecedented order, "Send in the F15s," they were shocked into silence. Saudi Arabia was not just going to war. It was leading the way.

Houthi rebels had been marching across Yemen, Saudi Arabia's neighbor, capturing one city after another. Their brazenness, support from Iran, and proximity to Riyadh made the guerilla force a perilous threat on the southern border.

For Saudi Arabia, no threat is greater than Iran, whose ayatollahs believe the Middle East is their strategic domain. It was Iran's supply of powerful missiles and military hardware that gave the rebels so much confidence in facing down the bigger and better-equipped Saudi armed forces. A day earlier, one of the rebel commanders declared that if Saudi Arabia intervened, the Houthis wouldn't stop their "expansion at Mecca, but rather Riyadh."

Mohammed wouldn't abide such threats. It was March 2015, and he was ordering the most ambitious military campaign in Saudi history. As with his own generals, the decision caught the United States by surprise. When the Saudis reached out to the White House on short notice and asked if they wanted to join the bombing campaign, "we were flat footed," one National Security Council official recalls.

In private gatherings with the king and the Royal Court's advisors in the week before the strikes, Mohammed pledged to make the engagement quick and brutal. "It will be over in a couple of months," he told Saudi officials and US State Department contacts alike.

The State Department and the Saudi generals were nervous. Though the United States had been encouraging Saudi Arabia to take control of its own security for years, the kingdom had never led a strike from the front, putting citizens in harm's way and its mettle to the test. In contrast to the aggressive young prince who had no prior military training, many of the generals had spent time at the US Military Academy at West Point or its UK counterpart, the Royal Military Academy, Sandhurst. They were wary of any show of force and knew that Yemen, with its mountainous landscape, fractious population, and committed fighters, had been a quagmire for any foreign power for a century.

US security officials accustomed to dealing with a long line of cautious and deferential princes suddenly realized they were dealing with a new kind of leader, one who seemed perfectly comfortable dropping bombs with or without US support. The

White House declined to get involved but began offering intelligence and targets.

Saudi jets streamed over the border, joined by fighters from the United Arab Emirates and other Arab allies, aiming laser-guided bombs at Houthi holdouts. Problems surfaced immediately. Though Saudi Arabia possessed high-tech weaponry, it didn't always have the expertise to use it.

Fearing putting citizens at risk in a ground war, the Saudi military pursued a strategy built around air attacks. Military officials would draw a grid over a map of the region of Yemen they were attacking. Then the Saudi military would march in foreign troops, some of them teenagers sent by the dictator of impoverished Sudan in exchange for Saudi aid, to clear civilians from each square of the grid. The bombers would follow, working under the assumption that anyone who remained was a combatant—and that the high-tech missiles and targeting intelligence, which the United States helped with, would result in precision attacks.

The strategy fell apart quickly. The foreign soldiers weren't diligent about clearing out civilians, and the bombing coordinates weren't always right. In some cases the planners were using different maps from the pilots. Even when the coordinates were right, the Saudi Air Force's ground radios sometimes couldn't communicate with its fighter jets. When that happened, pilots had to fly low to the ground so mission control could give them bombing targets over their cell phones. Laser guidance systems were often not properly calibrated, meaning bombs strayed far from their intended targets.

Operation Decisive Storm was a disturbing escalation of Middle East turmoil, but few observers at the time saw what an outright disaster it would become—and what a sign it was of the new directions in which Saudi Arabia was heading.

Mohammed made sure to send a message of strength inside the kingdom. Within hours of the first attacks, the Saudi government distributed photos of him with a resolute expression, studying maps and consulting with military leaders. The war reinforced that Mohammed was a new kind of leader. He wouldn't stand down in the face of provocation.

Not long after the Yemen bombing began, Tony Blinken, a security advisor to Vice President Joe Biden, flew to Riyadh to try to read the situation. He met the United States' most trusted Saudi contact, Mohammed bin Nayef, or MBN, who seemed dismissive. He didn't much want to discuss Yemen and implied it was a losing proposition. In fact, he told one former US intelligence official that Mohammed bin Salman hadn't even given him advance warning of the first Yemen strike. The war wasn't MBN's fight, and it seemed like he wanted to keep it that way. Blinken returned to Washington with more questions than answers.

It was clear to the White House staff that Mohammed bin Salman was a prince empowered to make decisions of geopolitical importance. And he was making those decisions quickly, maybe recklessly. There was a scramble in Washington to get up to date on his biography—even his birth date seemed a mystery. How had such an ambitious royal barely registered in their prince watching over the years?

After the Yemen bombing, the prince would be mentioned so frequently that he'd need a convenient abbreviation: MBS. As they delved deeper into his history, US officials and intelligence analysts found that Mohammed's rise was more unusual than they had realized. It turned out he learned brazenness not just from famous generals and warriors of history but from reading about American business tycoons.

What snapped Mohammed out of his teenage stupor, his indulgence in video games and fast food, was money, or rather his perceived lack of it. Speaking to a cousin one day, the fifteen-year-old prince learned that his father, one of the most powerful Al Saud family members, had not amassed a serious fortune—by Saudi standards—over his decades in office. Even worse, he had become dangerously indebted to princes and businessmen, opening up a profound vulnerability for the Salman clan.

That made Mohammed anxious about the future of his branch of the family. "It was the first shock and challenge that I faced in my life," he said later. Soon after, Mohammed approached Salman with a strange request for a prince. "I want to open a store," he said. Salman laughed. Just do your schoolwork, he replied, not understanding the anxiety underlying his son's proposal.

In any conventional sense, Salman and his children lived a life of extraordinary wealth. They had palaces in Saudi Arabia, a sprawling vacation residence in Marbella, Spain, where the gardeners cut "SALMAN" into the grass, and another palace complex the size of a university campus on the coast near Tangier in Morocco. Each had dozens of staff waiting to satisfy any princely whim. The problem was that Salman had spent, and not saved or invested, much of his share of oil profits, and he hadn't started lucrative side businesses like other, more entrepreneurial princes. He didn't control a license to sell Mercedes-Benz cars or distribute General Electric products—typical means princes used to grow their income.

While Salman had achieved great political might, he had relatively little wealth by Al Saud standards. His close family had some investments in companies and real estate but lived what amounted to a lavish hand-to-mouth existence, dependent on payouts from the king and treasury. When that money was slow to come, his staff might go unpaid. Friends and family members were shocked in the first decade of the 2000s when word spread through Paris that contractors and employees of Prince Salman and his family hadn't been paid for six months. To offer the generosity a prince typically shows to commoners who come with pleas for assistance, Salman would often write checks from a local bank, whose owner, a friend of Salman, would have to foot the bill.

The missing fortune would become a serious problem for the children of Salman if they should be pushed further away from the center of power. Their income would get smaller and spread among a growing number of descendants, and they would be dependent on the good graces of whoever was king. Mohammed realized he was far from power and nowhere in the line of succession. The only solution, he figured, was to become the family businessman. His shop plans abandoned, a few years later he became interested in petrochemicals.

During a trip to Kuwait at the time, he asked a government official if the Kuwaitis could process bitumen, a by-product of oil refining, for him as part of a new business idea he was cooking up. When they came back to him, they said they could only do 40 percent of the volume he requested. "Not good enough," he told them. "My plan is to be richer than Alwaleed bin Talal in two years."

Alwaleed was the most famous Saudi in the world at the time. He was on TV inside and outside Saudi Arabia, a recognized name on Wall Street and in popular media. He lived the over-the-top life people expected from a Saudi prince. Even Alwaleed's son, who sat far down the totem pole from Mohammed, raced Lamborghinis around Riyadh. CEOs wanted to meet these princes, and celebrities wanted to be seen with them, so long as the princes were paying the bills. No one was clamoring to live it up with Salman, who went to bed after nothing more exciting than a nightly session of *baloot*, a card game with four players similar to the French game of *belote*, and woke up at 7 a.m. each morning.

Mohammed also became interested in stock trading. For years he had been stashing some of the gold coins his father and his uncle King Fahd used to give him as gifts for the Eid al-Fitr holiday at the end of Ramadan. By the time he was sixteen, Mohammed had about $100,000 after selling the gold and a few high-end watches he'd received as gifts. It became the starting capital for his new career as a trader. He bought, he sold, and ultimately, he would later say, he "went broke."

But first, briefly, his portfolio's value went up. Mohammed would keep chasing the thrill of making a fleeting profit on a grander scale. He had ambitions to go abroad after university in Saudi Arabia and then to go into banking, telecommunications, or real estate.

Those ambitions were subverted by a more pressing need at home. When Mohammed was seventeen, his oldest half brother Fahd died suddenly; the Royal Court blamed heart problems, but Fahd had been a healthy man. Fahd was Salman's oldest son, born when his father was just nineteen. He'd been a government official, a businessman, and a racehorse owner. His sudden death left Salman heartbroken.

Two months later came the September 11, 2001, terrorist attacks and subsequent scrutiny of Salman's support for Islamic charities, some of which were found to have diverted money to terrorist activities. Then, the following July, almost a year to the day after Fahd's death, Salman's son Ahmed died at forty-three of heart failure. Another prince, a cousin, died in a car accident in Riyadh on his way to the funeral.

It was an almost unbearable series of tragedies for Prince Salman, and Mohammed stayed by his side throughout. At an age when many Saudi princes would leave the kingdom for an education in Boston, London, or Paris, Mohammed turned his attention inward. He attended King Saud University and spent much of his spare time scribbling in his notebook as an observer in his father's *majlis*, or gathering room for advisors and petitioners. Salman had another reason for keeping his favorite son in Riyadh: After seeing his older sons lose some of their Saudi identity abroad, Salman wanted to groom Mohammed and his brothers in his image at home. "I did not go to the Sorbonne to learn how to be a prince," Salman once told an American visitor.

It wasn't just Salman. Ibn Saud once said that "to be a leader of men, a man has to receive an education in his own country, among his own people, and to grow up in surroundings steeped with the traditions and psychology of his countrymen."

As governor of Riyadh, Salman had a lower international profile than some of his brothers, but he ruled over the central region called the Najd, ancestral homeland of the Al Saud tribe. He controlled real estate transactions, dealt with the religious leaders who propped up the ruling family, and presided over arrests and executions in Riyadh's Deera Square, known as Chop Chop Square for its frequent beheadings. He disciplined wayward princes, mediated disputes between feuding family members, and was keeper of the family genealogy, tracing familial relations with Saudi tribes back generations.

Salman was also a standard-bearer for his family's long allegiance with the Wahhabist religious establishment. He directed money to Islamic schools around the world. And he took a jaundiced view of the kingdom's most important international relationship, harboring a belief that the Saudi-US alliance was essentially transactional and not the deep friendship that princes who focused on foreign policy professed to their American counterparts.

A US official based in Riyadh remembers the first time Salman summoned him to meet in his *majlis*, a cavernous room lined with long sofas where each week the prince accepted entreaties from members of the public. A staffer led the American into the space roughly half the size of a football field, with intricately woven rugs and a crystal chandelier.

Salman held court at the center of the back wall in a large chair. A line of petitioners sat to his right. The prince motioned for the diplomat to sit in a chair next to him. "You're most welcome here," he said. "I know Saudi Arabia and America will always have a special relationship." As the diplomat thanked him, Salman interrupted with a caveat: "as long as you keep selling us your weapons."

Another US official found himself sitting beside Salman, then Riyadh's governor, at a Riyadh dinner during a visit by then–vice president Dick Cheney. While Cheney spoke with the king, Salman asked the official a question: "Would you like to know how I've managed to keep Riyadh for the last 40 years?"

"Sure," the official replied.

"Every week I hold three *majlis*," Salman said. "One for the religious scholars and two for the people. I even let the Bangladeshi street sweepers come. Because the day I don't know what the Bangladeshi street sweepers think is the day we lose power."

Some evenings, Mohammed would go out with friends into the desert and have staff make up tents and a fire. Frequent attendees were his younger brother Khalid and two cousins, Badr bin Farhan and Abdullah bin Bandar. They'd race four-wheelers in the dunes, set up soccer matches, and play video games. Eating fast food from McDonald's or more traditional fare by the flames, Mohammed would tell them of his plans to become a billionaire. They'd talk about Steve Jobs and Bill Gates, men who built enduring legacies by focusing on results and being shrewder than their competition. And he'd talk with charisma, mission, and mounting frustration and despair about the Saudi youth. "We are the ones who can decide the future of our generation," he said one night, as an attendee remembered it. "If we don't step up, who else will?"

Mohammed also had an early fascination with Alexander the Great, consuming history books about him and relishing his bold empire building. Some of his closest friends from that time would later refer to Mohammed as their "Iskander," Arabic for Alexander.

One day, Abdulrahman al-Jeraisy, the septuagenarian owner of a Riyadh-based conglomerate that sells paper, telecom services, and furniture, got an unexpected message. Mohammed, Prince Salman's son, wanted to borrow a million riyals, or about $250,000. It wasn't quite arm-twisting, but it also wasn't a request that Jeraisy could just brush aside. His family business was based in Riyadh, and Prince Salman governed the city. It was probably better to pay the $250,000 than deal with whatever trouble could arise from saying no. Fahd al-Obeikan, whose family owns a Riyadh manufacturing company, got a similar request. Only Mohammed wanted $500,000 from him. The industrialist ponied up alongside others.

The prince sank the money into stocks in the United States, and a few years later, when Saudi Arabia opened its own stock exchange, he invested there too. Called the Tadawul, it was an easy place to make money for a prince. There weren't many companies on the market. Most were subject to government actions that someone who spent all day in the Royal Court could not help but absorb information on.

Mohammed also started creating companies of his own and acquiring stakes in others. He began a garbage-collection business and a group of real estate companies named after the scenic Tuwaiq escarpment southwest of Riyadh. He'd eventually hold shares in more than a dozen businesses in Saudi Arabia under his own name, something relatively rare in Saudi Arabia, where powerful people hold vast interests through proxies or confidential arrangements. The transparency was a sign of both earnestness and naivete.

The corporate registry shows Mohammed and his full brothers had a stake in a tech firm that got a coveted broadband license from the government, as well as ownership positions in fish farms, building developments, commodity trading, and restaurants. They had a Riyadh office park, and their holding company owned a firm that partnered with a Louisiana hospital to send Saudi patients to the United States for organ transplants.

Mohammed got into the real estate development business. One persistent problem Salman struggled with as Riyadh's governor was land speculation. With money pouring into Riyadh, businessmen and members of the royal family would acquire undeveloped land and hold on to it in hopes of selling it at a big profit down the road, rather than developing it themselves.

Mohammed was focused on housing, a result of his work for his father. He began making deals with wealthy landowners: If they contributed a portion of land, he would find a developer to build houses on it. The developer and landowner would then co-own the new development. And Mohammed would get a percentage for his family. It worked well, since there was huge demand for new housing, and no landowner or construction company could comfortably say no to the son of Riyadh's governor. It was a model he'd try to re-create later on a much grander scale.

Seeing some success at home, Mohammed began making foreign contacts. Knowing that more senior princes in the Royal Court had access to government surveillance information unavailable to him, Mohammed looked for ways to develop his own intelligence-gathering capabilities. Around 2006 he approached the Center for Advanced Defense Studies, a Washington, DC–based think tank that uses publicly available information to learn about illicit financing networks, and asked it to build a private institution with the prince's own office. The think tank's management declined.

The prince brought some foreign business contacts into his

family home, welcoming them into intimate discussions of life and philosophy with Salman and his retinue. The teenager was now a towering young man who tended to sit off to the side, listening intently but not saying much. When he did interject, it was often with an anecdote from a history book or a religious text. During one Paris conversation about the nature of space and of God, Mohammed chimed in with an unexpected reference to a passage from the Koran. He was also married by now to a cousin, Sarah bint Mahshoor, and immediately they started having children. He'd eventually be father to two sons and two daughters.

From his reading of history, Mohammed came to see the world in terms of confrontation. He chafed at the idea that a power like the United States could exert control over Saudi Arabia in a way that harkened back to the colonial era. "He kind of had to have an enemy in his head, and the West was sort of the Romans, or the Byzantines. The Ottomans," one confidant recalls. The Western powers, Prince Mohammed told him in the early 2000s, "are not doing well for us."

These conversations made Mohammed, who spoke only in Arabic, seem more traditionally "Saudi" than his westernized older brothers. But Mohammed drew these men in with what one American calls "a magnetism" that made him want to get even closer to the prince. Mohammed, this man found, engendered loyalty through his father's power and his own ambition, but more importantly through a politician's knack for making the people he welcomed into his orbit feel special.

Translating that charm into business opportunity, Mohammed, through intermediaries, persuaded US mobile giant Verizon to bring fiber-optic infrastructure to Saudi Arabia. The deal, finalized in 2008, saw Verizon take a minority stake in a joint venture whose biggest partner was one of Mohammed's many companies. Verizon's legal department, headed by William Barr at the time, sent a lawyer, Verizon's current chief counsel, Craig Silliman, to Saudi Arabia. Silliman sat down with Mohammed to finalize the deal. Barr later became the US attorney general.

The deal succeeded in building Mohammed's reputation. "My son made millions for the family," Salman boasted to one visitor after the deal closed. Government officials were happy because they'd been concerned that regional rivals were developing better fiber-optic networks than Saudi Arabia.

But Mohammed was still a young man and had little business experience. His company had none of the capabilities needed to carry through an international joint venture. About two years later, Verizon packed up and went home, writing off the investment as a loss.

Mohammed's local enterprises were more successful and began to throw off millions of dollars, lessening his anxiety and contributing to a new war chest that would be necessary for showing largesse to important tribes and religious causes—all prerequisites to building a following that would support a bid by his father to become king.

But then Mohammed, still in his twenties, was investigated in relation to market shenanigans. Regulators had uncovered a suspicious pattern in the trading accounts of a group of princes, including Mohammed. Just before big announcements, they were making bets on stocks, netting major profits. Regulators suspected insider trading rather than lucky stock picking. The loser in the trades was often the government.

Saudi Arabia's chief stock regulator at the time, Mohammed Al Shaikh, investigated. He grilled Mohammed and determined that a trader acting on the prince's behalf, rather than Mohammed himself, was responsible for the irregularities. Al Shaikh advised him that it was better practice to put his stock portfolio in an investment fund.

The incident incensed King Abdullah, who issued a decree

saying that even princes were not above market laws. Mohammed wasn't named, but he was stung by the experience, and his
position in the family took a fall.

He was impressed by Al Shaikh, chairman of the Capital
Markets Authority and former White & Case lawyer, who had
treated him firmly but respectfully, steering him away from
trouble. He placed the law above stature, a sharp break from the
old Saudi tradition of "the ruler knows best." Al Shaikh had been
educated in the United States and worked for the World Bank.
The prince realized the man tasked with investigating him could
one day be a powerful ally.

————

Islamic leader Salman al-Ouda didn't know what to make of the
young prince sitting across from him in his living room in October 2012. He didn't even know why Mohammed bin Salman,
whom Ouda knew as a princeling of uncertain influence in the
Royal Court, had invited himself over in the first place. Ouda
would have politely turned the meeting down, but he had already
rebuffed Mohammed once, about a year earlier, at a wedding. It
wasn't good practice to ignore the son of the crown prince.

So there was Mohammed, sipping coffee on the couch and talking about world history, while Ouda, one of the Muslim world's
most popular imams with more than thirteen million Twitter followers, sat listening. Mohammed shared his ideas about Islam,
Arab leaders, and how a ruler should run a country. They struck
Ouda as the shallow learnings of a recent graduate who hadn't
spent much time inside the library or outside the kingdom. Then
Mohammed said something that got the cleric's attention.

"My role model," he declared, "is Machiavelli."

Ouda remained silent. Mohammed's attempt to earn respect
with his knowledge, rather than his birthright, impressed the

cleric. But the substance of the message was troubling. This prince was quoting *The Prince*; it augured tumultuous times for the kingdom and later for Ouda himself.

By that time Mohammed, whose wide girth and hot temper and the scruffy beard running down his throat had earned him the nickname "Stray Bear" from his enemies, had been gaining a reputation up and down the royal family for having a sharp edge. In one oft-recounted story, always told with a new variation, he sent a bullet to a land official who had declined to give him title to a plot he demanded—gaining him another nickname, Abu Rasasa, or "Father of the Bullet."

Even in his official work, Mohammed established a reputation for pushing around powerful relatives. Showing up with buses full of Filipino workers, he told his own aunt, one of the wives of the late King Fahd, that she was being evicted from a palace needed for new purposes. The power would be disconnected by midnight, he told her. This was especially bracing in Saudi culture, where age and rank are held in the highest regard.

During late-night banter, well-to-do Saudis like to point to Mohammed's tribal heritage on his mother's side, suggesting that his character traits traced back to his Bedouin blood. His mother, Fahdah, hails from the Ajman tribe in the northeast of Saudi Arabia. Its most famous member is Rakan bin Hithlain, a revered fighter during the Ottoman era. On the other side, Ibn Saud, Mohammed's grandfather, was the consummate desert warrior: six foot, four inches tall; lusty; strategic; and bold. Mohammed was the convergence of those two lines. It was folklore, but it would be important later in creating a mythical backstory for young Saudis looking to champion a reformer prince speaking directly to their demographic.

Within the Al Saud family, Mohammed became known as ambitious and self-assured—and protected by his powerful father, Prince Salman.

In 2011, Salman's brother Sultan, the minister of defense for forty-eight years, died. Salman assumed the role, marking a major shift of power. The Sultan clan's control of the army gave it great power and huge amounts of money. Transferring it to Salman gave an already influential prince a new power base. Soon after, Salman made Mohammed an advisor to the military.

The young prince, still in his twenties, started ordering around senior princes who had been officers for years, including sons of the prior defense minister and King Abdullah. He finally crossed a line one day when he started berating a cousin some thirty years his senior, a prince named Khalid bin Bandar who had served as a general for years. The senior prince refused to take orders from Mohammed, who became angry.

By that time four senior military officers, all princes, one of them King Abdullah's son, had quit because of Mohammed, and the king knew he had to rein in the young upstart. He summoned Mohammed to his vacation home in Tangier. But when Mohammed arrived, he didn't get the stern warning Abdullah would usually give. Instead the king had Tuwaijri, his Royal Court chief, dress him down. It was humiliating. Tuwaijri was basically a servant, as far as Mohammed was concerned, and here he was talking down to the grandson of Ibn Saud. He returned to Riyadh and told his father about the incident.

Salman, who was crown prince in addition to defense minister at the time, was even more upset than his son. He called Abdullah and told the king that Mohammed was acting on his behalf, and if the king didn't like it, Salman would resign. Abdullah backed down, and Mohammed resumed his place in the ministry.

From his time sitting in the *majlis* with his father, day after day, he also learned the inner workings of power in Saudi Arabia. Salman had vulnerabilities, he realized, and it was up to him to protect his father and the family lineage.

Salman, then in his seventies, was in line to inherit the throne, but like Abdullah he suffered from health problems. After back surgery, he became addicted to painkillers. They made him bad-tempered and forgetful, traits Khalid al-Tuwaijri and his allies looked to use against him in the months leading up to King Abdullah's death.

Mohammed set to work on beating the addiction, staying up with his father around the clock and handing him pills identical to those he'd been taking for years. Only they were actually new ones specially ordered up by Mohammed with lower doses. Over a matter of weeks, he'd helped his father emerge from a long torpor. The two, already close, used their time together to talk of Saudi Arabia's ills and ideas for shaking things up.

"Notice anything different about the crown prince," Mohammed asked a family friend not long after. "Yes," the friend replied. "He wasn't yelling at me all the time." Mohammed gave his trademark grin, so big it forced his eyes nearly shut.

Foreigners were only just starting to notice the ambitious new face in the Al Saud family starting in 2011 and 2012. The clubby *Gulf States Newsletter*, written by former diplomats, spooks, and other prince watchers, reported on him overseeing a ceremony for the National Association of Retired Persons in Riyadh on March 21, 2011, when his father was still the governor. "The usually low-profile prince has recently had a more visible public presence," one news brief read. "Observers note that Prince Mohammed is regarded as particularly ambitious, with an eye on the governorship and control of other government entities."

That ambition was mostly focused on the economy, something Mohammed saw as his expertise after his dalliances in business and markets. He surrounded himself with a coterie of advisors with backgrounds in economics, business, and law. They spent hours spitballing and writing out what would later be the key thrusts of the National Transformation Plan and Vision 2030 for Saudi Arabia, attempts to shift the economy away from oil in just two decades. Few of the ideas were innovative, but in the context of the country's history of resisting change, they were revolutionary. Saudi Arabia was so change averse, it didn't outlaw slavery until 1962 under pressure from President John F. Kennedy.

As an experiment, Mohammed decided to create his own foundation that would require no approval from anyone except himself. It would be a chance to create from the start a modern Saudi institution. He called it the Mohammed bin Salman bin Abdulaziz Foundation, or MiSK. To avoid the pitfalls of the past, he issued a tender for consultants to help design it from the ground up. Western firms jumped at the opportunity.

Mohammed also aligned himself with his wealthy cousin Alwaleed bin Talal. In 2012 Alwaleed wrote a letter to King Abdullah's Royal Court chief Khalid al-Tuwaijri. Saudi Arabia, he said, could be heading for a crisis. Oil prices were high at the time, but the Saudi budget was straining under huge outlays for subsidies and a host of handouts to the population. Health care was mostly free, education abroad was sponsored by the state, and citizens got special benefits for every child born. A Riyadh resident could turn on a water tap for hours and barely suffer the consequences; yet Saudi Arabia is one of the most water-scarce countries in the world, having to desalinate 1.2 billion cubic meters of saltwater a year—more than any other country on earth.

The kingdom's population was growing, costs were rising, and the rest of the world was talking with more urgency about using less oil. What would happen when oil prices dropped? To ward off a catastrophe, Alwaleed argued, Saudi Arabia needed to diversify, invest in solar and nuclear energy, and start moving some of its oil wealth abroad so it would have diversified sources of income.

To do this, Alwaleed suggested turning Saudi Arabia's Public Investment Fund (PIF), a government-owned investor, into a giant money manager that could put Saudi oil revenue into other industries. It was the same model Saudi Arabia's own neighbors in Abu Dhabi, Kuwait, and Qatar followed with savings from oil. Alwaleed pitched the plan in a meeting with senior princes and other officials from Abdullah's Royal Court. "I'm with Alwaleed," Mohammed said. In a second meeting they brought the plan to King Abdullah.

But the king and his advisors were dismissive. Moving money out of oil and into other investments was a risk, and the Al Saud were allergic to risk. Saudi Arabia had never done it before. What's more, PIF was like a moth-ridden back closet of forgotten investments, a fund full of local companies whose owners, in some cases with royal links, got PIF money as a sort of bailout. The notion that it could become a world-class investor seemed like a fantasy. Plus, the old guard reasoned, the world still needed oil.

Mohammed also became close to a civil servant named Turki Al Sheikh, a police official who was a few years older, had a taste for ostentatious cars and watches, and hailed from the Al Sheikh family, direct descendants of the eighteenth-century founder of Wahhabism.

In early 2015, with Salman on the throne, all of Mohammed's ideas were suddenly the highest priority. The day after the funeral of King Abdullah, Mohammed was fully in charge of the Royal Court and sending out orders at 4 a.m. for prominent Saudi officials and businessmen to come for a meeting later that day. Among other questions, he asked them if there was any risk in upending governance in the kingdom by doing away with most of the committees and bodies that King Abdullah had used for decades. Some expressed the view that such a change should be made slowly to monitor for unforeseen impacts. "Nonsense," he said to them. "If it's the right thing to do, we do it today."

Within six days of his father's becoming king, Mohammed was named chair of a new entity called the Council of Economic and Development Affairs, one of two committees that would oversee just about everything in the country. He had carte blanche to shake up the country's financial and development plans, though he surrounded himself with a cast of advisors with little government background and encouraged them to argue with him into the night on policy ideas.

Within two months, he'd selected the Public Investment Fund as the institution to put the country on the global investing map and lead up many of the reforms. By April, he took over the country's money-making machine, Saudi Aramco. Mohammed was in control of the most profitable and biggest company in the world.

One of Mohammed's first courses of action was to hire international polling companies to survey people about their perceptions of Saudi Arabia, especially any negative views. The results were unsurprising: it's a closed society with homegrown terrorists, no cinemas or entertainment, highly restricted rights for women, and other well-known views. Mohammed created a task force to address each point with an action plan. It was time for Saudi Arabia to enter global society on an equal footing, he told aides. Time and again, he told aides that their country had everything it needed to be a powerful nation on the world stage with a strong economy no longer reliant on oil.

And most importantly of all, King Salman announced that his brother, Muqrin, was stepping down from the line of succession. Mohammed would be the new deputy crown prince, putting him second in line to the throne behind only his cousin, Mohammed bin Nayef. Mohammed had real power now. The moves sent shudders through cousins who saw Saudi Arabia entering a new

Salman-centric era that could go on for decades if Mohammed were to follow in his father's footsteps.

The moves happened relatively quietly with few big headlines but were without precedent in the country's history. Mohammed was deputy crown prince and commander of the armed forces, and he controlled the great gushing oil wells that could underwrite his wildest ideas.

Chapter 3

PARTY IN MALDIVES

July 2015

The models arrived first, one boatload after another of long-legged young women pulling up to the dock at Velaa Private Island. The resort's butlers and housekeepers were amazed. There were just so many of them, around 150 in all, and most had traveled for days, flying from Brazil or Russia to Male, the capital of the Maldives, a tiny nation in the Indian Ocean. From Male the women took smaller planes to a northern archipelago, where they boarded boats across a turquoise expanse of the Indian Ocean to Velaa. The resort had staffers on hand to greet each woman and politely shuttle her by golf cart to a medical center to be tested for sexually transmitted diseases. Only after the testing was done and the women had settled into their villas did the seaplanes carrying Mohammed bin Salman and his friends arrive.

It was the summer of 2015, and Mohammed was closer than anyone could have predicted to the Saudi throne. In the six months since his father had become king, he had hit Riyadh harder and faster than any prince in recent memory. Mohammed had taken charge of the economy of one of the richest nations on earth and was free to spend its money however he deemed fit. He was leading a war in Yemen and getting to know politicians in the world's capitals. And that came after three workaholic years of reforming his father's charities and building political capital with powerful Al Saud members. Now it was time to celebrate.

That required a discreet place in keeping with his outsized new status. The Maldives were the perfect choice: a stunning setting in the open ocean replete with tucked-away resorts that could be closely controlled for as long as the prince wanted, overseen by a government so sympathetic to the Saudis that it was discussing selling an archipelago to the kingdom.

Mohammed had first visited Velaa about a year earlier with his father's entourage and was taken by the resort. Its Czech developer acquired the rights to build up a pristine island and designed it to be one of the world's most luxurious and expensive destinations. Velaa's four dozen or so villas, many built on platforms over a coral reef, have private decks and swimming pools. Each comes with a butler. There's a disco and a snowmaking machine so revelers can frolic in a blizzard by a tropical beach.

Since the Maldives government prohibits resorts from putting up buildings higher than the surrounding trees, Velaa's developer installed extremely tall palm trees along one beach so he could erect a tower with a view over the ocean. Its roof just reaches the crowns of the transplanted palms. Beneath that tower is a cellar stocked with exorbitantly priced French wine. And that's separate from the resort's main restaurant, which is built over the water so diners can watch sea turtles swim below while eating meals prepared by a gourmet chef.

Velaa has a combination of service and secrecy hard to match anywhere in the world. The resort's general manager during Mohammed's first visit, an experienced hotel executive from Malta named Hans Cauchi, impressed the prince. His staff members were impeccably trained, some by the International Institute of Modern Butlers, and understood how to be simultaneously attentive and discreet. Even the back-office staff knew to bow whenever Mohammed or King Salman walked by.

By the time the 2015 party was being planned, Cauchi no longer worked for Velaa. Instead he was doing work for Mohammed, facilitating luxury deals like home and yacht purchases. Mohammed enlisted him to help organize the 2015 party.

It was a vacation fit for a prince, starting with what workers called a "buyout" of the resort. That meant Mohammed and his guests had the entire island to themselves for close to a month. The Miami rapper Pitbull agreed to attend, though he stayed at another resort on a nearby island. The Korean pop star Psy and Afrojack, one of the world's most popular DJs, came too.

Money wasn't an issue for Mohammed. His office agreed that each of the resort's three-hundred-plus employees would get a $5,000 bonus, a big deal for workers who made $1,000 to $1,200 per month. And that was before the expected cash tips.

To maintain the prince's privacy, Velaa managers told staff they were not to bring smartphones onto the island during the visit. Each could bring a basic Nokia 3310 or no phone at all. Two Velaa employees got fired on the spot for breaking the rule.

There was a good reason for secrecy. Mohammed knew that Saudi Arabia's young people were tired of decades of obscene spending by the ruling family and frustrated by online accounts of princes' ostentatious homes, spending sprees at Harrods, and sports cars racing through the streets of Mayfair. He was cultivating the image of a reformer and didn't want to be seen in the same light as the famously spoiled princes of his generation—like King Fahd's son Abdulaziz bin Fahd, for example, a powerful prince famous for traveling the world with an entourage of two dozen, which has been dogged by sordid tales of sex and violence described in court filings. In 2012 a member of his retinue was convicted of drugging and raping a woman at the Plaza Hotel in Manhattan, where Abdulaziz had rented out a block of rooms.

Such behavior carried a growing political risk for a family who cast themselves as benevolent and pious, ruling their growing country with generosity, a steady hand, and a longtime alliance with some of Islam's most conservative clerics. Flouting the rules of Islam while imposing strict religious laws on their people was an easy way to lose popularity at home. Every time a prince is seen blowing millions of dollars on parties with alcohol and scantily clad models, a fissure spreads in the existing network of fractures between the rulers and the ruled.

Mohammed believed the changing demographics of Saudi Arabia made the concern urgent. A sizeable portion of Saudis live near the poverty line, and even the well educated struggle to find work in the kingdom's smaller cities and poorer, Shia-dominated Eastern Province. The key ingredients for instability were already there, and Mohammed was careful not to stir them up with new resentment of the royal family. He'd seen what could happen during the Arab Spring, when the Muslim Brotherhood, a ninety-year-old Islamist movement, temporarily won the presidency of Egypt citing the high-flying, alcohol-drenched ways of Saudi royals as proof of the corruption of the Gulf regimes.

So it was especially important that the Saudi people not find out that Mohammed was paying Velaa some $50 million for a vacation with his entourage.

Once the guests arrived, Velaa's own servers were kept at the periphery; the prince's party brought service staff to attend to individual needs, apparently, two Maldivian workers said, because the Saudis didn't want to be seen drinking by residents of another Muslim country.

Velaa's butlers and cleaners and chefs were surprised by how few Saudis there were, compared to the huge number of non-Saudi women. Just a few dozen men came from the kingdom, all friends and relatives of Mohammed, staff were told. Once they arrived, they retired to their villas and pretty much stayed there until the evening, though Mohammed and some friends did take at least one jet ski ride. Workers weren't sure if they were afraid of being photographed on the beach by oceangoing paparazzi or were just hewing to the nocturnal schedule customary in the Saudi summer.

Once the sun went down and the entertainers arrived, the men emerged. A DJ (some nights a band) set up on the main dance floor, near the pool, while smaller acts set up on other stages around the island. One night Afrojack, a Dutch DJ who performs for stadium crowds, put on a show. He was playing electronic beats that started calmly and climaxed to throbbing dance grooves when an excited Mohammed climbed onto the stage. The men and models cheered when Mohammed took over the DJ table and started playing records of his choice while Afrojack skulked away muttering, careful to curse out loud only when he was out of the prince's earshot.

The parties continued until dawn, when many of the men retired to a villa. They'd emerge late in the afternoon.

Even during a time of revelry, Mohammed seemed unable to completely lose himself. Walking during the day in shorts and a T-shirt with a couple of friends, he seemed to turn inward, says someone who observed him there. While the other men spoke animatedly, Mohammed was silent, apparently thinking about something more serious than women and music.

Then all of a sudden it was over. News of Mohammed's visit leaked in a local publication, and Iranian-backed news picked it up. Less than a week after the trip started, Mohammed and his delegation were gone. The women left soon after.

Mohammed was also buying some serious toys. He rented the *Serene*—a 439-foot yacht that Bill Gates rented in 2014 for $5 million a week—for a half day after spotting it from the air. Mohammed loved it. The yacht had an underwater view-ing room, a jacuzzi, two helicopter pads, and a business-style conference room. It was sleek and luxurious, perfect for hosting VIPs, but it could also transform into a party palace for nights with close friends.

Over the subsequent six weeks, Mohammed's team negotiated with agents of Yuri Shefler, the owner. They finally reached a deal for 429 million euros, about double the original cost. His team also bought a garish French château near Versailles—with fountains, stately grounds, and even a moat—for more than $300 million.

The ultimate owner of the yacht and the French palace was Eight Investment Company, headed by Mohammed's close friend Bader al-Asaker. It's part of a constellation of companies in Saudi Arabia set up by Mohammed in 2014 as he started to make serious money. The company in turn was owned by Three Hundred Fifty Six Holding Company, the holding company for many of his personal assets that dated back to his stock-trading endeavors in 2012. The holding company in turn owned other companies given numbers for names, includ-ing Fifty Five Investment Company and Ninety Investment Company.

Over time, some of these assets would blend with those of the state. The *Serene* would at times act as a floating *majlis* for meetings with foreign officials and high-profile business delegations in the years ahead. Eventually, it would become the centerpiece of an eleven-boat flotilla that comprised an offshore palace for Mohammed to relax away from the watching eyes of his family.

Watching from Riyadh and their multi-million-dollar homes abroad, Mohammed's rivals were increasingly uneasy. This was no longer a game of waiting for King Salman to die so that a son of King Abdullah or the late Crown Prince Nayef, long-time minister of interior, could take the throne as the first of the Al Saud's third generation to become king. Mohammed was already running the show, with his father the king's blessing. Even though Mohammed bin Nayef, the crown prince, stood between Mohammed and the throne, the young prince was taking steps that made him the effective leader of the country with more power than any king had ever had before.

Mohammed bin Salman's appointment in May 2015 as chairman of a new government council overseeing Saudi Arabia's state oil company was particularly galling to many uncles and cousins. Aramco was the source of wealth for the entire country, and a chunk of its profits kept the Al Saud living in luxury. Plus, if Salman had wanted to put one of his sons in charge of Aramco, wouldn't Abdulaziz—for years a deputy oil minister well versed in international petroleum negotiations—be the obvious choice?

One of Mohammed's chief rivals was Turki bin Abdullah, the son whom the deceased King Abdullah insulted as fat from his hospital bed. A former air force pilot whom his father appointed governor of Riyadh in 2014, Turki liked to argue he was fourth in line to the throne. But if Mohammed ascended instead, the young king could rule until long after Turki had grown old and frail.

Since leaving the air force, Turki had grown ostentatious, often traveling in a convoy of two 737 jetliners with friends, advisors, and so much luggage it took hours to disembark. He also had a modern-day harem—a group of attractive women who lived lavishly all over the world on a monthly check on the condition that they pick up and meet him wherever on request. Even when paying an informal visit to the Riyadh palaces of his sister or brother, Turki would wear a tan or black *bisht*, a cloak embroidered with gold thread, the Saudi equivalent of a formal suit.

Believing himself a victim of his father's relatively miserly ways, Turki was also obsessed with money. And it had gotten him embroiled in scandals, including a distant but important role in the roiling 1Malaysia Development Berhad sovereign wealth fund debacle that was just coming to light in late 2015. He received tens of millions of dollars from 1MDB allegedly for his role in part of the scheme where his business advisor used his connections and name to make it look like Malaysia was entering a joint venture with the government of Saudi Arabia. The maneuver is said to have allowed the conspirators to pocket hundreds of millions of dollars. Turki and others implicated deny the charges.

As with many rich men, Turki's taste for power was growing. Speaking to his advisors, he saw Mohammed as a threat but felt he could put together an alliance to challenge Salman's son. His plan rested on Saudi Arabia's peculiar military structure.

As a way to balance power within the family, the kingdom's armed forces were split between three separate ministries, each commanded by a different son of Ibn Saud. For decades, the once-powerful Prince Sultan and his sons controlled the Ministry of Defense, which oversaw the army and air force. The National Guard was under the auspices of King Abdullah and his clan. Prince Nayef and his sons had long controlled the third branch, the Ministry of Interior. Salman put Mohammed in charge of the Defense Ministry when he took the throne but left the other branches with the families that had long controlled them.

Turki thought the young Mohammed could be kept in check. "He only has the army," Turki told an advisor. "He isn't as strong as he thinks."

But developing a plan to sideline Mohammed was fraught. He had a reputation for sidestepping plots against him and what one confidant calls "an incredible capacity to sense danger." Abdullah's sons feared he might be using wiretaps, much as princes years earlier were convinced that Salman was listening in on their private conversations.

Turki tried to quietly feel out the US government about a possible coup, meeting former intelligence agency lawyers in places like Los Angeles to avoid word getting back to Salman and Mohammed. He also avoided meeting with government officials directly, a move bound to get picked up somewhere. "I want to know if the government will support me if there is no choice but to take over," he told one lawyer, pitching a new government led by the sons of Abdullah and Nayef. Turki painted Mohammed as erratic, a despot in the making.

Mohammed bin Nayef was more deliberate. Like his father who led the ministry before him, the prince known as MBN was wary of doing anything that could upset the family balance. He also had a deep faith in Al Saud family inertia, which for decades prevented any big upheaval among its top ranks. And he'd been closer to US intelligence and security officials than perhaps any other Saudi for almost fifteen years, working as the kingdom's key contact on antiterrorism initiatives. The importance of the US relationship, MBN figured, should help keep him safe.

By mid-2015, Mohammed's powers were broader than ever, but he knew that meant little if he couldn't pull off his reform plans. Sitting around the long table with members of the Security and Political Affairs Council, which he had recently joined, he could see just how difficult those changes would be.

The members included MBN, who seemed to oppose any change at all, even if he didn't say so outright. With every proposal—women driving, opening up to tourism—he or his advisors would list the potential consequences. There was also Musaad al-Aiban, the official with the longest tenure, who was another force for continuity. Others like Saud bin Faisal Al Saud, the Princeton-educated foreign affairs advisor who was in his last days with Parkinson's disease and other ailments, seemed to focus on age-old conflicts like the Israeli-Palestinian issue. Miteb bin Abdullah, the saturnine son of the former king and owner of the Hôtel de Crillon in Paris, could barely conceal his contempt for Mohammed, his small brush of a mustache and double chin framing a seemingly perpetual frown. As Mohammed consolidated power, the council would gradually shed those he believed recalcitrant in the face of change.

Mohammed also understood that to strengthen his position, he needed to burnish his image. Radically remaking the country would require buy-in from Saudi youth, since more than 60 percent of the population was under thirty. They were the least powerful people in the country, many struggling to find jobs and chafing under the kingdom's difficult climate for entrepreneurialism. But they were the most educated and outnumbered the vested religious ideologues and sulking princes many times over. As the Arab Spring showed, discontented youth could also pose a threat to Al Saud rule. Or they could be co-opted by a reform-minded ruler and become the base from which his power sprang.

This stratagem seemed not to occur to Mohammed's rivals, who focused their efforts on the traditional means of building power: cultivating the old religious leaders and tribal elders. It would be his rivals' biggest mistake.

To get the youth on his side, Mohammed needed to connect with them where they spent their time: the internet. In a society that prohibited public interaction between men and women, drinking alcohol, dancing, attending concerts, moviegoing, or even smoking a hookah pipe, young people's online lives became a crucial outlet and a way to commune.

Perhaps just as importantly, the internet showed Saudi youth exactly what they were missing thanks to their ossified monarchy and its commitment to upholding fundamentalist religious laws to keep favor with the clerics who, for decades, helped keep them in power. Largely barred from mixing or seeking entertainment in public, they lived increasingly virtually, watching videos on YouTube and Netflix and following international celebrity culture through Facebook, Twitter, and Instagram.

Mohammed grasped the significance of social media long before the kingdom's geriatric princes. In a country without polling or elections, Twitter could reveal how the public felt about a policy or a leader and help an ambitious young prince prove to older princes that he had the public's support—an important consideration for a family living in perpetual fear of a people's uprising. On the other hand, negative sentiment on Twitter could undermine a ruler. In 2014, near the end of King Abdullah's reign, Mohammed became concerned about anonymous Twitter users spreading claims that his father had dementia. If it got out of hand, if the rumors became accepted as fact by Saudis and foreigners, Salman's brothers might feel pressure to elevate one of his rivals, cutting the Salman clan off from its claim to the throne.

So Mohammed had his deputy Bader al-Asaker—the man behind the yacht and château purchases and the head of his MiSK foundation—begin a years-long effort to unmask Twitter critics. The endeavor would eventually use cutting-edge Israeli spy technology but began with a much more conventional strategy: bribery. The account of the effort set out below is based on Justice Department legal filings, which at the time of writing amount to allegations since a court case was still underway in 2020.

Asaker, a kindly looking man with dark, rectangular glasses who wouldn't be out of place at an IT conference, wasn't really a government official in 2014. He worked for Mohammed personally. But as an employee of the crown prince's son, he could gain access pretty much anywhere. On June 13 of that year, Asaker traveled to San Francisco to meet Twitter's head of

Middle East partnerships, an Egyptian American named Ahmad Abouammo.

It was framed as a routine visit by an important figure from an important Twitter market. Abouammo showed Asaker around Twitter headquarters in San Francisco's South of Market district. Asaker explained that he worked for an important prince who used Twitter extensively. The men exchanged contact information and arranged to follow up in London in the fall. During that meeting, Asaker gave the Twitter employee a gift: a Hublot watch worth at least $20,000.

Then came the ask. Twitter users were making trouble for Mohammed, including one nicknamed Mujtahidd, who had been brazenly criticizing the royal family and publishing rumors about senior members that often had a kernel of truth. It was a political mess, but it wasn't criminal or terrorist in nature, so Twitter wouldn't reveal the identity of such users to Saudi law enforcement. Asaker asked if Abouammo could help them find information on the people who registered these accounts.

Abouammo complied, using his access to internal systems to find Mujtahidd's email address and phone number. It was a potentially reckless move by the Twitter employee, possibly unmasking critics of a government that locked up dissidents.

Such requests continued for months. Over that time Salman became king, Mohammed became crown prince, and Asaker found himself working for one of the most powerful men in Saudi Arabia. Asaker would pay more than $200,000 to Abouammo, deposited in a Lebanese bank account that Abouammo had a relative open for him. "Proactive and reactively we will delete evil, my brother," Abouammo texted Asaker after one deposit of $9,911.

Abouammo had limited technical skill, and a single mole was hardly a reliable way of ensuring consistent access to Twitter users' private information. Asaker wanted a better spy. As luck would have it, Twitter had hired a young Saudi named Ali Alzabarah, who was educated in the United States on a Saudi scholarship.

Living in San Francisco, Alzabarah struck his friends as a typical software engineer—a "nerd," one friend called him admiringly. He didn't seem interested in things other than software and didn't speak much until the conversation turned to programming or the future of technology. Away from work, Alzabarah seemed to spend most of his time at home or socializing with a small group of expat Saudis who worked at tech firms in the Bay Area.

In February 2015, Asaker had an intermediary reach out to Alzabarah. It turned out that the engineer felt deeply patriotic toward Saudi Arabia and wanted to help the kingdom however he could. And while Alzabarah's job entailed maintaining systems to keep Twitter working properly and not accessing user accounts, Twitter allowed him access to private user information. For many users, that included phone numbers and email addresses as well as IP addresses, which can identify the physical location where a person logs in. That meant that in some instances, Alzabarah could not only help unmask an anonymous regime critic but also pinpoint the person's location.

A few months later, Asaker traveled to the United States as part of an official Saudi delegation and asked Alzabarah to meet him. "I am traveling to Washington at the request of the office of Mohammed bin Salman," Alzabarah told his wife in a text message.

Soon after that meeting, Alzabarah began using internal Twitter systems to comb through the account information of more than six thousand Twitter users. Mujtahidd, in particular, was an ongoing target. He was tweeting out what he claimed was private information about the royal family, and some of it, like the looming dismissal of King Salman's brother Muqrin as crown prince in April 2015, turned out to be true. The following month, Mujtahidd posted embarrassing documents from France detailing how the widow of a former crown prince was refusing to pay millions of dollars for luxurious hotel stays.

Days later Alzabarah accessed Mujtahidd's account and got his phone number and IP address at Asaker's request. Further requests for other users followed. Alzabarah told Asaker that one user split time between Turkey and Iraq. Another was based in Turkey. A third, a Saudi, was "a professional" who used encryption to conceal his identity, though once he signed in without encryption, and Alzabarah was able to track his IP address.

The Twitter engineer realized he was providing valuable information to Mohammed's men—some of the accounts he was accessing were, the Royal Court suspected, connected to terrorism, and Saudi officials announced a $1.9 million reward to anyone who helped avert an attack. In his private Apple Notes account, Alzabarah drafted language to ask Asaker about whether he could claim that money.

Alzabarah spoke by phone with Asaker on June 18 and the next day accessed the Twitter account of Omar Abdulaziz, a Saudi man who had obtained asylum in Canada after the kingdom cut off his schooling in retribution for public critiques of the government and who would form a strong bond with a Saudi journalist and regime critic named Jamal Khashoggi.

As the surveillance efforts gained momentum and sophistication, Alzabarah took a trip to Riyadh, where he continued accessing user accounts from Saudi Arabia. Now that the one-time "nerd" had become an international man of mystery, he wanted credit from the Saudi government and some reassurances of aid if he got into trouble. "Where am I, and how is this going to affect me?" Alzabarah contemplated in another Apple Notes entry, wondering whether he could get government help for his troubled father or business training from Mohammed's foundation. With the risks he was taking for senior officials, he wanted a "permanent" job, "something that secures my future and my family's."

Alzabarah returned to San Francisco and to Twitter and continued providing information to Asaker about Mujtahidd, the government critic. Soon after, he scored an apparent victory: Mujtahidd's account was shut down, and Mujtahidd claimed online that Twitter had told him the account was "compromised," though he was able to recover it days later.

Alzabarah continued his work for Asaker and was promoted to a higher engineering position at Twitter. "As much as I am happy for the position, I am happier with and very proud of my work with you," he wrote in an apparent draft of a letter to Asaker.

Understanding that human assets like Alzabarah would come and go—that they could get scared, or get caught, or lose their access to valuable information—Mohammed's men developed other ways of spying under the auspices of another of Mohammed's confidants, Saud al-Qahtani, a former employee of King Abdullah's Royal Court who quickly became enamored with Mohammed and later one of his most trusted minions. In June 2015, Saud sent an email to the head of Hacking Team, an Italian company that developed cloak-and-dagger software for governments to spy online. The king's office, Qahtani wrote, "would like to be in productive cooperation with you and develop a long and strategic partnership." A trove of internal Hacking Team documents that leaked online shows the Saudi government ended up paying millions of dollars for the spyware.

Qahtani told Mohammed that he could go much further than seeking out individual critics and could harness Twitter to gain support for his reforms and assess how his popularity compared with that of other members of the royal family. It turned out that an obscure group funded by the Ministry of Education was already working on a project that could be turned to those purposes.

Under the auspices of a Saudi computer scientist named Nasir al-Biqami, a group of programmers led by an American who worked for Lockheed was using artificial intelligence to understand how ideas and strategies developed on Twitter. Qahtani brought the group under his auspices in the Royal Court and had the programmers examine Twitter sentiment about Mohammed and some of his key rivals, including some of Abdullah's sons and the crown prince, Mohammed bin Nayef.

Saud determined that Mohammed needed a wider presence, a stronger effort to burnish his image and attack those trying to tarnish him. In an office in the Royal Court buildings in Riyadh's Diplomatic District, Saud assembled a group of specialists who created thousands of fake Twitter accounts with photos and names that appeared to belong to regular young Saudis. They tweeted praise of Mohammed and his plans and criticism of rivals.

Remarkably, Turki bin Abdullah's team had also hit on the importance of social media, which they were viewing more as a weapon. They hired a consultant in Switzerland who flooded Twitter and Instagram with propaganda against Mohammed bin Salman.

Qahtani struck back with even more aggressive and better-funded efforts, using accounts that appeared to belong to foreigners tweeting support for Mohammed. Some accounts were fake. Others, like those of Americans, including a deceased meteorologist, a TV financial commentator, and an Olympic skier, were real accounts taken control of by the Saudis, a British professor based in Qatar found. Qahtani also started keeping track of people who criticized the prince, sometimes attacking them with armies of Twitter bots. He earned the nickname

"Mr. Hashtag" for his aggressive Twitter presence, and his army became known as the "flies" among young Saudis.

Qahtani's efforts came to overshadow Asaker's alleged Twitter infiltration just as Asaker's well was drying up. His mole, Alzabarah, turned out to be less careful than one might expect a worried tech expert to be. He spoke with Asaker on an open phone line and communicated via email. US intelligence agents picked up on it.

It was a sensitive situation. Intelligence agencies don't work with the goal of developing criminal cases in US courts. They're focused on things happening outside the United States, and using the vast amounts of data they gather to mount court cases opens up all sorts of potential problems, including revealing who's being listened to abroad.

But sometimes they come across things that clearly deserve an examination by prosecutors. A US company's employees taking cash from a foreign government to access user information is one example. So intelligence officials passed the information on to the Justice Department, where it found its way to the San Francisco FBI office.

Late in 2015, an FBI agent walked downhill from San Francisco's Kennedy-era federal building in the squalid Tenderloin, down a block littered with syringes, to Market Street, where Twitter has its headquarters. The agent sat down with company lawyers and broke the news: Twitter had a mole.

By that time Abouammo had left the company, but Alzabarah was still active. The situation was sensitive, the agent explained, and the investigation was at an early stage. The agent asked that the company not tell Alzabarah what was going on—it could imperil the case if he got wind of the investigation.

But Twitter's lawyers were skeptical of the feds. Like many in the tech community, they resented law enforcement's presumption that it could get whatever private information it wanted. User data was sacrosanct as far as the Twitter lawyers were concerned. Even if the US government was requesting the data in an effort to bust someone who was giving it to a foreign government, Twitter was reluctant to cooperate. So rather than follow the FBI's request to keep things quiet to assist the case, Twitter lawyers brought Alzabarah in the following afternoon, accused him of improperly accessing user accounts, and told him he was temporarily suspended.

Alzabarah went home and called a friend, a Saudi-born venture capitalist he'd met in the Bay Area tech community. His friend picked him up a couple hours later, and Alzabarah told him he had a problem. He'd been "curious," started looking into some user accounts, and got busted. Now he was suspended from Twitter and figured he had to head back to the kingdom.

"Why?" his friend asked while they sat in his car. "I don't think that this is serious." If there were some sort of legal or security concern, he told Alzabarah, he would've been detained by the police or something, not allowed to leave on his own.

"No," Alzabarah said, "I need to go." He called Asaker on his friend's phone, and eventually Asaker got in touch with the Saudi consul in Los Angeles, phone records obtained by the FBI show. After a long back-and-forth, Alzabarah got on the phone with the consul general shortly after midnight. Less than seven hours later, Alzabarah and his wife and daughter were on a flight to Riyadh via LA. From the flight, he sent a resignation email to his bosses at Twitter.

Justice Department officials were livid. Twitter had blown up their case, tipping off a man they'd hoped to arrest—a man they would accuse of violating Twitter's rules and compromising the privacy of its users in the name of espionage for a foreign government. Now he was out of reach. As for Alzabarah's concerns, Asaker helped secure his future by giving him a job with Mohammed's foundation. Alzabarah's responsibility, according to Justice Department court filings, was "to monitor and manipulate social media" for the benefit of the kingdom.

———

Mohammed's Twitter push seemed to be working. Many Saudis seemed genuinely impressed by his fast-moving reforms, even some who had historically been willing to criticize Saudi policies. Jamal Khashoggi, a veteran journalist and former Saudi government official with more than one million Twitter followers, was initially among the converted. In an interview with *Middle East Monitor* in 2015, he defended Operation Decisive Storm as an important sign that Saudi Arabia wouldn't tolerate Iran's efforts to control the region. And he seemed enthusiastic about Mohammed's reforms. "Saudi should be part of this renaissance to freedom," he told an interviewer. "I want my country to be on the side of history."

Khashoggi, with a tidy white-and-black beard and a wry smile when telling a good story, had been hovering around the Saudi Royal Court since the 1980s. He had seen a lot in his career, embedding with Osama bin Laden and his band of jihadists in Afghanistan and serving in the Saudi embassy in Washington, DC, and he had veered in and out of favor with senior royals.

Though Khashoggi had once praised bin Laden for his efforts in Afghanistan, the journalist opposed his international terrorism. After bin Laden was killed, he wrote on Twitter, "I collapsed into tears a while ago, heartbroken for you Abu Abdullah," using an intimate nickname for bin Laden that referred to him as the father of Abdullah. "You were beautiful and brave in those beautiful days in Afghanistan, before you surrendered to hatred and rage."

His political alliances and criticisms of the Al Saud sometimes veered toward the edge of what was acceptable; sometimes he crossed the line. An interview with a Bahraini activist caused authorities to shut down the Al Arab television channel, which he cofounded, hours after it began broadcasting.

But Khashoggi was treated almost like an eccentric family member, always seeming to come back into favor even after episodes that would have ended the careers of other journalists. He once accepted a payment of $100,000 from a Saudi business partner of Turki bin Abdullah to write fawning articles about the prime minister of Malaysia—a small incident in the larger 1Malaysia Development Berhad scandal that wouldn't come out until later. But in 2015, as someone who had previously criticized the kingdom's leadership, his praise of Mohammed carried weight with foreigners who had influence. He was a charming and wily character, part journalist, part public relations officer, and later part dissident.

Buffing his popular reputation was one part of Mohammed's image-making effort. Just as important was his private campaign to show foreign leaders that despite his youth, inexperience, and rank as second in line to the throne, the prince was a person who mattered in the new Saudi Arabia.

So, after taking over as defense minister, starting the bombing campaign in Yemen, and gaining control over Saudi Arabia's oil company, Mohammed decided to start acting like a head of state. At about 10 p.m. one evening he sat down with a trusted intermediary, US ambassador Joe Westphal, in his Riyadh office.

Westphal, an affable veteran of American military administration, was the archetype of an old-school diplomat: warm and disarming but slyly perceptive. With a round face and easy smile, he could lower the temperature of a tense meeting with a goofy joke or self-deprecating story. Whenever he visited the United States, he made sure to buy children's books at a favorite bookstore in Greenwich Village that he'd bring back to King Salman—they were unavailable in the kingdom, and the king loved to read them to his grandchildren.

Once Westphal brought Salman a copy of "Rip Van Winkle." "It's a story that should resonate with you," he told Salman. "Imagine if a man fell asleep when you became governor of Riyadh and awoke 48 years later, when you left the role? You would see an unrecognizably modern place."

While he flattered and laughed, Westphal was also zeroing in on Mohammed long before Salman's coronation, reporting back to White House officials that the young man possessed a curiosity, ambition, and work ethic rare in the Royal Court. Mohammed responded to Westphal's attention. He felt the ambassador listened to him, and as he gained power, he increasingly used Westphal as a sounding board and a conduit to Washington, DC. That meant regular late-night meetings with the ambassador.

At that 10 p.m. meeting, Mohammed told the ambassador that President Vladimir Putin had invited him to the Kremlin to meet in person. But, Mohammed said, he would prefer an official visit to the United States first. An invitation would have to come from President Barack Obama, Westphal replied. In the meantime, he added, if Mohammed did meet Putin, the ambassador would love to hear about it.

Mohammed coveted the US meeting since it would show, unequivocally, that the upstart prince had become a world leader who respected the special bond between the two countries. But the US president generally met with other heads of state, not their heirs. And Mohammed wasn't even the heir. At that point, Crown Prince Mohammed bin Nayef was first in line for the throne. Mohammed bin Salman came after him, making him two steps removed.

So Mohammed decided to meet Putin first but also figured

out a back door to the White House. With tensions high due to negotiations the United States was conducting with Saudi nemesis Iran to curb its nuclear ambitions, Obama officials decided to convene the United States' Persian Gulf allies at Camp David to discuss the region. King Salman declined to attend, and Obama staffers worried it was a snub until learning the king was feeling unwell. In his place he sent the crown prince, Mohammed bin Nayef, and his son Mohammed bin Salman.

MBN, by age and title, was the senior prince. But a security official who attended meetings with both princes during the trip says Mohammed "was not deferring to MBN," a dynamic the Americans took close note of. Mohammed offered his thoughts on just about anything US officials asked about without the normal submissiveness to an older, more senior official that is characteristic of Saudi culture. Obama asked for improvements in Saudi Arabia's human rights record.

Mohammed used the trip to unveil his aggressive economic reform strategy to Obama's key deputies. He'd been working on it for more than two years, since Abdullah was king, and now he had a chance to show it to leaders of the world's biggest economic power. In the West Wing's Roosevelt Room, under a portrait of FDR, who had laid the foundation of the Saudi-US alliance with Ibn Saud aboard a ship in 1945, Mohammed detailed to officials including Treasury Secretary Jack Lew his plan to move the Saudi economy away from oil.

The plan was slickly put together, clearly polished by American consultants who knew how to make a near-utopian project sound realistic. The kingdom, Mohammed explained, would institute local taxes for the first time, cut subsidies for electricity, and encourage private-sector hiring of Saudis rather than foreign laborers. It would redirect oil wealth into foreign investments to move away from the near-total reliance on petroleum income.

The ideas sounded fine, but the numbers, especially the

assumptions about how quickly the Saudi economy would grow and how many new jobs it would produce, seemed extraordinarily optimistic. When Lew asked follow-up questions, Mohammed's answers seemed shallow. "It was clear that he couldn't really go more than one layer down in the substance of the economic plans," says one person who attended the meeting.

Lew nodded and listened while the prince talked, and afterward he told another White House official that Mohammed had unusual confidence for someone so young and so new in government. Another White House official at the meeting had a less diplomatic takeaway: The math behind the prince's economic assumptions was wrong.

And that wasn't just a problem for Saudi Arabia. If Mohammed was really going to cut handouts to his people, impose new taxes, and increase their utility bills without the economy creating the new jobs he projected, Saudi Arabia could be thrown into turmoil that could destabilize the region.

Days later, Mohammed traveled to Russia, met with Putin, and signed several government-to-government deals of relatively little consequence.

Over the ensuing summer, White House officials noticed a shift in their conversations with the Saudi ambassador to the United States, Adel al-Jubeir, who had been a fixture in Washington circles for close to two decades. Jubeir began speaking more and more about Mohammed in casual meetings and in formal talks like one with Secretary of State John Kerry at his house in Nantucket that August.

Jubeir was "selling MBS as the future 50-year king of Saudi Arabia," recalls one former US official, "which was confusing." Mohammed was second in line to the throne. Why would he be spoken of as the future king when his cousin MBN was supposed to be next?

"We discounted it a little bit, because he just seemed like the guy who hooked Adel," the official says, suggesting the Saudi foreign minister had simply been taken in by the charismatic prince rather than that there had been a genuine power shift. Staffers in the White House and State Department found the conversations awkward—they didn't want to get involved in some kind of domestic battle in the House of Saud. "It's not our job to pick the next ruler of Saudi Arabia," they told one another.

In September, Mohammed returned to the White House, this time accompanied by his father—recovered from the flu—for a more formal meeting with Obama. By then, the United States had finalized its nuclear deal with Iran, and Mohammed made his frustration clear. After dinner at Kerry's Georgetown home, Mohammed walked over to Kerry's baby grand piano and started playing Beethoven's *Moonlight Sonata*, a performance so surprising to guests that it was included in an official report the State Department sent to the White House. He later told an advisor that he had taught himself to play several piano compositions.

Mohammed also shed the polite acquiescence Americans were used to hearing in face-to-face meetings with Saudi princes, who typically avoided direct confrontation. Without raising his voice or losing his temper, sometimes with a smile, Mohammed told Kerry that Obama had made three key mistakes in the Middle East: abandoning Egypt's Hosni Mubarak during the Arab Spring, failing to use force when Syria crossed the "red line" with its use of chemical weapons, and negotiating the Iran nuclear deal without Saudi buy-in. But when Salman made public statements with Obama on the trip, the king expressed support for the Iran deal, not wanting to show a public rift between the allies.

It was a dizzying summer for Mohammed. He'd been a senior official for less than a year, and he was treading into a thicket of geopolitical difficulties. Obama, the leader of Saudi Arabia's strongest ally, seemed standoffish, skeptical of the monarchy, and willing to negotiate with Saudi Arabia's sworn enemy, Iran. The United States' longtime antagonist in the Kremlin seemed calculating and transactional, a leader without much to offer Saudi Arabia. Mohammed expressed dismay to a friend in Riyadh upon his return.

But in an important sense the visits were a victory: News agencies around the world, and most importantly in Saudi Arabia, showed Mohammed bin Salman having serious talks with the leaders of other countries. The images of him talking with Putin and Obama were evidence of his importance abroad and made him look fit to be king.

Mohammed's rising profile may have helped boost his status with the young Saudis he was targeting. But it made his enemies at home anxious and increasingly desperate. One rival, identifying himself only as a grandson of Ibn Saud, decided to take a stab at the jugular. He penned searing anonymous letters to senior members of the royal family that he also posted on Twitter, where they were shared and read millions of times. Newspapers, including the *Guardian* in the United Kingdom, wrote prominent stories about the anonymous letters.

The criticisms were harsh. King Salman, the writer said, was "incapacitated," and the kingdom was being run by "juvenile fools" operating "behind the facade of a helpless king." Chief among the fools was "the corrupt and destructive thief of the homeland, Mohammed bin Salman," the writer said. He called for Salman's surviving brothers to depose the king and appoint someone older and more experienced than Mohammed to run government affairs. "We are calling for the sons of Ibn Saud from the oldest, Bandar, to the youngest, Muqrin, to make an urgent meeting with the senior family members to investigate the situation and find out what can be done to save the country, to make changes in the important ranks, to bring in expertise from the ruling family whatever generation they are from," he wrote.

Outwardly nothing happened in Saudi Arabia. There was no comment from the Royal Court and no official confirmation that the letters had been read or received by the king. But Mohammed was enraged and ordered an investigation into who was leaking. His enemies were getting bold, so he'd need to show them he was stronger and more driven.

Chapter 4

I AM THE MASTERMIND

September 2015

Mecca had end-of-world vibes just after 5 p.m. on September 11, 2015. The sky grew dark with sand and rain, with whistling, sixty-mile-per-hour winds. Suddenly, almost in slow motion, one of the more than a dozen cranes standing over the Great Mosque of Mecca began to tip over. As the crane's 620-foot boom—bigger than the Washington Monument—crashed over its walls, the crane seemed to melt under its own crushing weight. Inside the courtyard, the home of the black cube called the Kaaba that Muslims direct themselves toward in prayer, the buckling metal crushed the bodies inside, killing 111, many of them Egyptian and Bangladeshi pilgrims on their once-in-a-lifetime journey to the center of Islam. More than four hundred others were injured. There was blood and broken marble everywhere.

It was an unspeakable tragedy, the worst crane accident in recorded history. The blame abruptly turned toward the company overseeing the refurbishment of the Great Mosque, or Masjid al-Haram. The Saudi Binladin Group was one of Saudi Arabia's biggest privately owned conglomerates. Its namesake, Mohammed bin Laden, born on the coast of southern Yemen, hitched his wagon to the increasingly wealthy royals during the early years of the kingdom, building palaces and villas and handling high-profile, delicate work in Mecca itself.

Mohammed became the richest nonroyal in the country, and his fifty-six children carried on the legacy after he died in 1967. One of those sons was Osama bin Laden, who founded the al-Qaeda terrorist group that drew America into a series of wars in Iraq and Afghanistan after he coordinated the hijacking of the jetliners that struck the World Trade Center and Pentagon.

The Saudi Binladin Group, owned by sons of Mohammed bin Laden, was overseeing a multiyear renovation of the Great Mosque when the accident took place. Salman and Mohammed were livid. It was a catastrophe for all the people injured and their families, but it was also a blow to the reputation of Saudi Arabia and the ruling Al Saud. The king is the caretaker of Islam's holiest sites, and here was a calamity in the center of Islam itself.

Mecca and Medina, the holy cities, are also the second-largest sources of revenue for the government of Saudi Arabia after oil, bringing in billions of dollars a year. In theory, the money they brought in was the closest thing the country had to a nonoil economy, but even that was a mirage. Mismanagement meant the Saudi government actually paid close to $10 billion a year to keep the holy cities operating at the highest standard. Nonetheless, the royal family rested on its promise to guard the mosques as a pillar of its legitimacy.

For Mohammed bin Salman, the tragedy was an opportunity to expand his already immense powers. Since his father became king, he had held meetings with Bakr bin Laden, the then-sixty-nine-year-old scion of Saudi Binladin Group, about participating in his economic-rejuvenation plans for the country. "We need you to bring your company public," he told Bakr, explaining that expanding the size of the Saudi stock market was a key part of his reform plans. "We can be partners."

Mohammed, aided by consultants, had come to see the family conglomerates as bulky relics of the past. He wanted ownership separated from management, public disclosure of financials, and a vibrant capital market. This also seemed like an easy win, an objective that wouldn't shake the bedrock of Islamic conservatism that seemed to obstruct other projects like letting women drive cars.

But Bakr, a pious and understated man, was wary of change and steeped in the old way of doing things with Saudi royals, particularly King Fahd, who died in 2005, and King Abdullah. Like Saudi Oger Ltd., owned by the Lebanese Hariri family, Binladin Group grew large thanks in part to a keen understanding of what the Al Saud wanted. If that meant building a palace for a new wife in a matter of months, they'd get the job done. Payment could come much later or never at all; the bin Ladens wouldn't make a peep. But here was a young prince with a bigger ask: He wanted to have a say in core business decisions.

Politely, Bakr rebuffed Mohammed, saying the market conditions were not yet ideal. Mohammed was annoyed, suggesting this decision was unwise, considering that the review of all megaprojects could lead to cancellations and a slowing down of work. Bakr called his brothers to discuss his fears.

After the crane collapse, Binladin Group was under attack. King Salman issued a royal decree pausing all contracts with the company, pending an investigation. The business was thrust into the cold, cut off from all further government contracts with payments on existing projects stopped. With some three hundred thousand employees at the time, most of them workers from India and Pakistan, the business quickly burned through its cash and reached a crisis point. Mohammed also made it personal for the bin Laden clan, issuing travel bans for top executives connected to the crane incident and some of the brothers.

Seeing the depth of their problems, Bakr tried everything,

including handing control of the business to a brother as a way of taking full responsibility for the crane accident. He hired a team of Western businessmen led by a German financier to restructure the company, but nothing worked. The deep freeze continued.

Saudi Oger's Saad Hariri, a dual citizen who also happened to be the prime minister of Lebanon, was struggling to keep the cash flowing too. The Oger business was poorly managed, so it had little cushion for a slowdown in payments. Saad desperately tried to win Mohammed bin Salman's approval, building an extension to King Salman's expansive seaside palace in Tangier for Mohammed. And when Mohammed suggested he'd like a more direct passageway in the Royal Court to access the foyer of his cousin Mohammed bin Nayef's section, Saad himself stayed up through the night with workers to cut through marble and concrete to get the job done. Mohammed thanked him but clearly felt no exchange had taken place. Saad hadn't won any goodwill.

Growing up under Kings Fahd and Abdullah, Saad was shocked to find the rules of Al Saud interaction had changed. His family company had made fortunes several times over by getting government business in exchange for building palaces for kings, princes, and high-ranking government officials. Now he was struggling to figure out how to save his family's empire. And King Salman loathed Saad, considering him an obsequious weasel.

Worse yet, Saad was close to the entourage of now deceased King Abdullah, especially to Khalid al-Tuwaijri, the head of Abdullah's Royal Court. For months after his coronation, Salman and his son Mohammed heard tales of the huge sums of money the Hariri family received from Abdullah's sons. Inside and outside the Royal Court, people chattered about the suitcases of cash Saad would take from Riyadh to Beirut or Geneva on his private plane. On one flight in the early 2000s, Saad told a friend riding on the plane that a ten-foot-by-ten-foot stack of leather briefcases full of hundred-dollar bills was for shopping expenses in Switzerland.

What Mohammed found after Abdullah's death, when he finally had full access to the bank accounts of the government and of King Abdullah and his family, was astonishing. Abdullah, who was—for a Saudi king—relatively frugal with his children during his life, left huge sums to his kids. Each daughter got more than $1 billion, and sons got at least twice that much. A literal pile of cash—in the form of hundred-dollar bills—amounting to more than $1 billion was found in one of Abdullah's palaces. Billions of dollars also flowed into the King Abdullah Foundation, a charitable organization set up by the king that his sons now controlled.

And then there was the money that flowed to the people around Abdullah, in particular Tuwaijri, and Abdullah's head of protocol, Mohammed al-Tobaishi. Each man was extremely wealthy for a civil servant and suspiciously close with the Hariri family.

Mohammed had known that Tuwaijri was an enemy for years by the time Salman became king. But Tobaishi managed to keep his job for the first few months of Salman's reign, until he was caught on video slapping a journalist. Salman fired him immediately, and Mohammed dug deeper into Tobaishi's finances. How did a man who was essentially the king's head butler acquire a huge ranch outside Riyadh, a horse farm, a stable of luxury cars, and enough money to partner in a London investment fund with two of King Salman's children? And how could he afford to build an Arabian horse stud farm staffed by foreign racing experts and veterinarians?

A large chunk of that wealth was tied to the Hariris. Rafic, Saad's father and the man who built the family company, Saudi

Oger, and served as prime minister of Lebanon before his son, had carefully cultivated Tobaishi for years, since before Abdullah became king.

Mohammed escalated his clashes with corrupt civil servants and private-sector operators who built their fortunes through bribes. Appointed by his father to lead an economic transformation, the prince expected businessmen and royal family members to fall in line as a patriotic duty, even if this meant taking financial losses. It was a huge shift in a country where, for decades, things simply did not change. The same wealthy companies paid kick-backs to the same royals and government officials, and no king or prince was willing to make the enemies that changing the system would require.

The one thing you'd never hear, at least in public, was a complaint. Privately, the children of the deceased King Abdullah would grumble. Sitting with his sisters, Turki bin Abdullah— the would-be heir to the throne fast being marginalized by Mohammed—complained that Salman had always been strange. He said that Salman had been Riyadh's governor for forty-eight years because he was too unpredictable to lead an important government ministry. But Abdullah's children were careful to keep the complaints private—so careful that after he died, they made a habit of leaving their cell phones in another room when they talked, for fear that Mohammed's men might be listening in on conversations in their own homes. Sometimes they were, it would later emerge.

The bin Ladens and Hariris took Mohammed's hits on the chin. One Western businessman explained the philosophy succinctly: "You get completely fucked over, but you still smile."

At the same time, Mohammed seemed to think he could do his own business deals in direct competition with the private sector but with all his governmental powers behind him. Coming up against him was the equivalent of bringing a butter knife to a gunfight. He'd win every time. In his eyes, he just had better ideas.

One of Mohammed's best business schemes also focused on opportunities connected to Mecca and its annual pilgrimage, the Hajj. Each year, as many as 2.5 million Muslims from around the world travel to Mecca to circle the Kaaba in prayer and fulfill their faith's commitments. For the 1.8 million or so who come from outside the kingdom, Saudi Arabia's state-run airline, Saudia, has a near monopoly on travel into the nearest airport in Jeddah.

Despite having the world's largest pilgrimage as its captive clientele, Saudia couldn't turn a profit. The carrier was famous for poor management and the skimming and procurement schemes that riddled the rest of the Saudi government. The airline also underinvested in planes, and its decrepit fleet made maintenance a constant challenge. A series of foreign turn-around experts couldn't manage to bring it into the black.

Soon after Salman assumed the throne, Mohammed decided to take on a major piece of the Saudia challenge. He wanted to bring the airline a new fleet of planes. It would be a giant deal, perhaps worth $10 billion or more. But there was a hitch: Shortly before King Abdullah died, Saudia had already made a deal with European plane maker Airbus. Saudia agreed to buy fifty of Airbus's new passenger jets, and the Saudi Public Investment Fund was planning to finance it. It was a good deal for the airline. Agreeing to buy so many planes up front earned a big discount.

From Mohammed's perspective, though, there was a big problem with the deal: It didn't involve him. That was especially problematic because, in the months prior, a company tied to his family had gotten into the airplane business.

Through a series of transactions, Mohammed's younger brother, Turki, had in 2014 become the chairman and majority owner of a Dubai company called Quantum Investment Bank, though it was in fact Mohammed who ultimately controlled the investment. As a financial institution, Quantum hardly had a track record. But it was tied to a longtime Dubai financier deeply involved in Islamic finance.

Islamic rules forbid lending money in exchange for interest. Pioneering financiers in recent decades have developed a number of structures, approved by Islamic experts, that technically allow money lending without interest. In the simplest terms, these structures add fees to a contract as a substitute for interest payments. It's a specialized nook of the market, but with huge amounts of capital available from pious and oil-rich investors in places like Saudi Arabia, the United Arab Emirates, and Kuwait, it's become a lucrative niche.

The bin Salmans' bank, Quantum, joined another almost-unheard-of company in Dubai and came out with a surprising announcement: Together, they were creating what could be the world's biggest airplane-leasing company. The low-profile company arose from a milieu of slick financial operators hailing from Lebanon and Morocco who set up an office in Dubai to become conduits for money from the oil-rich Gulf states. Their strategy was to raise money from Islamic investors, buy planes with it, and then rent them out to airlines. The cost difference between the loan payments on the planes and the rental fees they got from the airlines would count as profit for their investors.

It was a particularly good deal for the Salman family's Quantum because the tiny bank was in line for fees as a so-called placement agent. That means Quantum was tasked with raising investor money for the fund and would keep a portion of the money it collected. Whether the leasing business succeeded or failed, Quantum was guaranteed to get paid. The fact that it was tied to the bin Salmans meant that potential investors looking to curry favor with the family could do so by making an investment.

The fund raised billions. Mohammed's task was to make sure it had a client willing to rent its planes.

That was easy once his father became king. Soon after Salman took the throne, Mohammed had an underling tell Saudia that it would no longer buy its planes directly from Airbus. Instead, the company associated with Quantum would buy the planes, and Saudia would lease them from the company. The terms of the lease had Saudia renting the planes at about the normal market rate for a new Airbus. "It's a good deal for everyone," Mohammed told friends. His family would make some money, and Saudia would get new planes at the going rate.

The problem, Saudia executives grumbled at the time, was that under the old deal, Saudia wouldn't have had to pay that going rate. It would have gotten the discount as buyers of the planes. Under the terms of the new deal, the discount of 60 percent or more from list price went to the fund tied to the bin Salmans' bank. And they were about to lease their discounted planes to Saudia at a no-discount rate. But Mohammed decreed it was to be done, and Airbus—despite concerns among some employees that the deal was borderline corrupt—agreed to move ahead.

Mohammed acted as if it were his first big business triumph since his father became king. "I am the mastermind behind this deal," he proudly told an audience at a palace gathering soon after.

Mohammed understood that money was the key to power in Saudi Arabia on several levels. For his close family, money gave Salman the ability to spread largesse among potentially adversarial tribes and give payments to upstart princes who might want more political strength but would settle for a big payout. On a higher level, control over the state finance arms allowed Mohammed to pick winners and losers in his new economy.

He could have kept giving construction jobs to Binladin and Oger. Instead, during that time he picked smaller construction firms whose owners were more pliant and less entrenched with rival Al Saud factions. But most important was the oil money. It propped up modern Saudi Arabia, and the question of how those oil fields would be managed in the future would determine the kingdom's direction.

Mohammed had a clear vision for how to manage that oil wealth. As long as Saudi Arabia pumped and sold oil as its main source of revenue, it would be captive to the old economy that lived and died on petroleum products. But as a technology-obsessed millennial, he felt sure that era was in decline, and his reforms were about shifting the country to more sustainable sources of income.

Mohammed told his father he had decided to pursue his most aggressive economic plan yet. He wanted to sell a chunk of Saudi Arabia's oil company—the world's largest corporation and the engine that turned a barren desert into a modern nation—and use the cash to invest in other businesses. With an investor as shrewd as himself at the helm, Mohammed reasoned, the strategy would provide better returns than oil alone.

While the prince sold the plan to King Salman as his own, it actually had its roots in the 2012 plan of his cousin Alwaleed bin Talal. The difference was that Alwaleed didn't have much sway over his uncle, then-king Abdullah. Mohammed, on the other hand, had plenty of sway by the time he proposed the plan. His father, after all, was king.

But to exercise that sway, Mohammed had to remain constantly vigilant about threats to his power. They occurred in the form of dissident princes and disobedient courtiers. The biggest threat was Mohammed bin Nayef, the crown prince and the Saudi royal with the deepest ties to the United States.

Since the September 11 terrorist attacks, Mohammed bin Nayef had been in charge of coordinating antiterrorism efforts with the United States. This turned out to be an essential task— if Saudi Arabia hadn't joined up with the American cause to rid the world of Islamic extremists, the country could have become ostracized by the most powerful nations. With so many Saudis part of the terrorist attacks, it was incumbent on him to prove Saudi Arabia was not just a reliable ally but one with conviction about the same principles. The Americans grew to like him. He was quiet and calm. He listened, didn't make unrealistic promises, and got the job done. That meant that if US intelligence picked up information about a wealthy Saudi backing extremists somewhere in the Middle East, Mohammed bin Nayef would help get more information, freeze funds, or make an arrest.

Mohammed bin Nayef had weaknesses that the Americans picked up on too. After suffering injuries in a 2009 attempt on his life, he seemed more tired than in the past. He would fall asleep at meetings, and rumors circulated in Saudi Arabia—and among US intelligence—about potentially compromising pleasure-seeking behavior in Europe. Once Salman became king, the rumors reaching America took on much darker tones. Some in the US government saw such compromising information as useful—it meant they always had leverage if necessary. Others, however, were disturbed: If this information was making it out of the kingdom, it could easily be used within the Al Saud to undermine MBN's claim to the throne.

Many in the American intelligence community maintained a deep respect for Mohammed bin Nayef because he seemed committed to one of the thankless tasks that other Saudi princes ignored: In a country where power is held by individuals, MBN seemed committed to building strong institutions.

A big weakness of Saudi Arabia, as an absolute monarchy, was that the king, and the men he directly appointed, controlled everything. A new king, or a new appointee in a key position, would put his own men in place, wiping out any experience or knowledge that had built up. Senior positions were gained through personal relationships rather than merit. To develop a stable and competent government, American officials kept telling their Saudi counterparts, the kingdom needed institutions with their own cultures and succession plans and continuity. The problem was that many members of the Al Saud seemed to view strong institutions as a threat to their family. They wanted power to remain with individuals, even if that wasn't best for the country. MBN seemed like an exception. "We would sit, the two of us, and talk about institution building, which I thought was very impressive," says David Petraeus, who over decades as a general and later as head of the CIA spent hours together with MBN in Washington, DC, and Saudi Arabia.

With his focus on building a strong security apparatus that transcended his own power, MBN put a trusted deputy named Saad al-Jabri, a pious man with an immaculately manicured beard, in a central role maintaining the antiterror relationship with the United States. Jabri, a career civil servant, spent years dealing with US intelligence requests. He built relationships of trust in the CIA, military, and State Department, where officials knew him as "Dr. Saad" for his graduate degree. Jabri spearheaded a project to help reform extremists that got positive reviews from US counterparts. And perhaps most importantly, he had discretion over a huge amount of money that he could spend without going through Saudi Arabia's famously inefficient bureaucracy.

In the years after the 9/11 attacks, fighting terrorists—often in collaboration with the US—became a top priority. To facilitate antiterror operations, the Royal Court approved a plan that let MBN's Interior Ministry keep a portion of the money it made on day-to-day functions like renewing passports and issuing speeding tickets. The money piled up. In the fifteen years or so after the attacks, close to $20 billion went into the fund. MBN let Jabri control how the money was spent, allocating it for clandestine flights, government-backed businesses, and operations carried out in tandem with the US. As with many other Saudi enterprises,

Jabri found roles for family members, appointing his brother and nephews to roles with companies he funded. And under MBN's watch, Jabri was free to keep a portion of the money for himself.

The ability to control spending decisions gave Jabri credibility with his US counterparts that few other Saudi officials had. And many in the US intelligence community came to trust Jabri in a way they could never trust a member of the royal family. Mohammed realized this and saw it as a way to gain access to and credibility with US counterterrorism officials. Soon after his father became king, MBS made sure Jabri was elevated to a cabinet-level position in the Royal Court. It was a promotion that neither Jabri nor his patron MBN requested, and Jabri's allies suspected that Mohammed was trying to co-opt his rival's deputy to get an in with influential US figures.

For the first months of Salman's reign, Mohammed consulted with Jabri on security issues, especially those involving the United States. But he was never accepted by Mohammed's inner circle. Longtime allies like Saud al-Qahtani were suspicious of the longtime MBN loyalist now in their midst. These men wanted Mohammed to be the next king and worried Jabri was aligned with his chief rival.

Mohammed's allies in the government of Abu Dhabi, one of the United Arab Emirates, were also sour on Jabri, the result of years-old ill will between MBN and Abu Dhabi's ruling Al Nahyan family. At an international arms-procurement conference in Abu Dhabi in February 2015, Crown Prince Mohammed bin Zayed Al Nahyan made a shocking allegation to Mohammed: Jabri was a secret member of the political Islamist group the Muslim Brotherhood, an Al Saud nemesis. It was an unfounded allegation that the Abu Dhabi leader would repeat to contacts in the US government.

Friction between Mohammed and Jabri began in earnest after the Yemen bombing campaign commenced. Jabri objected to it, fearing it would become a morass. Jabri offered to resign after Mohammed didn't heed this advice, but Mohammed wouldn't let him. So Jabri took an extended vacation, traveling between his son in the United States and Saudi Arabia for a few months while he waited for a resolution.

Mohammed briefly drafted Jabri back into service when White House and US intelligence officials asked to deal with him to smooth out disagreements between the United States and Saudi Arabia over the Yemen campaign. But increasingly Jabri felt marginalized.

Then, in September 2015, while King Salman was traveling and MBN was at home in Saudi Arabia as acting king, Jabri saw a shocking piece of news pop up on Twitter: He'd been fired. MBN was equally surprised, and he and Jabri agreed it was a double insult. To fire MBN's top deputy while MBN was acting king seemed intended to belittle the crown prince. Mohammed fired Jabri, saying he was under investigation for covertly meeting with UK and US officials, including CIA director John Brennan, without the king's permission. The Royal Court put together a commission to investigate Jabri's fifteen years of intelligence contacts, though King Salman disbanded it after MBN told him that Jabri was meeting with those officials on his orders.

Jabri's longtime associates in the US intelligence community were shocked, and MBN was livid. But Jabri advised him to let it go—the firing seemed geared to escalate tensions between MBN and Mohammed, and no good could come of that.

The firing of Jabri was a blow to Mohammed bin Nayef's US relationship and a warning sign that Mohammed bin Salman was undermining it.

For Jabri himself, it meant a life away from home. Afraid Mohammed would lock him up if he stayed in the kingdom, Jabri got in touch with old intelligence contacts in the West and fled to Canada.

Chapter 5

BRING ME MCKINSEY

January 2016

Inside Aramco headquarters on Saudi Arabia's Gulf coast, staff were in a state of quiet panic. A prepublication copy of an article in the *Economist* arrived early that morning in January 2016 with news that just about no one in the company was expecting. Mohammed bin Salman had decided to sell a chunk of the company to the public in the biggest stock offering in financial history.

"A shudder of silence" swept through the executive suite, one employee recalls. High-ranking officials at Aramco had been advising Mohammed on plans to diversify the Saudi economy, but they'd never considered selling part of the kingdom's financial engine. It was the kind of idea cooked up in a room full of people without any knowledge of just how difficult such a task would be.

About a dozen members of Aramco's public relations team convened with top executives to quickly devise a statement that made it seem like management had been consulted and was part of the discussions.

Chairman Khalid al-Falih, who privately opposed the initial public offering (IPO) in meetings with government officials, confirmed the company was considering selling shares and touted its excellent management. "Nobody has any concerns whatsoever with the company having any weaknesses whatsoever," he told the *Wall Street Journal* days later. That statement was untrue. Beneath its veneer of Exxon-style corporate efficiency, Aramco was riddled with accounting and management idiosyncrasies that could turn off international investors. Some of them would be considered red flags.

Companies that trade on the massive stock exchanges of cities like New York, London, and Tokyo must follow strict rules making them accountable to investors. Their books have to be transparent, and their accounting must follow internationally accepted standards. Aramco, in contrast, was basically the biggest mom-and-pop in the world. It was accountable to one man, the Saudi king, and under no obligation to follow anyone else's rules. Aramco's records were so disorganized that the expat accountants who kept its books couldn't consistently calculate profits and losses by the end of each financial quarter—the most basic requirement for a publicly traded company.

Outwardly, Aramco claimed to "voluntarily comply" with international accounting standards. In fact, it cut corners on the boring but important details that investors use to quantify an oil company's performance. Aramco's accountants would just make up the rate of depreciation of oil fields, for example, rather than follow the standard calculations that big companies like Exxon and Royal Dutch Shell use. What did depreciation matter to a company owned by the king? But for a corporation whose shares trade on international markets, fudging such details could be a crime.

The company lacked the kind of accountability Western investors expect in other ways. Its management and pay structure didn't pretend to be meritocratic. Top decision-making positions were occupied by Saudis, even if they were less experienced or qualified than expats working beneath them. And those expat

employees' pay and benefits were based largely on their ethnicity
rather than their achievements. American and British engineers
and accountants had higher salaries than those from India or
Pakistan. Professionals from Africa made even less.

And in an industry whose other big companies developed
an obsession with safety after paying gigantic fines and legal
settlements for disasters like the *Exxon Valdez* oil spill and BP's
Gulf of Mexico oil rig explosion, Aramco had never been held to
the same kind of standards. It was governed by the Saudi courts,
which were controlled by the same royal family that owned
Aramco. So it lacked the same incentive to avoid costly and publicly humiliating accidents. Just a few months before Mohammed
announced the IPO plan, Aramco suffered the worst disaster
the oil industry had experienced in years, an accident caused by
Aramco's willful disregard for basic safety measures.

The catastrophe occurred in a brand-new housing complex near
Aramco headquarters, which the company rented to house non-
American expat workers. The Saudi company that built and
owned the apartment buildings gave them the veneer of modernity, with a courtyard swimming pool and workout area.

Aramco sent a building-safety expert named Thomas Meyers
for a routine inspection before moving employees in. Meyers,
a reticent Coloradan who spent years as a building inspector
for local government and a consultant to private companies,
had been hired after a fatal fire in Aramco worker housing
years before. It was a cushy job that he could feel good about,
with good pay, easy life in an Aramco housing compound, and
an opportunity to bring his safety expertise to a country that
needed it.

What Meyers found in the new condo complex was shocking.
Each of its eight six-floor buildings had open stairwells that
would function like "a chimney" in a fire, sucking in oxygen

from below and carrying heat and embers to the upper floors, he wrote in a report for his managers. The buildings didn't have full fire sprinklers—a violation of Aramco's own rules—and lacked proper safety exits. Apartments had no smoke detectors. And the buildings' electrical wiring was shoddily slapped together with tape. The problems amounted to "major life-safety concerns," Meyers and his boss wrote to Aramco management, urging the company not to move workers in.

The managers ignored the letter and moved dozens of employees and their families into the buildings. Almost immediately, Pakistani geologists and accountants noticed construction and safety problems in their new homes. The fire alarms didn't seem to work, and there were no fire-safety lights, one resident complained to a housing manager in an email. The company didn't fix the problems.

At 4:45 a.m. on August 30, 2015, an electrical transformer in the parking garage below one of the buildings failed. A Filipino lifeguard who lived in a downstairs bunkhouse smelled smoke and woke his colleagues. They fanned out across the complex, trying to wake residents. But the fire moved faster than they could. Burning oil from the transformer ignited car tires, and within minutes booming explosions began shaking the building, one for each car that blew up underground.

The flames shot up a stairwell as Meyers predicted, and residents on the upper floors had no way out. A pregnant woman jumped from her window into the complex's courtyard pool, hitting her head on the concrete edge. She died instantaneously. Another family dropped a toddler from their balcony to a man waiting in the courtyard below with outstretched arms. A Pakistani husband and wife jumped from their window, each embracing a child, hoping their own bodies would absorb the impact of the fall. The man suffered a traumatic brain injury and broke both legs, but the children were spared.

Residents gathered in the courtyard for a head count and realized that Ahmed Razi, a Pakistani geologist, and his family were still missing. A friend called upstairs, and Razi's wife, Nighat, said her apartment was filling with smoke and her husband was unconscious. She waved a hand out her apartment window, but rescuers couldn't get cherry pickers into the courtyard because the complex's entry was too small.

A Sudanese petrophysicist, Mohammed Gebreldar, managed to escape with his two-year-old daughter. But when he went back to rescue his two other children, his wife, and her mother, the smoke was too thick. The wife, son, and two daughters of a Canadian engineer, Tariq Minhas, were also trapped inside.

Once the flames were out, rescue workers searched the complex. Nighat Razi survived along with two of her daughters. Her husband and another daughter were dead. So were Gebreldar's two other children and mother-in-law. Minhas lost his entire family. In the end, ten people died, making it one of the deadliest oil-industry accidents of the decade.

But Aramco faced nothing like the criminal and civil penalties that nearly brought BP, one of the world's biggest oil companies, to its knees in the United States. Workers were unable to sue Aramco in Saudi courts. The company paid relatively small sums to many, but not all, of the residents. Some were forced to pay for their burnt cars to be salvaged and to settle any outstanding debt on the cars as a condition of leaving Saudi Arabia.

Families that suffered deaths got modest compensation, but Nighat Razi, who asked to stay in Saudi Arabia because one of her daughters suffered permanent, debilitating injuries and was hospital bound, was deported to Pakistan with a $32,000 payout. Aramco later paid her substantially more after *Wall Street Journal* reporters asked the company about her situation.

Minhas, the Canadian engineer, got a different kind of compensation. He was a devout Muslim, and Aramco agreed to bury his wife and children in a famous cemetery near the holy city of Medina. The company gave Minhas about six months of leave and flew more than a dozen family members from the United States, Canada, and Pakistan to visit Mecca. Aramco said at the time that despite there being no "ruling of liability or financial responsibility" against the company, "the company also chose to provide relief and compensation to cover damages incurred, as appropriate." They said, "The safety of our employees, their dependents, and our contractors is of paramount importance." Yet the biggest settlement Aramco paid ended up going to the Saudi company that built the firetrap: It got $5 million because Aramco had broken its lease early when it moved employees out of the scorched complex.

Aramco's safety record was a red flag to investors: If the company went public, the perceived risk of accidents that could result in expensive litigation could hurt shares.

Another concern was the fact that Aramco did lots of things other than produce, process, and sell oil. The company's engineers and workers built much of Saudi Arabia's infrastructure. Crews from the company laid the kingdom's first modern road and constructed its schools, universities, and hospitals. Its analysts were quietly consulted about any investment or economic idea, even if it had absolutely nothing to do with oil. Soon after Mohammed bin Salman took it over, he began sending over requests for deep dives into ideas like bringing theme parks to Saudi Arabia.

It had a long history of such work. During the first half of the twentieth century, when the oil fields were new and Saudi Arabia still poor, Aramco workers eradicated malaria in the kingdom. As the most capable engineering and project-management company in the country, Aramco could design and deliver projects that no one else in Saudi Arabia could. It also subsidized the Saudi economy.

To keep the people happy under their totalitarian rule, the Al Saud had Aramco give away fuel. It sold natural gas at a loss, and in some cases its government customers didn't pay at all. In 2015, Saudi Arabia's largest electricity company reported that it had run up a $20 billion debt by accepting fuel shipments from Aramco that it had never paid for—for fifteen years. The free fuel made it possible for the electric company to give Saudi citizens nearly free electricity. How would foreign investors feel about buying into a company whose profits went to subsidize the Saudi populace rather than pay shareholders dividends?

Then there were the vanity projects. King Abdullah ordered Aramco to develop a $1 billion "sports city" with a stadium and a mosque. He was so pleased with it that shortly before his death, he ordered up thirty-five more—a decree abandoned after Salman took the throne because of the cost and the effort required. Aramco built a museum and performance space, the King Abdulaziz Centre for World Culture, in the desert near the oil fields, hiring a Swedish design firm that created a building that looks like a spaceship from one of the *Star Wars* movies. And around the time Mohammed announced the IPO, Aramco built a $55 million complex to house one of the prince's favorite traditional Saudi events: an annual camel beauty pageant. That was great for the royal family, but US and UK stockholders would much prefer a cash distribution. Capitalism doesn't incentivize charity unless it's a relatively small marketing expense.

One senior Aramco official worried at the time that the country's leadership didn't fully grasp the huge sums Aramco spent on non-business-related projects. "Does MBS understand the decimal points?" he asked.

After Mohammed's IPO announcement, Aramco leaders scrambled to come up with plans to untangle the company from the government and the royal family. A Saudi manager named Motassim al-Maashouq convened key staff in a meeting room and declared that the project would make Aramco more efficient and transparent. Then he set out an almost completely opaque process for achieving that. He assigned about twenty trusted employees to code-named teams, swore them to secrecy, and set them to work on different potential strategies. One conference room with a combination-locked door housed Project X, which developed a plan to take the entire company public. Projects Y and Z, each with its own room, focused on proposals to sell one piece of the company at a time.

Still, Mohammed kept relying on Aramco for nonoil matters. He asked planners inside the company to formulate key pieces of his plan to remake the country's economy. And for months he tasked Aramco oil-forecasting analysts to prepare ten reports a week on investment opportunities, including the Comoro Islands, Japanese investment firm SoftBank, and at least one amusement park company. One oil analyst recalls the confusion that set in at the company. "What does Six Flags have to do with oil?"

Selling part of Aramco was a huge departure from the old Saudi way and only the first step in Mohammed's strategy to move away from oil, diversify the kingdom's economy, and create new jobs and social freedom for its burgeoning youth population.

The key to convincing his father and the rest of the aging Al Saud leadership of this plan was to make the case that without it, an inevitable economic crisis would threaten the royal family's grip on Saudi Arabia. And that required turning the vision into a specific plan, with numbers to demonstrate how it would work and international buy-in to show that it would help boost the kingdom's global status. He knew where to turn for help.

Over the two-plus years since King Abdullah had given Mohammed permission to study economic reforms, he had found a ready collaborator in McKinsey & Company. The world's preeminent consulting firm had entered the kingdom in 1974 with a modest assignment to plan a new oil company headquarters. The American consultants had the good fortune of working with a young Saudi engineer, Ali al-Naimi, who would rise up to become oil minister, the most powerful nonroyal in the kingdom, in 1995. From Aramco, McKinsey branched out into the Saudi government bureaucracy. In recent years it had solidified its ties to the kingdom by hiring young Saudis. Some were relatives of government officials, including two sons of Khalid al-Falih, Aramco chairman and minister of energy and industry.

In December 2015, the McKinsey Global Institute, the consulting firm's research arm, published a paper, titled "Saudi Arabia Beyond Oil," that laid out a plan for the kingdom to reinvent its economy. Between 2015 and 2030, McKinsey wrote, Saudi Arabia could double its GDP and "create as many as six million jobs." McKinsey said the work was independent research funded by its own money, not Saudi Arabia. But the lead author was Gassan al-Kibsi, the McKinsey consultant advising the Saudi government. The report amounted to a giant McKinsey marketing effort on behalf of its most important client.

The stamp of authenticity conferred by consultants who'd worked for the world's biggest companies and governments gave Mohammed new international credibility. By the time he announced the IPO plan in January 2016, he had enough buy-in from the Royal Court and enough power granted by his father that even the skepticism of Falih, the oil minister and Aramco chairman, couldn't stop the IPO plan.

Mohammed bin Salman developed a fascination with consultants when he was setting up his own companies and his MiSK foundation before his father became king. One idea he loved was the creation of key performance indicators, soon to be known throughout the ministries and government-linked companies as

"KPIs." Mohammed didn't respond to strategies that weren't backed up by numbers. He had an impressive memory for them as well, often recounting to underlings forecasts they had showed him months beforehand to prove he had a strong understanding of the underlying issues.

McKinsey and a whole host of other consultants were ready to accommodate whatever big requests Mohammed made for his economic-transformation plan. To get his attention, they built PowerPoint presentations with slide after slide of projections, charts, and graphs. And they loaded them with numbers, statistics, and KPIs, just the way the prince liked.

Mohammed got to know McKinsey's lead partner in the country, Gassan al-Kibsi, who went to work in the Middle East after graduating from the Massachusetts Institute of Technology. Mohammed offered him a bold vision to polish: Saudi Arabia would untether its fortunes from oil and connect its once insular economy to the rest of the world.

The consultants could turn Mohammed's ideas into plans with credible metrics and benchmarks that would satisfy the World Bank and the International Monetary Fund, as well as skeptical older Saudi officials. He paid McKinsey and another firm, Boston Consulting Group (BCG), tens of millions of dollars to write reports on every aspect of his vision. McKinsey worked on economic modernization and bureaucratic reforms.

Mohammed began using KPIs as part of his attempt to reform the government. Ministers like Falih and those in charge of the economic transformation and even entertainment were given KPIs that they had to meet in advance of periodic reviews. If they failed, they risked dismissal. To give the ministers a further incentive to focus their energy on governance, rather than the old practice of skimming money from companies that signed government contracts, Mohammed changed the ministerial pay structure. In the past they had received about $10,000 per month, plus benefits and a bonus, and the king would generally turn a blind eye to kickbacks. Under Mohammed, the ministers would each get several million dollars a year. But they would have to meet their KPIs, and the government would no longer turn a blind eye to kickback schemes.

He also set his sights on the lazy and ossified cultures inside ministries like the Ministry of Finance, where just about everyone seemed to be coasting along a few years away from retirement. He empowered Mohammed al-Jadaan, a longtime corporate lawyer whom the prince leaned on for a variety of powerful jobs, to gut the Ministry of Finance and replace its ranks with younger staff with banking backgrounds. Gone were the days of easy hours, steady work, and guaranteed pensions.

The changing way of government life was most apparent in weekly meetings of the Council of Economic and Development Affairs, which Mohammed invented to replace an older, more bureaucratic predecessor. Instead of providing dry updates and patting themselves on the back and praising the vision of their glorious leaders, ministers were expected to present in stages a vision for their ministries, a strategy for achieving it, and then updates on their progress. Before they could even present, they had to get past a special group within the council that vetted presentations. The then-thirty-year-old Mohammed would ask questions and sometimes yell at an obstinate minister who was twice his age. As a minister steadily walked the room through a seventy-page presentation, Mohammed was known to ruffle the papers as he raced ahead to read the whole document and begin writing down follow-up questions.

"It was difficult for everyone at first," said Adel al-Toraifi, the then–culture minister who was present at the vettings. "This wasn't what people were used to."

Away from McKinsey and Aramco, Mohammed was presiding over actions that were far from Western norms.

———

Al-Awamiyah sits about thirty miles up Saudi Arabia's Persian Gulf coast from Aramco's headquarters, an oasis town of about twenty-five thousand that hasn't experienced the same relative peace and prosperity as the rest of the kingdom in the decades since it started pumping oil.

What sets Al-Awamiyah apart is that its residents are largely members of the kingdom's Shia Muslim minority. That's a problem in a monarchy allied with Sunnis. In the eyes of the clerics who have propped up the Al Saud since the kingdom's founding, Shia Muslims aren't real Muslims. They're heretics. And in the eyes of the Saudi government, any Shia is suspected of having sympathy with Iran, the kingdom's archenemy.

Saudi Shia historically have had trouble getting decent jobs and access to government services. For decades, Al-Awamiyah and neighboring towns have been the site of routine protests met by brutal crackdowns. Led in recent years by a Shia cleric named Nimr al-Nimr, residents have taken to the streets to demonstrate on local and international matters alike, violating Saudi laws against public demonstrations in the process.

Even worse than the demonstrating he incited was Nimr's message. "In any place he rules—Bahrain, here, in Yemen, in Egypt, or in any place—the unjust ruler is hated," Nimr said in one sermon broadcast on YouTube and viewed by 1.6 million people. "Whoever defends the oppressor is his partner with him in oppression, and whoever is with the oppressed shares with him his reward from God." In other sermons he called the king and his family "tyrants" and said, "We don't accept Al Saud as rulers. We don't accept them and want to remove them."

Mohammed had even less tolerance for Shia dissent than his predecessors. And like them, he was especially sensitive to those who questioned Al Saud's legitimacy to rule. That's why, on a morning in early January 2016, Nimr and forty-seven others were marched into a Riyadh square and killed, some by beheading, others by firing squad.

The executions attracted public outrage. The government claimed Nimr was killed for disobeying the Saudi state, taking up arms, and trying to get a foreign power involved in Saudi matters. One Saudi official said Nimr was responsible for a physical threat against the crown prince, Mohammed bin Nayef. But Amnesty International and other human rights groups said his real crime was simply criticizing the royal family. Nimr's brother was arrested for tweeting news of the execution.

The confrontations led to protests in Iran and incendiary statements from government officials there. Calling the remarks "hostile," Saudi Arabia expelled Iranian diplomats, and Iran reciprocated. With the execution and the war in Yemen, Mohammed had put himself on a collision course with Iran.

But inside the kingdom, many felt the message of Nimr's execution was clear: There were some things Mohammed was not changing. And one of those things was that people who questioned his family's rule could lose their heads.

On balance, though, Mohammed succeeded in convincing influential Westerners that he was the reformer they'd been waiting to see in Saudi Arabia for decades.

In January 2016, the same month Nimr was decapitated, retired four-star general and former CIA director David Petraeus took a trip to Riyadh. He'd been hired by the private equity firm KKR & Company for his expertise on international markets, and he and firm founder Henry Kravis were interested in potential investments in the region.

Petraeus had led several US efforts in the Middle East and was in charge of US Central Command, which oversees military efforts in the Middle East, from 2008 to 2010. He had a deep history with the kingdom and with members of the Al Saud. As a general, he had spent time with Kings Fahd and Abdullah. He knew Abdullah's son Miteb, who had been National Guard chief, and hosted Salman on a visit to the United States in 2012. In 2015 he met Mohammed in Washington, DC.

When Mohammed got word that Petraeus was in Riyadh, he invited him for a meeting. The prince wanted to show him something, Mohammed's emissary said. While Kravis continued on with his trip, Petraeus agreed to stay in Riyadh for the meeting.

Mohammed's men brought the former general to a palace, ushering him through one grand room to another and finally into Mohammed's office. Waiting there was a familiar face, Saudi Arabia's ambassador to the United States, Adel al-Jubeir. He was there to translate for Mohammed, who wanted Petraeus to be one of the first Americans briefed on details of the consultant-driven plan to remake the Saudi economy. The prince called it Vision 2030.

Petraeus was blown away. He'd spent years meeting with stooped old princes who lived in fear that change could upend their rule. Here was a thirty-year-old prince laying out a detailed plan to radically transform the Saudi economy starting immediately. Mohammed was tall and vital, with his prominent nose and wide smile. "Great features," Petraeus recalls thinking. "If you wanted to design a Saudi prince, that's what he would look like." Even more surprising in a country where leaders and progress moved glacially, "He conveys energy. He conveyed urgency."

Mohammed talked for two hours straight, giving astonishingly detailed financial projections from memory, never looking at notes. One by one, he named categories of the economy that could be built up, or invented from scratch, to reduce the Saudi dependence on oil, and he recited how quickly each of those categories could grow and how much income they could bring in. The plan blended practical changes—lower subsidies, new taxes—with seemingly outlandish ones, like a new state on Saudi Arabia's Red Sea coast with flying cars and robotic workers that wouldn't be unveiled for more than a year.

"Look, General," Mohammed said, "if we only achieve 60 percent of what it is that we are striving to accomplish, wouldn't that be extraordinary?"

"It would be extraordinary," the general said. "It would be phenomenal."

There were small signs on that visit that Mohammed was maneuvering to gain power over family rivals. Petraeus, like other US intelligence officials, had a long and warm relationship with Mohammed bin Nayef, the crown prince who stood between Mohammed and the throne. Petraeus asked Jubeir, the ambassador to the United States, to set up a meeting with the crown prince. But it never happened.

Petraeus figured the crown prince was busy. But when he returned to the United States, he got a puzzling message from a person close to Mohammed bin Nayef: "MBN missed seeing you. Why didn't you stop by?"

Wowed by the prospect of an early role in the world's largest IPO, bankers from the United States and Europe filed onto first-class flights to Riyadh to meet the prince. They included Achintya Mangla, a London-based banker at J.P. Morgan, and Jonathan Penkin, from Goldman Sachs Group. These were the top IPO bankers in the world, and like their bosses they were putting all their efforts into pitching the prince. There were not only hundreds of millions of dollars in fees for the taking but years of major transactions they could take part in. It was an investment banking gold rush.

Larry Summers, the former US Treasury secretary and Harvard

University president, came to visit. So did former House majority leader Eric Cantor. Both were working with boutique investment banks seeking a piece of the Aramco deal. Former UK prime minister Tony Blair was too. He had spent his years after government service advising government leaders—some widely considered despots—on reforms and consulting with companies working in totalitarian countries, amassing a fortune in the tens of millions of dollars. He spent an evening in a desert tent with Mohammed, discussing the philosophy of governance and power. Blair was working for JPMorgan Chase at the time, though one of his staffers said they didn't discuss banking.

Buzzing around the early-stage talk was Michael Klein, a former Citibank deal maker who worked closely with Alwaleed bin Talal for years. Operating as the proprietor of his own financial firm, he leveraged his contacts with Khalid al-Falih, the energy minister whom he knew from another deal, to get an early consulting role on Aramco. He soon ingratiated himself with the head of Saudi Arabia's sovereign investment fund and was among the first to suggest that international investors could value Aramco at $2 trillion.

When Mohammed told bankers from the United States and Europe in follow-up visits that he expected a $2 trillion valuation, they nodded and said yes. In fact, the prince would later tell people, one big European bank said it could be worth $2.3 trillion.

While titans of finance were gravitating toward the kingdom, Mohammed started to develop some nagging suspicions about the consultants he'd been relying on to formulate his vision. The McKinsey and BCG people were certainly smart, but such consultants were also mercenaries, and they had an intrinsic conflict of interest: It never behooved the consultants to say no. If the prince asked whether some outlandish scheme was feasible it would always be in their interests to say yes. Consultants make money by getting assigned to giant projects, not by telling their employers that such projects are bad ideas.

Mohammed understood this conflict of interest, and even as he had McKinsey and other consultants working on dozens of projects throughout the government, he told Saudi confidants that he believed the country leaned too heavily on foreign expertise. The expats whom Saudi Arabia paid generously for their knowledge of oil or engineering or economics had little personal stake in the kingdom's success or failure; they got paid whether their plans worked or not.

Mohammed started seeing examples of these conflicts in every aspect of the consultants' work. The prince loved KPIs, but some of the ones McKinsey came up with were fuzzier than he liked. And most of the consulting firms didn't have significant offices in Saudi Arabia. Instead they flew their experts back and forth from Dubai, since their American and European staffers didn't want to live in Saudi Arabia, where alcohol was illegal and women, under the law, were subordinate to men. How, Mohammed wondered, could he entrust the future of his country to a bunch of people who wouldn't even live there temporarily?

The project was supposed to help Saudi Arabia achieve certain goals by 2030. So Mohammed proposed he only pay the consultants based on results. "I'll pay you when you reach the KPIs"—in 2030, the prince said. The consultants balked. They'd be paid as they went, or they wouldn't take the job.

The expenses quickly grew. Over five years or so, a Vision 2030 effort to remake the Saudi military racked up $250 million in consulting fees without much change to show for it. The consultants recommended a complicated structure that imposed a large civilian bureaucracy over uniformed leaders, alienating officers who would have to buy into the plan for it to work. Frustrated by the stalemate, the official in charge of the transformation tried to address the problem by hiring a new consultant to evaluate the other consultants' work. The new consultant was dismissed after filing a report that concluded the entire effort was bound to fail and didn't address the kingdom's biggest military problem: Saudi Arabia spends about 10 percent of its GDP, an unsustainable amount of money, on the military, in part to provide jobs to members of powerful Bedouin tribes. Without trimming that spending, the new consultant said, Saudi Arabia would have trouble achieving the economic growth Mohammed sought.

For many in the US government, the Aramco IPO and other splashy achievements were far down on the list of priorities. While the US ambassador to Saudi Arabia, Joe Westphal, talked with New York Stock Exchange leaders and Mohammed about having the IPO in New York, he and others from the US government urged Mohammed to focus on the less publicly noticeable priorities of border security and developing an effective system to ward off attacks on Saudi oil installations.

———

It seemed like an April Fool's joke.

John Micklethwait, the Oxford-educated editor in chief of Bloomberg News, went on TV on April 1, 2016, to report that Saudi Arabia was going to start a $2 trillion investment fund. "An amazing thing," Micklethwait called it. "If you think about it, it's enough to buy Google, Microsoft, Alphabet"—Google's parent company—"the whole lot of them. Warren Buffett."

Mohammed had revealed the plan during a five-hour interview in which he outlined his strategy to reinvent the Saudi economy. His ideas made sense, in the abstract, to foreign economists and business leaders. Mohammed would use cash from the Aramco IPO to invest in new industries, giving his country new sources of income beyond oil.

But no one could figure out how it would work in practice.

Was it possible to pour that much money into global markets without inflating a giant bubble? And who would Mohammed put in charge of managing the investments? The man currently heading the sovereign fund, Yasir al-Rumayyan, was chiefly known, at home and abroad, as an easygoing luminary of the Riyadh golf community who had a taste for fine cigars and after-hours bars in Dubai frequented by long-legged, short-skirted Russian women.

Skeptical or not, the Western attention alone was a victory for the prince. By the end of April, he'd be on the cover of an issue of *Bloomberg Businessweek* magazine detailing the transformation plan for Saudi Arabia that the consultants had prepared. Vision 2030 had taken hundreds of Saudi and foreign consultants months to finish, and it laid out broad goals the United States and World Bank had been suggesting for years. An economy with incentives for entrepreneurship and innovation and freedoms for women to join the workforce would certainly create a stronger nation, the foreigners argued.

Mohammed's plan set an almost ludicrously ambitious timeline for reaching those goals, considering Saudi Arabia was a country with roughly the same economic structure as when oil money started flowing about a half century earlier. "All success stories start with a vision, and successful visions are based on strong pillars," the Vision 2030 statement said. The three pillars were making Saudi Arabia the heart of the Arab and Islamic world, becoming a "global investment powerhouse," and turning the country into a "global hub connecting three continents" and an "epicenter of trade."

Once the announcement was made, Mohammed knew he needed to show progress quickly. In the ensuing weeks he grilled Saudi officials and foreign consultants alike on how they could show their ideas were working. He'd lose patience with, say, the finance minister and turn instead to the Ministry of Economy and Planning for an urgent task. "The principles changed every week. The wheel gets reinvented every few days," a person working for BCG complained.

The sovereign wealth fund debut showed the world Mohammed was planning to spend. A month later he hosted US secretary of state John Kerry on his yacht the *Serene*. But he still needed a splashy deal to introduce the Public Investment Fund (PIF) as the new investor on the block.

Not long before, Mohammed had been introduced to Travis Kalanick, founder of the then-hot start-up Uber. The men developed a rapport—the prince would later call the entrepreneur a friend—and Mohammed saw Uber as an attractive investment. The business press fawned over the company. It was expanding quickly all over the world and could play a big domestic role in Saudi Arabia, with women still prohibited from driving. Mohammed and Kalanick discussed an investment. At the beginning of June, the fund wired a total of $3.5 billion to Uber. For that, Mohammed became the biggest investor in the world's hottest tech start-up, and he got his staffer, the fund's chief Yasir al-Rumayyan, on Uber's board. He'd proven the kingdom was doing something differently.

The investment would be the first instance of many in which Western businessmen, consultants, and bankers promised the world to the young prince but failed to deliver. Investing in Uber didn't earn him a financial return. Nor did Uber invest in Saudi Arabia in a big way. In effect, Saudi Arabia doled out $3.5 billion for the privilege of announcing it was an investor in Uber. It would likely get its money back, but without an impressive return.

A veteran of Middle Eastern sovereign wealth funds who has grown cynical over the years explains how it works for Gulf investors. All the best deals and opportunities are seized upon by big American institutions with the help of New York City banks.

The second-tier deals go to the Europeans. And the lemons are packaged up and rebranded for what derisive bankers call the "dumb money" in the Middle East. "They don't care about us," he says. "They only want our money."

Days later Mohammed headed to Silicon Valley.

Executives were eager to greet the prince. In pressed jeans and a blazer, Mohammed posed for photos with Mark Zuckerberg and visited Google's founders.

The reception was less effusive among the venture capitalists (VCs) whose ranks Mohammed wanted to join. While entrepreneurs were hungry for Saudi money, the VCs were a different breed. Often pompous, driving Teslas to their low-slung offices on Sand Hill Road in the hills above Palo Alto, they specialized in making small deals in early-stage start-ups that could pay giant returns in the unlikely event of success. Their industry was booming. The last thing the successful VCs needed was a prince with hundreds of billions of dollars inflating the valuations of new start-ups and telling them how to do their jobs.

"We don't need your money," one prominent VC told an emissary of Mohammed's ahead of his visit to California. "We've got plenty." Another explained that his firm already had Saudi money, irritating the prince's entourage since this money manager apparently didn't know the difference between money from some rich Saudi individual and the opportunity that Mohammed was offering to manage money for the Saudi state.

The only VCs who seemed truly eager to meet the prince were those at the other end of the spectrum, the ambitious up-and-comers who also upset the prince's entourage by boasting that they had an in with the Saudis. One was Joe Lonsdale, a cofounder of the data analytics firm Palantir who had worked with the successful VC Peter Thiel. Ahead of the visit, investors recall, Lonsdale told them he had Saudi investment, when in fact he had a modest sum from a son of the energy minister. It was far from a relationship with the kingdom's government. Asked about the claim, Lonsdale said it was "not appropriate to share" the names of people whose money he managed and that he never boasted about having Saudi investment. Lonsdale says he ended up not pursuing investments from the region. "It seems in those societies many make money by peddling connections, versus building things or applying intellectual rigor," he later said.

But the more established VCs' attitudes seemed to change at a dinner at the Fairmont Hotel atop San Francisco's Nob Hill. "I need a bridge between Saudi and Silicon Valley. I need you to help our reforms," Mohammed told a group that included Marc Andreessen, Peter Thiel, John Doerr, and Michael Moritz, titans of venture capital with decades of experience backing start-ups that turned into multi-billion-dollar corporations.

As the prince saw it, the venture capital model could be scaled indefinitely. If they made huge returns on relatively modest investments, imagine how much they could make if he boosted their capital tenfold. After the dinner, Doerr put his arm around the energy minister, Khalid al-Falih, and excitedly told him, "Together, we're going to remake the energy industry."

But the Silicon Valley VCs couldn't move quickly enough for Mohammed. They were set in their old ways of making small investments. Mohammed wanted to make giant investments, and he wanted to do it right away. Before the VCs could figure out a way to accommodate him, the prince met a like-minded maverick investor from Japan who promised to circumvent the Valley's old guard. First, though, there were some pesky voices that needed dealing with.

Chapter 6

CAPTAIN SAUD

February 2016

Something wasn't right about Captain Saud.

Sitting on a fine-grained leather couch in the custom wood-paneled cabin of his Boeing 737-800 in Paris, Saud had the outward appearance of a pilot. His uniform was crisp, his demeanor confident and friendly. He cracked jokes and showed pictures of his children to staffers of the VIP he was supposed to fly to Cairo, a Saudi prince named Sultan bin Turki II.

But little things seemed off. One member of the prince's entourage was a recreational pilot, and Saud couldn't keep up with his small talk about 737 pilot training. The captain's plane also had a crew of nineteen, more than double the usual number of staffers for a Paris-Cairo flight. And the crew was made up only of men, some a little burlier than you'd expect. Where were the leggy European blondes who were fixtures on Saudi Royal Court flights?

And then there was the watch. Saud was fascinated by the Breitling Emergency Watch the prince's companion was wearing. "I've never seen one of these," he said, in perfect English.

The $15,000 watch, which has a radio beacon to call for help in case of a crash, is a favorite indulgence of pilots with disposable income. What kind of airplane captain had never seen one?

And what kind of pilot wore the Hublot that Saud had on his wrist, a showy hunk of metal that would cost three months' salary for most pilots?

The watch, the nineteen men, the lack of flying knowledge—the dissonant little details added up. Sultan's security detail, sent to the plane ahead of him to assess the situation, warned the prince not to get on the plane. It was a trap.

But Prince Sultan was tired and lonely. He missed his father, who was waiting for him in Cairo. And Mohammed bin Salman himself had sent this plane. Sultan figured he could trust his newly powerful first cousin.

Prince Sultan bin Turki II, named because his father was the second of Ibn Saud's two sons named Turki (the first died at a young age), was born on the troubled fringe of the Al Saud's most powerful branch. His father, the full brother of former King Fahd and King Salman, seemed a candidate for the throne until he married the daughter of a leader of Sufi Muslims, who practice a strain of Islamic mysticism with which many of the Al Saud disagree. Shamed into exile, Prince Turki moved into a Cairo hotel, where he remained for years.

His son Sultan maintained a relationship with his powerful uncles and cousins in Saudi Arabia and married his first cousin, a daughter of then-prince (and later king) Abdullah. But she died in a car accident in Riyadh in 1990, and the prince, then just twenty-two, adopted the life of a libertine.

On his generous allowance from King Fahd, Sultan traveled around Europe with an entourage of security guards, models, fixers, and friends. The aging king had a tolerance—some would say a fondness—for high-living princes and an enduring affection for his nephew. When Fahd left a Geneva hospital after a 2002 eye surgery, Sultan was right behind his wheelchair, a privileged position among royals jostling for physical proximity to the king.

Sultan didn't have a role in the government, but he liked to be seen as a person of influence in his country. He spoke often with foreign journalists about his views on Saudi policy, taking a more open stance than most princes but always supporting the monarchy. In January 2003 he started veering onto a different tack. Sultan declared to reporters that Saudi Arabia should stop giving aid to Lebanon and claimed that Lebanon's prime minister, Rafic Hariri, was corruptly using Saudi money to fund an extravagant lifestyle.

Internationally, the statement didn't seem like a big deal. Hariri was widely suspected of being corrupt, though he was never publicly accused of any crime in Saudi Arabia, and the prince didn't really criticize the kingdom as much as Lebanon. But inside the Royal Court, it amounted to a Molotov cocktail. King Fahd's son Abdulaziz, a government official known as Azouz, was close to the Hariris, and Sultan's statement seemed directed at antagonizing his cousins. Sultan went a step further a few months later when he faxed a statement to the Associated Press saying he had started a commission to root out corruption among Saudi princes and others who had "pillaged the nation's wealth over the past 25 years."

About a month later, Azouz sent Sultan an invitation. Come to the king's mansion in Geneva, he said. Let's work out our differences. At the meeting, Abdulaziz and another Saudi minister tried to coax Sultan to return to the kingdom. When he refused, armed guards pounced on the prince, injected him with a sedative, and dragged him onto a plane for Riyadh.

It wasn't a graceful abduction. Sultan weighed about four hundred pounds at the time, and at some point during the ordeal, either the drugs or the process of dragging the unconscious man by his limbs damaged nerves connected to Sultan's diaphragm and legs. He spent the next eleven years in and out of prison in Saudi Arabia, often with travel restrictions, and sometimes in a locked-down government hospital in Riyadh.

In 2014 Sultan contracted swine flu, which led to a cascade of life-threatening complications. Assuming the prince, now a semiparalyzed, wheezing shadow of his antagonistic younger self, was no longer a threat, the government allowed him to seek medical care in Massachusetts. As far as Sultan was concerned, he was free.

Massive change swept the House of Saud during Sultan's time in detention in the kingdom. King Fahd died in 2005, and his successor, Abdullah, had less tolerance for ostentatious displays of princely wealth. Abdullah trimmed handouts to princes and censured the most profligate and ill-behaved of the bunch. The new king wouldn't countenance entitled young men who brought public shame to his family.

But Sultan seemed not to grasp that shift or the bigger one that happened in early 2015, after he'd recovered from his acute health problems, when the even more austere King Salman assumed the throne. Instead of fading into a low-key life, Sultan got liposuction and cosmetic surgery and started getting the band back together to resume his life of vagabond opulence.

Sultan reached out to security guards and old advisors and friends, people he hadn't spoken to since his kidnapping more than a decade earlier. The entourage reunited, Sultan set out for Europe like a stereotypical Saudi prince of the high-flying 1990s.

With armed security guards, a medical detail of six full-time nurses and a doctor, rotating "girlfriends" hired from a Swiss modeling agency, and an assortment of Saudi and European hangers on, his expenses amounted to millions of dollars a month. It was like a modern, ultraluxury caravan, one entourage member recalls. From Oslo to Berlin, Geneva, and Paris, they ate only the finest food and drank only the best wine. After a few days or weeks in a city, Sultan would grow restless and order the butlers to pack his bags and call the Saudi embassy for the escort granted to grandsons of Ibn Saud. They'd hop on a rented private plane and set out for the next city.

In mid-2015, Prince Sultan took over the most luxurious hotel on Sardinia's most picturesque beach, where he could swim in the Mediterranean each day. In the sea, Sultan's partially paralyzed lower legs could support his weight. It was the closest he could get to moving freely.

Along the way, the Royal Court kept depositing money in his bank account. But Sultan realized the payments wouldn't keep up indefinitely, and he didn't have other sources of income. Then he had an idea: Sultan decided the Saudi government owed him compensation. He'd been permanently injured, after all, in the 2003 kidnapping, and his disabilities made it difficult to, say, start a company or an investment fund the way his cousins could.

So Sultan appealed to someone who he figured could help, the new king's favorite son and his first cousin, Mohammed bin Salman. Sultan didn't know Mohammed well. He'd been locked up since the young prince was in his late teens. But he heard from family members that Salman's son had become the most powerful person in the Royal Court and was a decisive official who could deliver a payment rather than empty promises. So he asked Mohammed for compensation for his injuries.

It didn't work. Mohammed was unwilling to pay someone who had brought about his own troubles by airing family grievances. What kind of lesson would that teach other royals? So in the summer of 2015, Sultan did something unprecedented: In a Swiss court, he sued members of the royal family for the kidnapping.

His confidants were worried. "They abducted you once. Why wouldn't they abduct you again?" warned Sultan's lawyer in Boston, Clyde Bergstresser. Sultan would often listen to

Bergstresser's advice. The lawyer, a blunt New Jersey native who had no Saudi connections and was referred to Sultan during his treatment in Massachusetts, was more direct than members of Sultan's entourage and family in advising the prince, and the men developed a relationship of trust. But on this point Sultan was obstinate. He hired a lawyer in Geneva and, in July, sued. A Swiss criminal prosecutor started investigating. Newspapers picked up the story. Sultan's payments from the Royal Court abruptly stopped.

His entourage didn't realize the problem for several weeks until one day in Sardinia Prince Sultan decided he wanted room service. The prince and his retinue had been staying in the hotel above a turquoise cove for two months, running up $1 million or more in expenses. Now the restaurant was refusing to serve them.

It fell to a member of the prince's entourage to tell Sultan why. "You're absolutely broke," his staffer explained.

The hotel would have just evicted him but couldn't afford to write off the weeks of unpaid bills. The prince assured his staff that he could come up with a way to restore the Royal Court's payouts to him. They convinced the hotel to reopen the line of credit. And then Sultan took a gamble. He figured Mohammed bin Salman had angered so many powerful members of the royal family that he could outmaneuver the king's son.

Sultan sent two anonymous letters to his uncles, the surviving sons of Ibn Saud. King Salman is "incompetent" and "powerless" to rule, Sultan wrote. "It is no longer a secret that the most serious problem in his health is the mental aspect that has made the king the subject of his son Mohammed." Mohammed, he wrote, is corrupt and has been using his proximity to the king to enrich himself. Sultan alleged Mohammed had diverted more than $2 billion in government funds to a private bank account and was also stealing oil money. The only solution, he wrote, was to isolate the king and "convene an emergency meeting of senior family members to discuss the situation and take all necessary measures to save the country."

Sultan's unsigned letters were leaked to the *Guardian* newspaper in England. His name wasn't publicized, but the substance of the criticism—and the prince's history—made his authorship obvious to senior members of the Royal Court.

Prince Sultan awaited the fallout. Perhaps his uncles would try to rein in Mohammed. Or maybe Mohammed would offer him some money to stop making trouble. The combination of the lawsuit and the letters, Sultan hoped, would be such a distraction at a time when Mohammed was trying to sell his vision of reform that the Royal Court would just pay up. It could be a situation like his father's, Sultan reasoned, in which he could live in financially supported estrangement.

Amazingly, it seemed to work. Not long after the letters, as if by a miracle, more than $2 million from the Royal Court appeared in Sultan's bank account. He covered the hotel debts and renewed his travel plans. Even better, he soon got an invitation from his father to visit Cairo and hopefully patch up their strained relationship. As a bonus, his father told him, Sultan wouldn't even have to pay his own way there. The Royal Court was sending a luxury jetliner to fly the prince and his entourage to Cairo. It seemed that Mohammed bin Salman was bringing his wayward cousin back into the fold.

The prince's staff was dumbfounded. Some of them had been around the last time he criticized the Al Saud and found himself on a Royal Court plane. It ended with kidnapping, imprisonment, and a lifetime of health problems. Now the prince was criticizing the family again, and the Royal Court was again sending a plane. How could he even consider getting on?

But Sultan seemed to want to believe that it represented a

reconciliation. Perhaps Mohammed bin Salman really was a new kind of leader, one who wouldn't stand for thuggish behavior.

The Royal Court sent a specially outfitted 737-800—a plane that fits 189 passengers in commercial use—to Geneva, and Sultan ordered his staff to meet the crew and suss out the situation.

It didn't feel right. Captain Saud seemed off, and the nineteen-member crew seemed like security officials, not flight attendants. One of Sultan's staffers warned him, "This plane is not going to land in Cairo."

The prince brushed aside the concern. "You don't trust them?" he asked.

"Why do you trust them?" the staffer responded. Sultan didn't answer. But he wavered until Captain Saud offered to ease his fears by leaving ten of the crewmembers behind in Paris, as a good-faith gesture to show this wasn't a kidnapping. That was enough for the prince.

He told his entourage to start packing. With the butlers, nurses, security guards, and a "girlfriend" hired from a modeling agency, the retinue numbered more than a dozen.

The plane left Paris uneventfully, and for two hours its flight path to Cairo was visible on the screens around the cabin. Then the screens flickered and shut off.

Several members of the prince's entourage were alarmed. "What's happening," one of them asked Captain Saud. He went to check and returned to explain that there was a technical problem, and the only engineer who could fix it had been among the crewmen left behind in Paris. But there was no need to worry, he told them; they were on schedule.

By the time the plane started descending, just about everyone aboard realized it wouldn't land in Cairo. Looking from the window, they saw no Nile snaking through the city, no Pyramids of Giza. Riyadh's sprawl was unmistakable.

By the time Kingdom Center Tower, a skyscraper with a huge hole in the center that cynics said resembled the Eye of Sauron from the *Lord of the Rings*, came into view, pandemonium had broken out on the jet. Members of Sultan's entourage shouted. The Americans and Europeans asked what would happen to them, landing in Saudi Arabia without visas and against their will. Would they be detained? Would their governments have to get involved? Would they be allowed to call their embassies? Prince Sultan, weak and wheezing, decided it was time to take action.

"Give me my gun!" he shouted.

One of the prince's guards refused. Captain Saud's men had guns, and a shootout on the plane would almost certainly be worse than whatever was about to happen. So the prince and his people stopped shouting and sat silently until they touched down. There was no way to fight, and Sultan, helped by Captain Saud's men, was shuffled down the jetway. It's the last time anyone in his entourage saw him.

Security guards showed up and herded the prince's hangers on to a holding area at the airport and eventually to a hotel. There they stayed for three days, unable to do anything. They couldn't leave without a visa, so they just had to wait.

Finally, on the fourth day, guards brought the retinue to a private Royal Court office. One by one, the foreigners were summoned into a sprawling conference room with a huge table in the middle. At the head was Captain Saud, now in a *thobe* instead of his pilot's uniform. "I'm Saud al-Qahtani," he said. "I work at the Royal Court." Saud was no longer just Mohammed's Mr. Hashtag. He had become a central player in the Royal Court's security apparatus, someone Mohammed could rely on to accomplish sensitive, aggressive tasks.

Prince Sultan may not have been a powerful prince, but Mohammed felt he was a problem. He had taken sides against the family, and Saud showed how far he would go to deal with someone Mohammed considered a thorn. Saud asked the foreigners to sign nondisclosure agreements, offered money to some, and sent them back home. The operation was successful, and Saud would use the experience on similar missions to silence dissenters, including one almost three years later that would upend his own life and threaten Mohammed's reform project.

Chapter 7

BILLIONS

September 2016

For nearly two years, Nizar al-Bassam had been trying to do business with Mohammed bin Salman. Now, in Tokyo in September 2016, he was about to get his chance.

At Deutsche Bank, where he worked until late 2015, Nizar specialized in getting to powerful people through strategic charm offensives. Those efforts usually involved one of Nizar's specialties, sumptuous lunches where he sold his contacts on billion-dollar deals over numerous dishes that he liked to personally select for his guests. He was the consummate relationship builder, often working his way up from advisors and aides until he reached the oligarch or prince he was seeking.

Born in Dhahran, where his father, Nabil, was a senior executive and board director of Aramco until his death in 2007, Nizar grew up in the Aramco "camps," fenced-in residential areas modeled after a typical US suburb with front lawns, pee-wee baseball, and English as the dominant language. Attending school there as a child, then later Middlesex boarding school in Massachusetts and Colby College in Maine, he became just as culturally American as Saudi.

In Nizar's last months at Deutsche Bank, Mohammed bin Salman had burst into view with plans to turn the Public

Investment Fund (PIF) into a major sovereign wealth fund. Nizar immediately started trying to get to the key people around the fund, including its chief, Yasir al-Rumayyan, and made some progress, helping to set up meetings for the new PIF team at the St. Petersburg International Economic Forum in June 2015 and offering advice on bailing out the sinking construction company Saudi Oger, a former client. But he still couldn't get to the big man himself.

Hundreds of financial professionals, lawyers, and deal makers were trying—and sometimes succeeding—to take part in the opportunities yielded by the Vision 2030 plan and related projects. There were bond offerings, private placements, and all manner of transactions to get your teeth into, on top of advisory contracts and consultancy projects. The great financial gold rush of the decade was underway, and everyone wanted a piece of it. For Nizar, it was also the perfect next step—marrying his Saudi origins with decades as a high-flying banker.

Beyond the financial opportunities, Mohammed bin Salman was opening the country to tourism in a big way. For much of the country's history it has not been open for visitors, except those going on pilgrimages to Mecca and Medina. Mohammed felt it had huge potential as a vacation destination. The kingdom has a twelve-hundred-mile coastline on the Red Sea, including famous coral reefs that seem more immune than most types to warmer temperatures. And it has historic sites—such as two-thousand-year-old Madain Saleh, with ornate tombs carved into massive sandstone outcroppings by the Nabateans, the same culture that carved the ancient city of Petra in Jordan— that are not on most Middle Eastern tourist destination lists. The prince initiated projects, including a large cluster of beach resorts called the Red Sea Project, to open them up and build the hotels and transportation infrastructure to support them.

He also started building a mirrored concert hall by the Nabatean ruins in al-Ula and an "Entertainment City" nearly as big as Las Vegas outside Riyadh. Called Qiddiya and helmed by a former Disney executive, it is designed to have theme parks, racetracks, and typical Gulf-style projects like an indoor ski slope similar to the one in Dubai.

Here was a young prince, fully in control of his country, with huge amounts of cash to spend and even more on the way. He was everybody's favorite new Saudi ruler, even if he was just short of the title. Steve Schwarzman, founder of Blackstone, became an advisor to the prince. Bankers kept coming by the planeload, eager for a sliver of the action. Even Shane Smith, the tattooed founder of Vice Media, got on the bandwagon.

At first, Nizar wanted Deutsche Bank to be a banker of choice for PIF or the newly empowered Salman clan, but by late 2015 he was growing dissatisfied with the bank as it cut back its ambitions in so-called emerging markets. By May 2016, he'd left and was setting up an advisory firm with partners including former Goldman Sachs Group, Inc., banker Dalinc Ariburnu. One of their first ideas was tapping hidden pockets of money, especially in the Middle East, for a series of investment funds. In canvassing for partners, Nizar and his colleagues began talking to another old Deutsche Bank hand, the chain-vaping head of strategic finance at Japanese tech conglomerate SoftBank Corp., Rajeev Misra.

An arrogant financial engineer with a taste for debt and risk, Rajeev was a senior Deutsche Bank banker during the financial crisis, overseeing a team that eventually profited from betting against the housing market. He left soon after, making brief stops at UBS and Fortress Investment Group before landing at SoftBank.

Rajeev had reconnected with Masayoshi Son, SoftBank's

technology-obsessed founder, at a wedding in Italy a few months earlier and subsequently accepted a job trying to help Masayoshi develop complex debt structures to fund his ambitions. The two had worked together years earlier when Rajeev helped Masayoshi raise $16 billion to buy Vodafone Japan in 2006. SoftBank was pulling off major transactions and had run out of funding, but Masayoshi's ambitions were bigger than ever.

Masayoshi, a short, smiley Japanese man of Korean descent, briefly became the richest man in the world at the peak of the dot-com bubble in the year 2000, only to see most of his fortune plummet in days. But then a lucky $20 million investment in Chinese online marketplace Alibaba in 2000 grew to some $74 billion worth of stock when Alibaba went public in 2014. Using his massive war chest, Masayoshi wanted to bet big on his belief that the world was accelerating toward the "singularity," the moment when technological growth goes so far as to take on its own life, transforming the world as we know it.

Rajeev struggled to find his place at SoftBank, clashing with two other Indian executives who were closer to Masayoshi. He allegedly conspired with an Italian businessman to target them; the businessman set up a honey trap that failed and a fake shareholder campaign calling for them to be fired, though Rajeev later denied involvement. After less than a year, Rajeev was considering leaving. But in conversations with Nizar and his business partners, Rajeev became convinced there was more money waiting on the sidelines than he knew during his years as a banker specializing in the bond market. Then one of his rivals resigned, paving the way for him to begin consolidating power at SoftBank.

Sovereign wealth funds would pair perfectly with Masayoshi's billions. SoftBank and Nizar's new firm, FAB Partners (later rebranded as Centricus), worked together to create an idea, called Project Crystal Ball, for a $20 billion fund that would make investments in technology start-ups with money from SoftBank and partners willing to accept Masayoshi's gut-instinct style of high-speed investing.

They decided to pitch Qatar on the idea first. Nizar had strong ties there already, and the tiny Gulf peninsula had more savings per capita than any country on earth thanks to its massive natural gas fields and tiny population. But when Masayoshi arrived at 4 a.m. on August 28, 2016, in a private jet, Nizar was in for a shock as they sped toward the hotel. During the journey, Masayoshi and his aide had made some tweaks: The Crystal Ball fund was now planned at $100 billion, by far the biggest fund of its kind in history. "If I'm going to do a fund, it has to be big enough to disrupt the whole technology world," he said during the car journey to the hotel, adding that SoftBank could contribute tens of billions of dollars, some of it debt. That was a huge risk for Masayoshi. Most fund sponsors put in a token 1 percent and ask investors to supply the rest. Little did he know at the time that putting skin in the game was exactly the strategy needed to convince Gulf investors to join with a big project.

The Qataris were impressed with Masayoshi's conviction, but nothing came of the discussions. The team still needed huge amounts of money to reach the $100 billion target, and Nizar believed the Saudis, especially Mohammed bin Salman, would be the best bet. By luck, Mohammed was scheduled to arrive in Tokyo within days of the Qatar trip. Nizar hitched a ride on Masayoshi's jet back to Tokyo.

For months, the PIF team had expressed a willingness to meet Masayoshi, but nothing seemed to come together. Nizar sent a stream of messages to his contacts, hoping to at least get Masayoshi in front of key advisors and ministers traveling along-side Mohammed. Masayoshi had an office next to his cleared on the twenty-sixth floor of SoftBank's headquarters in Tokyo. They lobbied contacts as if they were on a political campaign.

The day Mohammed arrived, Nizar felt his phone vibrating on his chest. He had fallen asleep with it there. It was Yasir, the head of PIF, finally returning his call. Yasir could meet Masayoshi in less than four hours. Scrambling, the team prepared to receive him, knowing they'd have a window of half an hour to pitch him on Crystal Ball. "This is interesting. I need to discuss with the deputy crown prince," Yasir told them at the end.

The team went on to make the same pitch to Khalid al-Falih, the minister of energy and head of Aramco, and Majid al-Qasabi, the minister of commerce, who grilled them with tough questions. Finally, the call came through. Mohammed bin Salman agreed to see Masayoshi at the Geihinkan state guest-house. It was the last day of his trip to Japan, and the stakes were high. Without sovereign wealth, the fund could never reach the astronomically high level Masayoshi wanted.

The meeting was intimate and simple, just Mohammed and his key advisors together with a small SoftBank team led by Masayoshi in a brightly lit room with gilded furniture. Nizar waited outside. After Masayoshi went through the presentation on an iPad—his sixth time now—Mohammed said he had discussed the idea at length with his team and wanted to be the cornerstone investor in the new fund. He needed Saudi Arabia to be at the center of global technology transformation, and this was a way to attract innovative companies to his country while also earning returns to fuel the transition away from oil. In short, it was perfect for his Vision 2030.

Nizar was dumbfounded when Masayoshi relayed the news minutes later. He'd imagined they'd need to spend months getting a deal. Instead, they received a commitment for $40 billion. But just before the meeting ended, Mohammed said he'd like Masayoshi to spend a few days seeing Saudi Arabia. "I want you to see my country and fall in love with it," he told him. Masayoshi demurred, saying he could spare half a day. "In that case, maybe it's better you don't come," Mohammed said, a grin forming. The choice was obvious: Masayoshi agreed to come for three days.

The teams would go on to negotiate for nine months before they reached an agreement on the structure and terms of the deal, but Masayoshi liked to say with his typical flourish that it was a deal for $45 billion in forty-five minutes—$1 billion per minute. Not long after, Abu Dhabi agreed to join Saudi Arabia in the fund, committing $15 billion.

Project Crystal Ball, the PowerPoint presentation, was about to become the Vision Fund, the biggest private equity fund focusing on technology in the history of finance. It was an example of the powerful way Mohammed bin Salman was impacting the world through decisive action. Other world leaders controlled more powerful militaries and bigger economies, but he had more distilled power than just about anyone else on earth and a willingness to follow a gut feeling with action. No other investor, as a first big bet, would wager $40 billion on one money manager with a checkered investment record.

After visiting Aramco and the desert on his first trip to Saudi Arabia, Masayoshi settled down for lunch in the Al-Auja palace with Mohammed. Relaxing with his headdress off, revealing a receding hairline, his top button unbuttoned, the prince asked if Masayoshi and his team might be interested in hearing about another project he was planning, something called NEOM.

Over the course of an hour, Mohammed presented an idea more radical than the futuristic visions Masayoshi liked to daydream about back in Japan: an entire new city, built from scratch, with technology in its DNA, across 12,500 square kilometers of land in the north of the country, including a long strip of the Red Sea coast. The land was sparsely inhabited, and those living there would be moved, whether they approved or not.

"Would you like to be a part of this project," Mohammed asked.

"This is a work of art," Masayoshi replied, agreeing to be a founding advisor.

The prince convinced Masayoshi to come back a few months later to see NEOM's planned location in person. They flew into a tiny airport in the city of Tabuk and boarded helicopters that rose above a mountain range and over the coast to land on a rented cruise ship just across from the old fishing village of Sharma.

The prince envisioned an ambitious city that would be at home in a science-fiction novel. Along a sweeping stretch of coast would be a built-from-scratch city of skyscrapers served by flying robot taxis. A planned resort nearby would supplant the French Riviera as a destination for Saudis and Europeans drawn in by its unspoiled corals. An uninhabited island just off the coastline would host an animatronic Jurassic Park–style attraction featuring full-size, robotic dinosaurs.

Even more shocking, the plans seemed to be happening. Onboard the cruise ship were dozens of consultants from McKinsey, BCG, and Oliver Wyman, working on how to turn the NEOM idea into reality. It was a high-stakes bid for the consultants; the two losing teams were contractually obliged to turn over all their work to the winner, who would lead up what was supposed to be a $500 billion project.

Unlike other projects for reforming the Saudi economy, NEOM wasn't concocted by foreign consultants or economic experts. It was a vision that came to Mohammed in a moment of inspiration.

In the days after his father became king, Mohammed was no longer consumed by questions of succession and palace intrigue. He had time to step back and consider what a re-invented Saudi Arabia should look like and what realizing that vision would take.

The task was daunting. King Abdullah had tried to institute social, economic, and educational reforms, but when he died after a decade-long reign, women still weren't allowed to drive. There was just the beginning of an entrepreneurial culture. And a young man still couldn't sit at a café with a young woman unless the two were siblings or spouses. There was little to boast about in the Saudi economy—no innovation to speak of or national champions. The big projects, like King Abdullah Economic City, seemed like feeble imitations of similar developments in Dubai and Singapore.

The economy was dependent on oil and as isolated as ever from the rest of the world. No one wanted to invest in the kingdom. Between 2009 and 2016, annual foreign direct investment fell by 85 percent, consultants for MBS found. And things seemed to be getting worse. In 2011, the consultants said, Saudi Arabia was the world's tenth-easiest country for international companies to do business in; in 2016 it had fallen to eighty-second.

Unlike its tiny neighbors, Saudi Arabia had a big enough population to support a serious economy with homegrown industries. But those with money tended to leave the country to spend it, going to Dubai for entertainment; Paris for tourism; and London, Switzerland, or the United States for medical care. There were few Saudi "staycations."

Mohammed viewed this as "economic leakage." And he became obsessed with the concept that Saudi dollars being spent elsewhere were draining the kingdom's economy. The government was lavishing its citizens with subsidies and jobs, but the benefits were fleeing the country rather than recirculating among domestic businesses and retailers.

Saudi Arabia, Mohammed realized, had been stuck in the same old habits for a half century. It pumped oil, sold it, and spent the money buying things from elsewhere. Only now the kingdom's population was growing rapidly, while the oil—or at least the international demand for it—was running out.

One evening, while mulling those challenges, Mohammed opened a Google Earth map of the kingdom on his computer screen. Staring at an image of his country from space, he scanned the Arabian Peninsula, from Jeddah and Mecca in the west, across the Empty Quarter, to the eastern oil fields of Dhahran, and wondered what he was missing. What opportunities for progress might be hidden in the desert?

And it struck him: The region north of Jeddah, where the mountains along the Jordanian border slope down to the Red Sea, was a blank slate. There was just one small city in the area, and it was surrounded by sparsely populated desert. Mohammed summoned a helicopter to bring him and some friends to the site.

What he saw from the air was inspiring. He had been there before, but he was seeing it with the fresh eyes of a first-time visitor to the kingdom. He flew over mountains so high that snow fell in winter and deserted white beaches lining a placid bay. Offshore coral reefs rivaled those of Egypt's nearby diving resort, Sharm El Sheikh, but with virtually no development.

And while the area had obvious challenges, including a near-total absence of freshwater, it had a great advantage: As it had few people and little significance to Saudi Arabia's religious or economic establishment, Mohammed could make massive changes with little resistance. The area's locals were largely seminomadic Bedouins who had been roaming that stretch of desert for generations. They could be cast out with financial enticement and minimal threats of force.

Perhaps most importantly, the region was largely free of the decrepit infrastructure, ossified bureaucracy, corrupt government officialdom, and rigid religious courts that held back social change—and turned off foreign investors—in established Saudi cities.

Remaking Riyadh and Jeddah, reforming ineffective governance, and getting rid of Islamic judges who ordered lashings and harsh prison sentences that Western allies complained about was a huge task, with entrenched resistance. There would be no pushback in a model city built from scratch in his newly declared frontier. And if it succeeded, if NEOM was as innovative and livable and prosperous as he envisioned, it could pull the rest of the kingdom into a more optimistic future. This was similar to creating the MiSK foundation early in his career—his own company, custom built from scratch with help from foreign advisors—but on a gargantuan scale.

Mohammed decided to build not just a city but a mini kingdom. It would have cutting-edge technology and medical care, all powered by solar energy rather than oil. Nearby would be prime spots for beachgoers and yachts and mountains for hang gliding, rock climbing, and even skiing once engineers started producing snow to supplement the dusting the mountaintops received in winter. Its courts would be Islamic but not Wahhabist. Women wouldn't have to hide their hair or bodies, and alcohol might even be allowed. And everyone—the judges, the bureaucrats, the financial authorities—would report to Mohammed.

He pulled together a board of directors that included the Saudi housing minister, a former Riyadh mayor, a Royal Court advisor, and Mohammed Al Shaikh, the onetime securities regulator who became a trusted ally of the prince. Also on the board was Yasir al-Rumayyan, the banker in charge of Saudi Arabia's sovereign wealth fund.

Mohammed served as board chairman and brought on foreign consultants to assist in the planning. Early on they settled on the name NEOM, a portmanteau of "new" in Greek and "future" in Arabic "because the project represents a civilizational leap for humanity. So the name shouldn't be from a specific civilization,"

Mohammed would later tell a Bloomberg interviewer, though he told another contact that NEOM was actually meant to signify "neuron city," since one of its aims would be to harness the power of the human brain.

When he convened NEOM's first board meeting in August 2016, Mohammed made clear to the consultants that their job was to turn his outlandish instructions into plans that could be implemented in the immediate future. While the board included capable Saudi bureaucrats, none had experience in technology or large-scale planning. It was the consultants' job to figure out what was feasible, then to come up with a plan for how to get those things done.

But the instructions to the consultants for how to plot out the futuristic city-state were fuzzy. Sitting in a gray *thobe*, his head uncovered, at the end of a long boardroom table, Mohammed offered aphorisms too abstruse to be of much use to the consultants.

"NEOM will represent a new generation of cities, combining all innovative ideas in one city," he declared.

How would the consultants deliver this?

"Consultants should check media, cultural content, books and literature to look for ideas" about imagined futures, the board resolved at one meeting, essentially ordering the experts to base the futuristic city on what people in the past thought the future should be.

"Leverage Tomorrowland as inspiration to what future cities might be," it suggested at another, ordering consultants to study the Disney theme park attraction that has included a 3D Michael Jackson video, a monorail, and a film titled *Honey, I Shrunk the Audience*.

Mohammed did identify some ambitious priorities, including the prevention of economic leakage. NEOM could provide the resorts, medical care, and even automobiles on which Saudis spent billions of dollars abroad, Mohammed reasoned, keeping that money within the Saudi economy.

Another fixation of the prince was the difficulty foreign businesses had operating in Saudi Arabia. The kingdom invested billions of dollars in foreign companies. Now Mohammed wanted those companies to invest in the kingdom. The world's biggest tech firms, automakers, and aerospace companies would come to NEOM and build offices and factories, Mohammed said. This would require new legal structures circumventing Saudi Arabia's Islamic courts, where there was no functional bankruptcy law, and even simple business disputes could turn into a Middle Eastern Bleak House.

And Mohammed was deeply aware of the kingdom's other big challenge: No one from the West wanted to move to Saudi Arabia. Its climate was too harsh and its restrictions on entertainment and women's rights too uninviting. That, too, would have to change in NEOM.

And lastly, it had to be better than regional rival Dubai.

Turning those edicts into a credible plan seemed impossible for the consultants. But with Mohammed promising to spend $500 billion on it, they knew it could be the commission of a lifetime, potentially bringing tens of millions of dollars to whoever got the lead role.

In those initial NEOM meetings, McKinsey consultants and their rivals from BCG and Oliver Wyman sat opposite their Saudi counterparts at the long boardroom table and presented ideas for what NEOM's focus should be. They identified nine areas ("clusters," in consultant jargon) that NEOM's board agreed would form the foundation of the city. These were unsurprising, including things like energy, technology, manufacturing, and entertainment. Then, at a meeting the consultants called an "ideation session," Mohammed announced there would be a new

cluster, "Cluster 0," which concerned the notion of "livability."
NEOM had to be the world's most pleasant place to live.

Through board meetings over the course of months, Mohammed threw seemingly endless ideas at the consultants. NEOM
needed flying cars and a multi-billion-dollar bridge to Egypt.
Was it possible to create an artificial full moon that would rise
each night? And about that beach in the resort area: "I want the
sand to glow," Mohammed told one of the planners. Commercial
space travel would be a good industry to bring to the city. Also
farmers' markets.

NEOM had to "pioneer and lead all sectors of the future,"
Mohammed told the Saudis and Westerners around his boardroom table. It would have the world's highest per-capita GDP
and an unrivaled work-life balance.

Some of his requests were seemingly contradictory. The Saudi
government was going to spend $500 billion on NEOM, but
the project would not be "built on subsidy," the board declared.
"NEOM will ensure equality and fairness for all," said Rumayyan,
the sovereign wealth fund chief, at one meeting before discussing how NEOM would have full-time surveillance of everyone
within its borders so criminals could be caught instantaneously
and, later, how only Saudis with certain qualifications would be
allowed in.

Latham & Watkins, a US law firm that agreed to be NEOM's
"legal partner," identified problems in the existing Saudi legal
system and suggested fixing them by implementing a new structure in which every judge was appointed by, and reported to,
Mohammed. The firm declined to comment on its work when
the *Wall Street Journal* reported on it.

In more than two thousand pages of planning documents, the
consultants came up with an answer for everything. NEOM,
BCG declared, could stop up to $100 billion in annual economic
leakage. The prince's notion of "livability," formerly a matter of

personal preference, could now be quantified through a groundbreaking new system that McKinsey invented specifically for NEOM. It was "based on empirical evidence and leveraging big data to measure citizen satisfaction, happiness, and engagement," the consultants wrote in explanation of how they had devised a way to objectively measure a city's pleasantness. NEOM, they promised in presentations to their Saudi clients, would be the most pleasant of them all.

The consultants turned NEOM's apparent weaknesses into strengths. The region might not have any freshwater, but it had "unlimited access to saltwater" and could become a "global water champion" by developing desalination plants. And perhaps, BCG suggested, NASA would partner in developing the prince's artificial moon, which would be the biggest in the world.

After four workshops over a series of months, the board and its consultants arrived at a vision statement for the project: "The land of the future, where the greatest minds and best talents are empowered to embody pioneering ideas and exceed boundaries in a world inspired by imagination." It was a masterclass by the consultants in telling an ambitious prince exactly what he wanted to hear.

After visiting the cruise ship full of consultants off NEOM's coast, Masayoshi told Mohammed that he was a visionary and agreed to have SoftBank partner on one of NEOM's most ambitious projects: "A new way of life from birth to death reaching genetic mutations to increase human strength and IQ," as the consultants later described it.

Speaking later, Masayoshi referred to Mohammed bin Salman as the "Bedouin Steve Jobs."

Rajeev, the SoftBank executive, had his own enormous task at hand. The Saudi and Abu Dhabi money made him change his mind about leaving SoftBank. Now he had more financial firepower than just about anyone on earth and a fly-by-the-seat-of-his-pants boss who was happy to make multi-billion-dollar investments with a quick meeting and a "gut instinct." The only problem was that the Vision Fund had about twenty employees and no investment procedures or compliance apparatus. Even worse, though it had already started investing money, it had to temporarily hold money on SoftBank's balance sheet while the fund's team was getting built up.

The team members at PIF were skeptical of the Vision Fund their boss had signed on to, but they were in no position to oppose it. Instead, they started pushing for details and proof the firm was ready to accept so much cash.

The official closing for the Vision Fund was still months away, but on another visit by Masayoshi, Nizar, and Rajeev to Riyadh, the prince appeared concerned. There was a dinner on the beach full of excited discussion about NEOM and Masayoshi's utopian vision of including one million robots in the city to handle all the domestic tasks, leaving humans to free to do more important things. It was typical Masayoshi: a nice round number and flashy concept without much substance.

Afterward, Mohammed pulled aside Masayoshi for a walk along the water to ask him to consider looking at investing in Uber. The company was in the news for all the wrong reasons, including governance and safety issues and a scandal involving senior executives spying on rivals. Uber was the Public Investment Fund's first big deal, and he didn't want it to go belly up—such bad public relations could harm the public view of his fledgling investment record.

"I'm very worried," Mohammed said. Masayoshi had wanted to avoid ridesharing but agreed to take a closer look.

———

Mohammed bin Salman's worries didn't stop there. He had deftly taken power, set the country off on the biggest transformation project since the discovery of oil almost eighty years earlier, and started spending billions of dollars on foreign investments. But war was still raging in Yemen, and the long-entrenched elites he'd knocked out of orbit were plotting behind his back. To survive, like his uncles and grandfather before him, he'd need support from the United States, where an upcoming election could be a huge boon to the kingdom.

Neither Donald Trump nor Hillary Clinton seemed like a natural ally. Saudi leaders had long found Clinton an irksome counterparty when she was secretary of state, with her insistence on pressing the king and his deputies on human rights issues and demanding more freedom for women in the kingdom when they met. Donald Trump seemed even more problematic, with his naked Islamophobia and criticism of President Barack Obama for attempting to block a law that would let people sue Saudi Arabia in US courts for the 9/11 attacks.

But Mohammed, with the help of allies in the United Arab Emirates, came to believe that Trump was the better choice. He seemed inclined to scrap the Iran nuclear deal, which the Saudi leadership loathed, and appeared to care little about the human rights issues that preoccupied Clinton.

So Mohammed was furious when, three weeks before the presidential election, a distant cousin of his showed up in Los Angeles with a prominent Democratic donor and posed for photos with Representative Adam Schiff, a powerful congressional Democrat. It looked to the world like a member of the Saudi royal family was supporting the Democrats.

The cousin, Salman bin Abdulaziz bin Salman Al Saud, was technically a prince. But he wasn't a descendant of the kingdom's founder, Ibn Saud, as Mohammed was. Salman was descended from a relative of Ibn Saud, so he wasn't in line for the throne.

Salman was handsome and fantastically wealthy, largely because his father, a former advisor to King Fahd, had built a huge family fortune. He and Mohammed had known each other since they were young. When they were in their teens, Salman used to tease Mohammed, who was overweight and spent his time playing video games while Salman was becoming fluent in French and traveling abroad. When they were in their twenties, Salman dismissed Mohammed as uncultured and unpleasant, telling friends he was the cousin whom other young Al Saud tried to avoid.

Now they were in their thirties. Mohammed was the most powerful man in the kingdom next to the king himself, and his cousin Salman was, in Mohammed's eyes, a self-aggrandizing clown. Attracted to wealth and power, Salman started the grandiosely named "Visionary Movers Club," an attempt to unite world leaders behind charitable initiatives that betrayed his claim to be fluent in English.

Appearing in posed photographs with neatly trimmed stubble and finely tailored Italian suits with lapels so wide they bordered on the preposterous, Prince Salman chased political leaders and press coverage, trumpeting his education at the Sorbonne and promises to fix global problems like access to clean water.

A Dubai businessman had introduced Salman to a Democratic donor, California executive Andy Khawaja. He in turn had Salman meet Schiff, who later told CNN that all he recalled of the meeting were general discussions of Middle East politics. Salman told a member of his entourage afterward that his talks with Khawaja and Schiff focused on his charitable efforts. (Separately Khawaja has since been indicted in the United States on charges of funneling illegal campaign contributions to Clinton in a scheme connected to Mohammed bin Zayed; Khawaja said he "never took money from any foreign leaders. It's all lies.")

But Mohammed was furious. Why was this no-name prince making it look like the royal family was backing Clinton? He called Salman, who assured him the meetings weren't political. That night, an official with the Royal Court called Salman's father. "Why is he in the US?" the official asked. Cowed, Salman decided to lay low, at least for a while, and he wrote a letter to the Royal Court saying he was just in the United States for business and social engagements, not politics. But for Mohammed the upcoming election was a crucial moment, and his cousin's appearance had been inopportune.

Chapter 8

LITTLE SPARTA

December 2016

Discarding his white robes for a buttoned-up dress shirt and aviator sunglasses, the muscled crown prince of Abu Dhabi, Mohammed bin Zayed, arrived for a secret meeting at Manhattan's Trump Tower looking like an Arab James Bond.

The group receiving him was unlike anything he'd seen in his years of diplomacy with the United States, his closest Western ally and protector. On one side was Steve Bannon, the former banker and right-wing media executive whose fraying fleeces over two or three layers of collared shirts, reddened cheeks, shaggy gray hair, and tendency to pontificate on the ancient past gave him the air of a rumpled, though deeply reactionary, professor. Then there was Jared Kushner, the trim real estate heir married to Ivanka Trump, who once told Bannon on a flight that he didn't think experts with a deep understanding of the past were necessarily the best people to plot out the geopolitical future.

"I don't believe in that," Kushner said.

"You don't believe in what?" Bannon responded.

"In history," Kushner said. "I don't read history. It bogs you down."

And between them was Michael Flynn, a decorated former lieutenant general who was just coming out of a private-sector career as a consultant and lobbyist for foreign governments. They all worked for real estate tycoon Donald Trump, who had just, against all the odds, won the presidency of the United States in part by rallying nearly half the voting populace around a doctrine of "America First." At times, his policies were outright hostile to the Muslim world.

But Mohammed bin Zayed, known as MBZ, suddenly felt deeply at ease as Bannon got to talking.

"I'm only here to talk about the Persians," Bannon said.

Mohammed bin Zayed broke into an astonished smile. "Did you say Persians? I've been looking for an American like you for twenty years."

Bannon was speaking in a way the Emirati leader understood. "Iran" was a nation whose government President Barack Obama had trusted enough to negotiate a nuclear deal with. "The Persians," on the other hand, were an ethnic group and longtime enemy of the Arabs. And as far as MBZ and Bannon were concerned, they were a threat to the United Arab Emirates and Saudi Arabia—and their allies in the West—if they decided to rebuild the Safavid empire that had dominated much of the region three centuries earlier.

In a discussion with Admiral Kevin Cosgriff in June 2007, Mohammed bin Zayed summarized his cultural viewpoint succinctly. "Any culture that is patient and focused enough to spend years working on a single carpet is capable of waiting years and even decades to achieve even greater goals," he told Cosgriff, according to a leaked State Department cable. Iran's goal was "a new Greater Persian Empire wielding the influence of a nuclear weapon."

Mohammed and Bannon went on for another hour, talking about history, security, and frustration with what they saw as Obama's dangerously naive Iran deal. Then the Emirati made a suggestion: The Trump camp should meet Mohammed bin Salman. "He's the key to your plans in the region," he said.

The suggestion was just one way that the Emiratis were bolstering the credentials of an upstart prince in the massively larger Saudi Arabia. Since its founding in 1971, the UAE has had complicated relations with the Saudis and their association with the Wahhabi strain of Islam. While the princes along the Persian Gulf (or, as they call it, the Arabian Gulf) quickly built international cities of renown like Dubai, Abu Dhabi, and Doha, the aging kings of Saudi Arabia and their Wahhabist supporters appeared to be obsessed with a status quo dating back to the early twentieth century. Modern Saudi Arabia's history—and the Al Saud's claim to legitimacy—was intertwined with the conservative religious establishment and the custodianship of the holy cities of Mecca and Medina.

Yet Saudi Arabia was the Gulf country with a real population and serious size. It was the only country in the region that really mattered on the world stage. But it had long refused to lead, preferring instead to rely on the United States to maintain regional security while it spent billions of dollars spreading Wahhabism, a worldview holding that going to the movies or listening to music was evil, through the far reaches of the Muslim world.

Many of the same ingredients are present across the Arabian Peninsula: huge petrochemical deposits and the requisite wealth, conservative social norms, tribal customs, and desert topography. Still, the differences between each Gulf city can be profound. The Al Maktoum family of Dubai are the consummate mercantilists, focusing their efforts over the years on creating a futuristic trading hub that is home to millions of expatriates who live much as they would in Sydney, London, or New York. The Al Sabah of Kuwait allowed democratic-style institutions to rise in their country before any of their neighbors, even permitting rowdy newspapers that criticize government officials, something unseen elsewhere in the region. The Al Said of Oman have developed a reputation as low-profile diplomats, operating as

important go-betweens in discussions between Western countries and Iran, for example. And the Al Thanis of the tiny
peninsula of Qatar have propped up Islamists, including the
Muslim Brotherhood, and other similar groups across the Arab
world even when their fellow Gulf states see them as the biggest
threats to their absolute monarchies. Though one of the smallest
countries, Qatar has one of the most aggressive foreign policies
in the whole region.

Mohammed bin Zayed, the crown prince of Abu Dhabi, was
one of more than a dozen living sons of the founder of the country, Zayed Al Nahyan. After his father died, he quickly became
one of the most powerful sheikhs. When his elder brother,
Khalifa, who was the president, became ill in 2014, MBZ took
over as the day-to-day ruler of the country. Other brothers held
top positions across the government, including foreign minister,
national security advisor, and minister of interior.

A former helicopter pilot, MBZ is a man of contradictions. He
presided over some of Abu Dhabi's most ambitious efforts, including setting up a peaceful nuclear energy program, building a
New York University outpost that accepts mainly students from
abroad, often on full scholarships, and the creation of a Louvre
museum on an island near the city's main island. But he also
surrounds himself with people of dubious character, including
former US and UK spies and men like Erik Prince, founder
of the infamous private security contractor Blackwater. MBZ's
aspirations to make the UAE a legitimate player in military conflicts, including sending special operations soldiers to help the
United States in Afghanistan, earned Abu Dhabi the moniker
"Little Sparta" from retired US Marine Corps general James
Mattis, who ran US Central Command from 2010 to 2013.

In the same morning, MBZ could be convening in his office
with Will Tricks, a former MI-6 officer who advises him on
intelligence matters, and taking a stroll through a giant aviary

filled with exotic birds within his palace compound, talking about history with Zaki Nuseibeh, his father's erudite former translator whose homes are lined with thousands of books. To Western friends, he's a philosopher king—unpretentious, worldly, unafraid of criticism, and bold in confronting enemies. To those caught up in Abu Dhabi's security dragnet, he is a brutal autocrat who some even claim is willing to get his hands dirty, allegations he denies.

Mohammed Zawahiri, brother of top al-Qaeda leader Ayman Zawahiri, alleged in an interview that when he was arrested in the Emirates in 1999, he was bundled off to Abu Dhabi where Mohammed bin Zayed handled the interrogation himself, beating him in the process. The Egyptian claimed he was then packed into a wooden box with holes and sent to Egyptian security, which threw him in prison without acknowledging his existence for seven years. Sources close to MBZ have denied these claims.

Despite a personal wealth of billions of dollars, MBZ is known as remarkably low-key, often wearing a baseball cap in his office, driving himself around the city or eating at his favorite café in Abu Dhabi, an Australian import called Jones the Grocer, for lunch with a visiting diplomat.

Having written off the geriatric leaders of Saudi Arabia for years, MBZ focused much of his effort on dealing with the United States, relying on an athletic, completely bald Emirati called Yousef al-Otaiba, who quickly became the most connected Arab in Washington, DC, when he arrived as ambassador in 2008.

Otaiba's skill rested in large part on his ability to connect with Americans on a cultural level, including cheering on sports teams over beers and barbecue at his lavish ambassador's residence outside the capital or treating more refined guests to special dinners prepared by Wolfgang Puck and other renowned chefs.

The UAE had a long history of relations with the Saudi royal family and was technically a close ally. When Abdullah was on his deathbed, Mohammed bin Zayed bet that his son, Miteb bin Abdullah, was on his way to the throne. It was only when Mohammed bin Salman forced himself onto the scene and emerged as a new force that Abu Dhabi started paying attention.

Much about MBS turned out to be attractive to the Emiratis. He was a young technology enthusiast who wanted his country to undergo a similar transformation as the UAE. Abu Dhabi had a 2030 plan built by management consultants long before Riyadh, and Abu Dhabi's development convinced the world to start treating the city as a sort of Middle Eastern Washington, DC, with diplomats, businessmen, spies, and powerful people regularly descending on it for conferences and strategy meetings.

In Mohammed bin Salman, MBZ saw a once-in-a-lifetime opportunity to forge a deeper alliance with his much bigger, more powerful neighbor. Not only could Mohammed put an end to Saudi Arabia's regressive ways, but together they could be a major force in global foreign policy and perhaps begin to build a better future for the region.

The problem, as MBZ saw it, was that MBS had not yet solidified his power and influence in the face of Al Saud rivals—some of whom, like Crown Prince Mohammed bin Nayef, had bad blood with the Emiratis. (MBZ once effectively called the crown prince's father, Nayef, an ape to US diplomats.) So MBZ set his extensive lobbying and influence operations into motion with the goal of getting the word out to the West: Someone exciting was on the rise in Saudi Arabia, and they needed to meet him. This was especially important in the United States, where officials had a long-standing relationship with Mohammed bin Nayef. Now, with a new US president and an ascendant prince in Mohammed, there was an opportunity for MBZ to gain more influence.

Otaiba was a key component in this campaign, as was MBZ's brother Tahnoon bin Zayed, the national security advisor (arguably the country's de facto spy chief) and jiujitsu champion who often wore sunglasses indoors because of light sensitivity and relaxed by floating in an isolation chamber. Tahnoon would be a frequent intermediary between the men, meeting Mohammed in Tangier; Washington, DC; and, frequently, Riyadh. Tahnoon would go on to have a big impact on Mohammed, convincing him to try the ketogenic diet preferred by a doctor called Peter Attia and to pare back his love of McDonald's fast food. When John Kerry met Mohammed on his yacht in the Red Sea in 2016, Tahnoon was lounging around on his own boat anchored nearby.

Khaldoon Al Mubarak, the man in charge of Abu Dhabi's sovereign wealth fund Mubadala Development, also worked with his Saudi counterparts on economic diversification plans.

Back in Washington, DC, Otaiba started spreading the word to his network of former US government officials, who in turn started talking about MBS to their old colleagues in the State Department, Pentagon, and White House. David Petraeus, the retired general, first went to see Mohammed bin Salman at Otaiba's urging.

"Incredible, frankly. Breathtaking vision. And some of it already in execution. If just half materializes, will be extraordinary," Petraeus wrote afterward, according to an email from a cache hacked by a group calling itself Global Leaks.

"MBZ shares that exact assessment," Otaiba wrote back. "Now you need to convey that to an extremely anxious and wary administration of MBS I've been urging them to invest in him the way we have."

The Mohammed bin Zayed meeting in Trump Tower set off alarms in the Obama White House, which would be in place for another two months. Off-the-books meetings between foreign leaders and an incoming administration don't normally happen.

America had been Saudi Arabia's most steadfast backer since US geologists discovered crude in the desert almost a century ago. American companies built the foundations of the Saudi oil industry and provided the kingdom with weaponry and military training. In exchange, Saudi Arabia became the United States' most reliable ally in the region. Even after the 1973 oil embargo, the 9/11 terror attacks, and the innovation of fracking that ended America's reliance on Saudi oil, the relationship remained strong through the early 2000s, thanks to old hands in the US State Department, the CIA, and Saudi Arabia's intelligence and security services.

But the friendship soured under the presidency of Barack Obama. Leaders from the UAE and Saudi Arabia chafed at his decision to negotiate a nuclear deal with Iran, their biggest enemy, without consulting them. To make matters worse, the negotiations were held next door in Oman, one of the six Gulf Cooperation Council countries. When Obama paid a 2015 condolence call to Riyadh after Abdullah's death, a still obscure MBS stood up in a meeting of ministers and cabinet members and chided Obama for turning his back on the kingdom. Some in the American delegation had no idea who the assertive young prince was.

Later on, Mohammed would complain to a group of Americans, "Obama stopped supporting us." It was a gross oversimplification—the United States had sold billions of dollars' worth of weapons to Saudi Arabia during Obama's presidency— but it reflected the view throughout the Saudi Royal Court and the region. In Mohammed's eyes, Obama's nuanced approach to negotiating with Iran while maintaining the Saudi alliance amounted to a betrayal.

Even with Obama out and Trump coming in, primed for

a favorable introduction to Mohammed, he had another big problem: His rival, Mohammed bin Nayef, had much stronger relationships with US officials, friendships that sank much deeper than the political level into America's intelligence, military, and diplomatic institutions. That remained true even after Mohammed cast MBN's former deputy Saad al-Jabri into exile.

After two decades as Saudi Arabia's antiterrorism chief, MBN knew all sorts of people inside the State Department and CIA. Many considered him a friend. Information from his army of agents and informants had revealed threats to Saudi and American interests alike.

Donald Trump's election offered a chance for Mohammed to reset the US relationship with himself as the focal point. On the surface, Trump's surprise victory seemed like a defeat for the Muslim world. His campaign's Islamophobia shocked even Americans as he spoke of banning Muslims from entering the United States.

MBS saw that as bluster. It had nothing to do with how Trump actually felt about Islam, he'd assert later. Rather, the prince figured, it was what Trump needed to say to get elected. Beneath the bombast, MBS calculated, was a man who could be won over with a bit of flattery and some nine-figure deals for US companies. What's more, Mohammed sympathized with the hatred of Islamic ultraconservatives: they'd given the religion a bad name with their over-the-top displays of religiosity and ignorance of the rest of the world. Skeptical Westerners were still writing with ridicule about Abdulaziz bin Baz, the former Saudi grand mufti who denied that the Earth orbits the sun until a Saudi, King Salman's older son Sultan, returned from a voyage on a US space shuttle and assured bin Baz that the Earth does indeed rotate on its axis and revolve around the sun.

Mohammed's two willing partners in the remade US alliance would be the same men MBZ met in Trump Tower, Steve

Bannon and Jared Kushner. They realized they needed to erase the Islamophobia charge to get Arab support for their top Middle East priorities. For Bannon that was punishing Iran, while Kushner needed backing for a Palestine peace deal. The young real estate executive loved the idea that he could find a way to bring peace to the Middle East with old-fashioned business sense and horse trading. It would be a hallmark of the Trump presidency. For every problem, there was a transaction that could solve it.

The Saudi courtship of Kushner began early on. Mohammed sent two senior emissaries, security official Musaad al-Aiban and then–energy minister Khalid al-Falih, to Trump Tower. They wanted Trump's first visit as president to be to Riyadh. It seemed like a good plan all around. For Mohammed, it would show that he was reinvigorating the old US alliance. For Trump, it would help banish the Islamophobia charge. Leaders from both countries understood that such a visit would be seen as an aggressive stance against Iran.

"If you want to have a good relationship with President Trump," Kushner told Aiban and Falih at the meeting, "it's very simple: stop terrorism. Modernize. Stop extremism." Also, he added, it would be good for Saudi Arabia to make progress normalizing relations with Israel.

And Kushner said that if Trump was going to make the visit, the Saudis would have to make some changes to show good faith to the United States. "You have to start letting women drive and give them more rights," Kushner told the men. They assured him that Mohammed was planning to do those things, since he believed they were good for the kingdom.

It turns out that MBS already had women's right to drive on the top of his agenda. To most in the West, it seemed like the simplest of decisions, but king after king had taken steps toward rectifying the backward tradition and then stopped at the last minute. A new law had been drafted and redrafted for decades, but geriatric royals felt it was too risky. MBS, with his focus on the sentiment of the burgeoning youth population, felt it was no longer such a risk—indeed that it was a bigger risk to continue alienating young Saudis and Western allies with the restriction. Later in 2017, the king issued a royal decree that women could drive starting June 2018. Kushner and others felt they were having a positive influence, even if MBS already had the change on his agenda before he'd met them.

In the weeks after the inauguration, others in the new Trump administration worried about the visit. Secretary of State Rex Tillerson and some staffers for the National Security Council objected. They had bigger foreign-policy priorities and more reliable allies that they needed to meet. They warned about the risk of appearing to favor MBS at a touchy time for Saudi Arabia. The United States' most trusted Saudi contact, MBN, was sandwiched between a king with Wahhabist sympathies and his favorite son, who had clear ambitions for the throne. Some staffers worried that a visit could play into Mohammed's plans to usurp his cousin and position himself as the king-in-waiting.

Tillerson told other officials that he was especially worried about undermining MBN. And he argued that the promises the Saudis were making, to improve the situation of women and fight extremism, were unreliable. "Saudis, they'll always let you down," Tillerson told Kushner in one meeting. "They'll never come through."

Postpone the plan until May 2018, Tillerson's staff told Kushner, who delivered the message to Bannon in a White House meeting.

"You've got to be fucking kidding me," Bannon said. He dismissed the career officials as the "deep state," a term that originally described unelected actors in Turkey's government who supposedly ran the country from the shadows. Such staffers' priority, Bannon argued, was to maintain their own power and prop up their own allies abroad. They couldn't be trusted to support the kind of new order Trump's advisors envisioned.

Kushner argued that the White House should give the Saudis the opportunity to deliver, and Trump staffers set up a call between the new president and King Salman.

"I'm a great admirer of you, Mr. President," Salman said.

"Okay, King," Trump responded. He said he would put Kushner, his son-in-law, in charge of organizing the trip. Salman responded that he had tasked Mohammed with taking care of the Saudi end and offered the former reality TV star a flattering flourish. "If you don't think he's doing a good job," Salman said, "you can tell him, 'You're fired!'"

Kushner and Mohammed began communicating, sometimes via WhatsApp messages, and got along well. Kushner liked Mohammed's explanation that he wasn't trying to modernize Saudi Islam; he was actually trying to restore it to its more moderate roots. Mohammed had explained to many foreign politicians and journalists that Saudi Arabia had been on the road toward a more liberal society until a 1979 terrorist attack on the Grand Mosque in Mecca prompted the Al Saud to cede power to conservative religious elements.

In fact this was an oversimplification: The Al Saud had come to power through their alliance with Wahhabist fighters, and the political descendants of those fighters were the kingdom's religious establishment.

But Mohammed gave Kushner confidence that he was a new kind of prince, one who understood the importance of the world of money and technology and wasn't interested in age-old grievances. In comparison, MBN seemed stodgy and change averse.

Facing doubt from Tillerson and members of the political establishment, Kushner called Mohammed and told him he wanted all the Saudi promises surrounding the trip put in writing. The prince responded by sending Aiban, the security official, to Washington for several weeks. In meetings over that period, he and Kushner worked through the US requests and the Saudi promises and put them all in writing. Once Aiban returned to Riyadh, Mohammed told his well-organized group of deputies to start planning a series of lavish public ceremonies. In Washington, Kushner didn't move as quickly.

In February, a cherub-faced former presidential advance man named Steve Atkiss got a surprising call from the White House. "It looks like the president's first trip overseas may be to Saudi," an aide named Joe Hagin told Atkiss, a former colleague. "No one here has any knowledge of how to plan a trip, and no one has any knowledge of Saudi."

Atkiss offered to help. He had planned a trip to the kingdom for George W. Bush and accompanied the then-president to Riyadh. He was also along for a visit King Abdullah made to Bush's Texas ranch. Atkiss said he'd work for the Trump White House as a volunteer—it was an opportunity to help Hagin, an old friend, and wouldn't be bad for his consultancy, Command Group. He had a meeting with Kushner and began reaching out to his Saudi planning counterparts.

A few weeks later, Mohammed bin Salman came to Washington to meet Pentagon officials in his capacity as Saudi defense minister. He arranged a brief sit-down with Trump that turned into seven hours of lunch and conversations after German chancellor Angela Merkel had to cancel a planned White House appearance due to a snowstorm.

The press photos of Mohammed with Trump sent a signal back home. MBN, the crown prince, wasn't on the trip. Mohammed, who was supposedly his deputy, was forging a new alliance with America.

What Mohammed found was encouraging. In his first trip to

the White House without the skeptical Obama administration crowd, he received a much warmer reception, especially when he criticized Obama. The big problem with the former president, Mohammed told Trump, was that he had a fundamentally flawed view of the Middle East. He wanted to empower Iran and the Muslim Brotherhood and to cut Saudi Arabia out of the mix. And Trump nemesis Hillary Clinton, Obama's first secretary of state, had been disrespectful to Saudi Arabia, Mohammed said.

In the weeks after that meeting, Mohammed would understand he was dealing with a much more receptive, and pliant, White House than any the Saudis had previously seen. And compared to his own operation, he would realize, the Trump White House was extremely disorganized. That would play to Mohammed's advantage.

Once trip dates were finalized, Mohammed's staffers began working day and night to carry out the prince's plans to host the trip. He wanted to fly in top chefs, and his staffers arranged that. He wanted Trump and King Salman to hold a public ceremony to sign commercial deals so that Trump could take credit for bringing in billions of dollars of Saudi spending.

To show Trump that he—not MBN—was the most fervent fighter of terrorism in the Saudi government, Mohammed brought engineers and a construction crew to a decrepit Royal Court hotel and had them turn the lobby into a *Battlestar Galactica*–style "war room" for a new anti-extremism center under Mohammed's control. He even brought David Petraeus to see it while construction was underway. It seemed potentially impressive, though somewhat redundant since MBN had been working for years on anti-extremism programs. As later became clear, it was more a made-for-TV set for world leaders to convene on than an indicator of any kind of significant shift in Saudi priorities.

And to show Trump that Saudi Arabia loves America, Mohammed had staff arrange for performers like the Harlem Globetrotters to be in Riyadh when Trump arrived. Flying in celebrities from a visiting leader's own country was an unconventional strategy, but Mohammed figured it might appeal to Trump's apparent unease with anything too exotic.

The Americans, on the other hand, seemed to have no such detailed vision. The day-to-day life of the Trump White House was America's greatest soap opera, complete with rumors of ill-fated romances, firings, and polarizing policies, such as building a wall on the Mexican border. Kushner and Bannon were in the middle of it, but they knew that they wanted the Saudi visit to happen right away—and that they, not the "deep state," had to control it. As far as Trump's closest advisors were concerned, there was no such thing as a government staffer who existed to carry out the president's orders—the longtime staff, they suspected, were liberal ideologues who would undermine the Trump agenda.

So Kushner and a deputy national security advisor named Dina Powell took on lead roles in the planning. An Egyptian-born, Arabic-speaking former Goldman Sachs banker and George W. Bush aide, Powell was seen in the White House as a bridge to the Middle East.

Powell and Kushner sat down with Atkiss, the ex-presidential advance man, to start arranging logistics. He was set to depart for Riyadh the next day and needed instructions. One priority, after safety and working out logistical kinks, was making sure the president wasn't put in any embarrassing situations.

As a longtime advance man—someone who prepares the groundwork for the massive moveable circus that is a presidential entourage—Atkiss had a seemingly clear role. The White House and its commercial, military, diplomatic, and security people would come up with a detailed list of plans, and he would go to Riyadh ahead of time to arrange logistics, assess risk, and work out whatever details were necessary to carry out the White House's instructions and make sure the trip went safely and smoothly.

But Powell and Kushner gave vague instructions in their White House meeting. They basically just provided a list of things the president and the Saudis wanted to do, including the ceremony to sign US-Saudi business deals. How long would the ceremony be? They didn't know. An hour-long meeting would present different security concerns than a ten-minute sit-down. What deals would be signed? Who had to be brought in for the meeting? Did the CEO of Boeing need to be flown in? The chairman of GE?

"Hmm, I don't know," Kushner responded. "Who's the keeper of the list?" He, Powell, and Atkiss stared blankly at one another. "Could you be?" Kushner asked Atkiss.

It was a strange request of a volunteer, since lists of attendees on an official visit are typically kept by the National Security Council. But this was the White House asking, and Atkiss agreed to do it. When he arrived in Riyadh, he went to the fortresslike US embassy and sat down with staffers there to discuss. "It's on us to come up with a list of every possible deal between the United States and Saudi Arabia that could be signed at this event," Atkiss told them.

There were other awkward requests from the Royal Court. The Saudis, for example, wanted to gather leaders from most of the world's Muslim countries in a room to meet Trump. This had the makings of a debacle. Trump was brand-new in the presidency and couldn't be expected to know much about the fifty-plus heads of state who would likely be there. Was it really a good idea to put an inexperienced president in a room with the leaders of Turkmenistan and Burkina Faso, Jordan and Mauritania and just hope for the best?

"The Saudis want to do it," Kushner responded. The idea was greenlit. So was a Saudi plan for King Salman to place a medal in the shape of a collar around Trump's neck, a request that concerned some White House staffers because Trump doesn't like being touched by strangers.

Atkiss checked into the Riyadh Ritz-Carlton with plenty of busy work to do—making sure Donald and Melania Trump got the separate suites they requested, for example, and figuring out where the emergency exits were in each meeting place.

On his first morning, Atkiss dialed into a video conference that would start a monthlong cycle in the tradition of *Groundhog Day*. On his screen were Powell and Kushner, the point people for the White House. They asked questions about meetings and logistics. Then Atkiss made his one major query: "Who's working on the list?" He needed to know what business deals Trump and the king were going to sign. He'd given the embassy-generated list to Kushner and Powell to review. "Where are we on the list?"

"I don't have it," Kushner said.

Each day, for another nineteen days, Atkiss would ask the same question. And each day, he would receive a similar response. It wasn't clear who was responsible for the delays. Kushner and Powell were both working on multiple priorities, and Secretary of Commerce Wilbur Ross, whose office also had a role reviewing the deals, didn't seem engaged.

Atkiss had no such trouble getting much more specific direction from his Saudi contacts. During daily meetings, Aiban or another of the government officials working on the trip would brief Atkiss on a detailed plan and ask for US feedback. Sometimes MBS's younger brother Khalid would come to meetings, and the older ministers would all defer to the soon-to-be ambassador to the United States, waiting for him to speak. Breakfasts and dinners and tours for the president were scheduled. A princess arranged to take Melania around Riyadh.

At the king's executive office, a grand white building in the modern Islamic style called the Royal Diwan, workers removed each cobblestone in the driveway surrounding an immaculate grass courtyard and laid it back down, ensuring the path was perfectly smooth. One day the king's head of protocol, Khalid al-Abad, brought Atkiss to scope out Ibn Saud's old fortress Al Murabba, which is now a museum. They did a walkthrough of the tour Trump would take of the renovated mud-walled building. Abad showed him the entrances, exits, and security checkpoints. "And here," he said as they entered a museum gallery, "we will have Toby Keith."

Atkiss paused. The country star who sang "We'll put a boot in your ass, it's the American way" to would-be terrorists after 9/11 seemed like a strange person to bring to Riyadh. But in his enthusiasm to embrace America, Mohammed had his underlings offer several million dollars for the singer—who had performed at Trump's preinaugural celebration—to drop everything and surprise the president in Ibn Saud's former home.

Late at night, Mohammed's deputies would call Atkiss, passing on inquiries directly from the prince. And during the day, Atkiss would keep working out the details and pestering the White House to give him the list of agreements. A few days before the trip, Aiban asked once again for the list of business deals. Atkiss promised he wouldn't come back to Aiban until he had the list.

On May 18, two days before the trip, Atkiss logged onto his final video conference with the White House. "Let's go over the schedule," Kushner said.

"No," Atkiss said. "We're not going to go through the schedule." He had promised the Saudis he would have the list of deals, and he needed it right away.

Kushner looked at him awkwardly.

"Steve," Kushner said softly, "we're just not going to be able to do it. You have to do it."

That meant a volunteer was in charge of figuring out which multi-billion-dollar agreements the president of the United States and the king of Saudi Arabia would sign.

A surprised Atkiss rushed to the US embassy and, together with a career foreign service official named John Godfrey, reviewed seventy-some potential deals the officials had earlier put together. They divided them into categories—bilateral agreements, commercial deals, and military sales—and picked out the ones that sounded best. They ended up with a list of nearly a half trillion dollars' worth of deals for weaponry, nuclear plants, and other strategically important projects.

The Saudis were speaking Trump's language.

Chapter 9

GOLDEN GAMBIT

May 2017

Donald Trump couldn't have been more pleased when he arrived at Riyadh's Ritz-Carlton on May 20, 2017, to find a fifty-foot-tall projection of his own face staring sternly at him from the palatial hotel's sandstone facade. Next to his giant visage was that of a gently smiling King Salman, with a pair of hands clasped in the middle. Billboards around the city trumpeted, "Together We Prevail," with their images side by side. American and Saudi flags hung all over the place.

It was Trump's first foreign visit as president, and the Saudis were treating him like a king. Mohammed had carefully orchestrated the Ritz arrival, along with every other aspect of the visit. The prince knew just how to deal with Trump. He'd grown up in an extended family dominated by striving, geriatric princes who were terrified of humiliation, desperate for respect, and obsessed with adding to their inherited wealth. And Mohammed had learned to ingratiate himself with those fragile, old men. Until his father became king, making himself indispensable to them was the only way to gain power in the Royal Court. Now he had to do the same with an American version.

Bringing Trump to Riyadh would be the most prominent step yet in Mohammed's march toward the Saudi throne. Over that

time, the prince had built the fortune his father Salman needed
to become king. He had outflanked would-be usurpers to ensure
Salman inherited Abdullah's crown. And he had gained control
of the Saudi military and the economy, sidelining cousin and
rival Mohammed bin Nayef. After all that, he had proclaimed
that the kingdom would no longer squander its oil money on
maintaining the brittle status quo. And of course he was now
rich beyond belief.

Now he was bringing the US president to Saudi Arabia for
his first foreign visit. This sent a message at home and abroad
that Mohammed had the support of the world's most powerful
country. And it showed his family that he could do what Tony
Pfaff, who had served as a Middle East–focused military advisor
to the State Department and on the National Security Council,
calls "kingly things."

Mohammed was barely thirty-one years old. With his path to
the throne blocked by the much older Mohammed bin Nayef,
"establishing legitimacy to the Saudi throne" required public displays of leadership, says Pfaff, who is now a professor at the US
Army War College. Things like bombing Yemen and promising
economic renewal helped, but none was more important than
proving he could be the man to revitalize the strained US-Saudi
relationship.

The visit to Riyadh, part of a three-city journey through
religious centers that continued on to Israel and the Vatican,
wasn't Trump's first trip to the Gulf. He'd visited Dubai, where
a developer bought the rights to use his name on a residential
golf course real estate project that went up for sale in 2014. And
while he had never traveled to Saudi Arabia, he'd had a number
of run-ins with Saudis, including members of the bin Laden
family, during his career.

Trump attended a White House dinner with King Fahd in February 1985, hobnobbing with princes including Saud bin Faisal

and Bandar bin Sultan, the US ambassador at the time. During the same period, one of Osama bin Laden's half brothers, Shafiq, lived in Trump Tower a few floors below Trump himself.

Trump subsequently struck up a relationship with Salem bin Laden, a scion of Binladin Group, that led to Trump's sending a team to Riyadh to consider helping build a luxury project there. He had one strange requirement: The bin Ladens must pay him $10,000 to conduct the study. He told them that he liked to require such a payment to ensure his business partners actually read the proposal.

Even in those days, he had strong views about the US alliance with the Gulf states, telling *Playboy* that "the Saudis, the Kuwaitis walk all over us" and that Arabs spent a lot of money in his casinos. "They lose a million, two million at the tables and they're so happy because they had such a great weekend," he said. "If you lost a million dollars, you'd be sick for the rest of your life, maybe. They write me letters telling me what a wonderful time they had."

He sold the Plaza Hotel to a group of investors including Alwaleed bin Talal in 1995. Three years later, he bought a $30 million yacht from Adnan Khashoggi, an arms dealer, once one of the richest men on earth, and uncle of journalist Jamal Khashoggi. It famously included a discotheque with laser beams that projected Khashoggi's face on the ceiling and an operating room complete with a morgue. Trump renamed it the *Trump Princess*.

King Salman was on the tarmac to greet the president when Air Force One taxied in at 10 a.m. The festivities began immediately, with a tea ceremony in the royal airport terminal. Trump was wearing a dark suit with a bright blue tie dangling far below his waist, and Melania wore a black jumpsuit with a gargantuan golden buckle and belt and a matching gold necklace.

Afterward, King Salman presented Trump with Saudi Arabia's highest honor for a foreigner, the Collar of the Order of Abdulaziz Al Saud. During the ceremony, Trump, not wanting to bow to the king as Obama appeared to do on an earlier visit, lowered himself in an awkward curtsey so that Salman could place the medal around his neck.

Trump and Salman sat at side-by-side tables in the middle of a giant, carpeted room, their delegations in armchairs along the wall, while they signed what Trump would later call $350 billion worth of deals, including weapons sales and Saudi investments with big US companies like the money manager BlackRock Inc. (It later turned out that many of the deals were just preliminary agreements.)

They visited Mohammed's new antiterror center that day, touring the hotel lobby-cum-state-of-the-art-control-room, where some two hundred Saudi computer analysts used what they said were "artificial-intelligence programs" to sift through social media posts looking for clues to new targets or shifting ideologies. The actual programming was spearheaded by an American contractor working out of an office building in downtown Riyadh. The center was mostly for show.

Trump was impressed and, huddled with Melania, King Salman, and Egypt's authoritarian president, Abdel Fattah el-Sisi, placed hands on an illuminated globe in the center of the room. The Malaysian prime minister, Najib Razak, tried to edge into the photograph. He was at the center of a major Department of Justice investigation into billions of dollars stolen from a Malaysian fund and allegedly spent on lavish homes, including for his stepson, so a photograph with the US president would go a long way with voters back home.

Standing on the sidelines was Ali Alzabarah, the alleged former Twitter mole. Since returning to Riyadh, he had been working for Mohammed's MiSK foundation. He told a friend that his name, along with those of dozens of other Saudis, had been provided to US officials ahead of Trump's visit for a security check so he'd be allowed to spend time near the American delegation.

A Royal Court photographer captured a shot of the leaders gathered around the orb, Trump smirking and Salman gazing out in blank-eyed wonder. Mohammed bin Salman stayed out of the scene, letting his father take public credit while he continued to orchestrate from the background. The Saudis would later give the orb as a gift to the US government, which eventually stashed it out of sight in the embassy in Riyadh.

Trump walked hand in hand with Salman from one meeting to the next. But when the stage was set for the summit of Islamic leaders, the king had to be the focal point. So courtiers walked Salman to a desk atop an intricately patterned carpet in the middle of a high-ceilinged octagonal room, where he waited for Trump to arrive.

The scene struck a chord with Trump. "Wow," he said to his Secret Service detail. "Wow. Get Melania over here! She's got to see this!" His bodyguards and their Saudi counterparts scrambled to fetch the First Lady from her tour with a princess.

The summit took some awkward turns. In a traditional Arab move, it started with the Muslim leaders sitting on chairs along the wall on the periphery of a gilded, velvet-trimmed room. This is the typical layout of a *majlis*, where older Gulf royals conduct much of their business, going from person to person without any schedule or program.

Trump looked befuddled sitting on a chair as servers filled the Arab leaders' porcelain cups with cardamom-perfumed coffee—and Trump's porcelain cup with his preferred beverage, Diet Coke, poured from a traditional coffee pot. He recognized chiefs of some major powers, like Egypt's Sisi and Turkey's Recep Tayyip Erdoğan. But the rest were a blur. Could anyone blame the president for not knowing the Gambia's Adama Barrow or

Uzbekistan's Shavkat Mirziyoyev? White House officials cringed when Trump asked the name of a man who turned out to be Ashraf Ghani, the US-backed president of Afghanistan. At one point, a leader of one of the smaller African countries stood up and walked toward Trump; the others lined up behind him, forming a receiving line to greet the president.

During the preparation, a member of Trump's security detail gave the advance man, Atkiss, a tip: "The president fucking hates Toby Keith." He passed that on to the Saudis, who arranged for the country star to be whisked away to perform elsewhere in Riyadh, rather than in front of the president.

For Mohammed, those ceremonial events were much less important than the dinner he and his wife hosted for Kushner and his wife, Ivanka Trump. Secretary of State Rex Tillerson, who was along for the trip, was supposed to take the lead in US foreign policy. But MBS didn't invite him, and Tillerson only learned of the dinner after it happened. It was a shrewd move, since it allowed Mohammed to sell his vision, and his version of Saudi history, to a US official with none of the skepticism or allegiance to MBN that Tillerson had.

"My father's generation, they came from really nothing, and they look at where they are today, and it so far exceeds their dreams," Mohammed told his guests. "But my generation looks and sees unlimited potential. And we're not so patient." Kushner was sold.

During other gatherings over the course of the trip, Mohammed and his deputies told Kushner and the president about their problems with Qatar, a tiny, gas-rich nation that occupies a peninsula off Saudi Arabia's east coast. As a leader striving for a bigger seat at the international table, Qatar's emir had made decisions that infuriated Saudi Arabia. One of the most aggravating was starting international news channel Al Jazeera, which

Ibn Saud, the grandfather of Mohammed bin Salman and founder of Saudi Arabia's ruling dynasty, as pictured in 1942. (*Bob Landry/The LIFE Picture Collection via Getty Images*)

King Abdullah with then-prince Salman, father of Mohammed and long-serving governor of Riyadh, in 2007. (*Hassan Ammar/AFP via Getty Images*)

Mohammed bin Salman, crown prince of Saudi Arabia. (*Bandar Al-Jaloud/ Royal Court*)

Turki bin Abdullah, son of the late King Abdullah, tried to see if the US government would support a coup of King Salman and his son Mohammed. *(Dmitry Astakhov/AFP via Getty Images)*

Former police official Turki Al Sheikh became a close associate of Mohammed bin Salman in his rise to power. *(Fayez Nureldine/AFP via Getty Images)*

Mohammed bin Salman and his father pushed Miteb bin Abdullah, another son of King Abdullah, out of the line of succession and later detained him in the Ritz-Carlton in Riyadh on corruption charges. *(Fayez Nureldine/AFP via Getty Images)*

Mohammed bin Zayed, the day-to-day ruler of the United Arab Emirates and crown prince of Abu Dhabi, was an early supporter of Mohammed bin Salman's rise to power. (*Odd Andersen/AFP via Getty Images*)

A horrifying crane accident in Mecca in 2015 caused a rift between Mohammed bin Salman and the construction company responsible, Saudi Binladin Group. (*Ozkan Bilgin/Anadolu Agency/Getty Images*)

In the early days of King Salman's reign, Mohammed bin Salman vied for influence with his older cousin Mohammed bin Nayef. President Barack Obama was reluctant to help empower the younger prince. (*Olivier Douliery/Corbis/VCG via Getty Images*)

Mohammed bin Salman found an ally in Steve Bannon, chief strategist of President Donald Trump. (*Mandel Ngan/AFP via Getty Images*)

Mohammed bin Salman connected well with Jared Kushner, son-in-law of President Trump. (*Mandel Ngan/AFP via Getty Images*)

SoftBank's Rajeev Misra and Masayoshi Son with the Public Investment Fund's Yasir al-Rumayyan. (*Bandar Algaloud/ Saudi Royal Council/Handout/ Anadolu Agency/Getty Images*)

Egyptian president Abdel Fattah el-Sisi with King Salman and President Donald Trump at the launch of Saudi counter-extremism center in Riyadh. (*Bandar Algaloud/Saudi Royal Council/Handout/Anadolu Agency/Getty Images*)

Qataris write comments on a wall bearing a portrait of Qatar's emir, Sheikh Tamim bin Hamad Al Thani, in Doha. (*Karim Jaafar/AFP via Getty Images*)

Prince Alwaleed bin Talal, Saudi billionaire and founder of Kingdom Holding Company, following his release from eighty-three days of detention in the Ritz-Carlton hotel in Riyadh. (*Guy Martin/Bloomberg via Getty Images*)

Mohammed bin Salman pushed aside his older cousin Mohammed bin Nayef to become heir apparent. (*Olivier Douliery-Pool/Getty Images*)

Lebanese Prime Minister Saad Hariri was detained by Saudi officials. *(Hasan Shaaban/Bloomberg via Getty Images)*

Mohammed bin Salman was the secret buyer of the world's most expensive painting, the *Salvator Mundi* by Leonardo da Vinci. The final price, including fees, was more than $450 million. *(Timothy A. Clary/AFP via Getty Images)*

Badr bin Farhan, a close friend of Mohammed bin Salman from childhood, bid for the painting and later was appointed to run the kingdom's culture efforts. *(Valery Sharifulin/ TASS via Getty Images)*

Saudi Arabia began plans to open up long-closed archaeological sites to tourists, including the historic city of al-Ula. (*Fayez Nureldine/AFP via Getty Images*)

Women's rights activist Loujain al-Hathloul was arrested and allegedly tortured in Saudi Arabia. (*AFP via Getty Images*)

Mohammed bin Salman and Donald Trump meeting in the Oval Office during the prince's three-week visit to the United States. (*Mandel Ngan/AFP via Getty Images*)

Jamal Khashoggi, a longtime regime-friendly Saudi journalist who became a leading antagonist to Mohammed bin Salman, was murdered by Saudi agents in the Saudi consulate in Istanbul. (*The Asahi Shimbun/The Asahi Shimbun*)

Turkish President Recep Tayyip Erdoğan drip-fed information about Jamal Khashoggi's murder to the press, punishing the Saudi Arabian government. (*ADEM ALTAN/AFP via Getty Images*)

Despite the scandal of Jamal Khashoggi's murder, Mohammed bin Salman re-emerged and wielded more power on the world stage than any Middle East leader in a generation. (*Kim Kyung-Hoon/Pool via Bloomberg*)

brought Western-style accountability journalism to the region, especially amid the Arab Spring from 2011 to 2013. Many of the journalists were former BBC producers and came from other high-profile companies. Their coverage of the region's politics was in-depth, hard-hitting, and illuminating.

They also had a crack investigative team headed by an American, Clayton Swisher, a former marine who served for a time as a bodyguard at the US State Department for Madeleine Albright and Colin Powell before turning to Middle East–focused journalism. Gulf leaders were annoyed about American and British media criticizing their policies and digging into affairs they'd like to keep quiet, but they couldn't imagine why one of their supposed Arab allies would allow it.

Qatar also supported the Muslim Brotherhood, the group dating back to Egypt in the 1920s that had grown to be a powerful force across the Middle East, with a deep antipathy for the Gulf monarchies. The UAE and Saudi Arabia backed a military coup in 2013 against the first democratically elected president of Egypt, Mohamed Morsi, a Brotherhood leader. MBZ had already told other White House officials, including Bannon, that Qatar was destabilizing the region and supporting terrorists.

Over the course of the trip MBZ and Mohammed made it clear that they were deeply at odds with Qatar. The problem for the United States is that Qatar is host to America's largest air base in the Middle East. While Saudi Arabia is the United States' biggest ally in the region, Qatar is arguably more strategically important when it comes to military operations.

Qatar is tiny, just a thumb-shaped spit jutting into the Persian Gulf. But its enormous oil and gas reserves and population of just 2.6 million give it fantastic amounts of money to spend. It has bought trophy assets around the world, including the Shard and Harrods department store in London. And it has bought goodwill. The US Army base in Doha was built using Qatar state

funds, and the deal included unlimited electricity, oil, and gas—
an arrangement worth billions of dollars to the United States.

Tillerson appreciated this and valued the alliance, and at a
lunch for Gulf country leaders during the trip, he got the sense
that something was off. The seating chart Tillerson received
in advance showed him sitting at a table with Qatar's foreign
minister. But when he arrived, the minister had been moved to a
table near the kitchen. Based on this and another apparent slight
at a meeting of heads of state on the trip, Tillerson concluded
that something was happening with Qatar, he would later tell a
congressional committee.

The Saudis would present Trump with a pile of lavish gifts—
bejeweled sculptures, swords, daggers, headdresses, and a robe
lined with white tiger fur among them—and Trump and his
staff would return to the United States claiming a foreign-policy
victory of resetting ties with Middle East allies.

The importance of the meeting wouldn't become clear for
another two weeks. With the Trump delegation back in the
United States, a newly emboldened Mohammed launched a
Qatar offensive and initiated a domestic coup that would propel
him to the top of the Saudi government.

The pinnacle of the two-day gathering was Trump's speech.
Obama had given one of his most memorable speeches at Cairo's
Al-Azhar University, the center of Sunni Islamic learning in the
Arab world eight years earlier. He told the audience of scholars
and politicians he'd come "to seek a new beginning between
the United States and Muslims around the world, one based on
mutual interest and mutual respect, and one based upon the
truth that America and Islam are not exclusive and need not be
in competition." He lamented how colonialism fueled conflicts
in the region and created the conditions that allowed terrorist
groups to grow.

Trump, speaking in a lavish conference hall with crystal chandeliers next to the Ritz-Carlton, made no apologies and described the conflict before them as a black-and-white matter. "This is a battle between barbaric criminals who seek to obliterate human life, and decent people of all religions who seek to protect it," he said. "This is a battle between Good and Evil."

Later in the speech, he almost lambasted his audience. "A better future is only possible if your nations drive out the terrorists and extremists. Drive. Them. Out. DRIVE THEM OUT of your places of worship. DRIVE THEM OUT of your communities. DRIVE THEM OUT of your holy land, and DRIVE THEM OUT OF THIS EARTH."

There were multiple standing ovations. Bannon looked on with pride. This was the real, new beginning. No more apologies.

Masayoshi Son and Rajeev Misra also flew in during the Trump visit to sign the paperwork on the $100 billion Vision Fund. When they finally got in to see Mohammed bin Salman, they were astounded to find him alert and going strong despite having not slept in more than twenty-four hours.

After staying up late talking to Jared Kushner, Mohammed had gone straight to several events for a business conference taking place alongside the summit of Arab leaders. Trump had brought along an assortment of thirty American CEOs and top executives, many of them conservative donors to his campaign.

One morning they were brought into the palace for public announcements with the prince himself and relinquished their cell phones to security guards on the way in. But the prince didn't appear for hours, leaving the executives to sit together with no way of communicating with anyone outside.

The scene was a bit awkward as stark competitors like NASDAQ's Adena Friedman and the New York Stock Exchange's Tom Farley, Raytheon's Tom Kennedy and Lockheed Martin's

Marillyn Hewson, J.P. Morgan's Jamie Dimon and Morgan Stanley's James Gorman sat making small talk. They were some of the most important executives in the world, but they were willing to forgo communication even with their chiefs of staff and family members for hours on end for a chance at the MBS bonanza.

It was the peak of excitement among bankers and other businesses to take part in the Aramco IPO, which was still described as selling 5 percent of the company at an overall valuation of $2 trillion. The total fees on such an event could top a billion dollars.

Finally, the announcements began, with Trump looking on fondly as eye-popping commitments were made—in all $200 billion worth of business deals and $110 billion worth of arms purchases over a decade. The numbers were wildly inflated. Very little of the money was coming anytime soon, if ever, but it served Mohammed bin Salman well. This was a US president who formed foreign policy on a transaction-by-transaction basis, and he'd announced deals worth more than the GDP of Greece in 2017.

During the Vision Fund signing, there was so much excitement that Misra left the signed paperwork behind on a table in the room, and they had to send aides rushing to find it.

Blackstone founder Stephen Schwarzman had not been a full Trump supporter in the run-up to the election, but he remained neutral and began providing advice to the White House soon after Trump won. The Saudis, seeking to establish closer ties with businessmen in the Trump orbit, struck a deal with Schwarzman during the conference as well. The Public Investment Fund would contribute $20 billion to a special infrastructure fund mostly devoted to projects in the United States.

This was a savvy move by Mohammed. It got him closer to a Trump advisor, would contribute greatly to the US economy as a sign of goodwill, and should earn a hefty financial return in the end. It was the kind of arrangement that Mohammed wanted to make his signature deal.

Immediately, momentum for such agreements picked up. Word got out among US business leaders that Mohammed bin Salman was ready to deal, and they clamored to meet the prince. Ari Emanuel, Hollywood's most powerful agent, met with Mohammed. "You're the best at what you do," the prince told Emanuel. "I want you to do your best here."

Mohammed was eager to bring business and investment into the kingdom, but Emanuel—like Schwarzman and the other US businessmen who came to meet the prince—was there for another purpose. He wanted Saudi money, and by the time the trip was over, he had the outlines of a deal that would bring Emanuel's firm, Endeavor, nearly a half billion dollars from the kingdom.

Chapter 10

"BLOCKADE"

May 2017

Early on the morning of May 24, 2017, as Donald Trump was wrapping up the Israel leg of his first overseas trip as president, several bizarre statements from the emir of Qatar popped onto the website of the Qatar News Agency (QNA). It took just seconds for regional media in Saudi Arabia and elsewhere to pick up the news and broadcast it far and wide, amplifying the reach so that millions of people saw the reports.

"Iran represents a regional and Islamic power that cannot be ignored and it is unwise to face up against it," Qatar's ruler Sheikh Tamim bin Hamad Al Thani told a military graduation in Arabic, according to the QNA accounts. "It is a big power in the stabilization of the region." The statement amounted to treason among the most influential Persian Gulf states, which see Iran as the greatest threat and aggressor in the region.

Only it was all a ruse. Tamim had never given the speech or issued such a statement. Other reports were also false, including descriptions of tensions with US president Donald Trump, whom Tamim allegedly said might not last a full term; of Qatar's good relationship with Israel; and of the emir's admiration of Palestinian militant group Hamas.

Roused from bed, the thirty-seven-year-old Tamim ordered a statement issued denouncing the fake messages, and his ministers managed to get one out within forty-five minutes. But it was too late to stop the flood of Arabic news coverage on Saudi Arabia's Al Arabiya and the United Arab Emirates' Sky News Arabia.

The Qatari royal family knew immediately that their government systems were compromised, and they felt certain their increasingly assertive neighbors in Saudi Arabia and the UAE were involved. It took weeks for forensic evidence to emerge showing their systems had been infiltrated by a Russian cyber-mercenary group that had been hired for the job.

The ruling Al Thani had been on thin ice with their bigger neighbors for years, building on tensions lasting decades, but they hadn't seen the sneak attack coming and initially under-estimated the resolve of their adversaries. The old Gulf spats involved flare-ups, followed by mediation sessions led by the emir of Kuwait or sultan of Oman, after which the regional alliance was patched up with some grumbling. This new conflict was sudden and all-encompassing.

Within thirteen days, Saudi Arabia, the UAE, and their closest allies, including Egypt and the tiny Comoro Islands, moved in lockstep to impose a full boycott of Qatar. They ejected Qatari citizens from their countries, severed financial ties, and refused to allow Qatari planes to use their airspace. Grocery stores ran out of food because the country had relied on land-based trade with Saudi Arabia for dairy products and other key produce. Even camels grazing just over the border were ejected.

Mohammed bin Salman, feeling emboldened by the Trump visit, even mulled invading Qatar by land if the country didn't yield to a set of demands that included dismantling the Al Jazeera television channel and completely ceasing any foreign policy agenda diverging from that of its neighbors. In a culture that values saving face, he and his cohorts were demanding that Qatar return to its old status as a semi-independent vassal state.

It was a type of outward aggression not seen between Gulf states, and that successive US ambassadors to Saudi Arabia had tried to prevent through personal diplomacy, for decades.

There had been near constant tension between the kingdom and Qatar, its tiny and extremely wealthy neighbor, since the mid-1990s. Saudi rulers were especially incensed by Qatar's foreign policy, which seemed to them based on making friends with Saudi enemies like the Muslim Brotherhood. Saudi Arabia, the UAE, and Bahrain pulled their ambassadors out of Qatar in 2014 over such issues as Qatar's support for the Arab Spring protests.

But that flare-up had passed, and in his near-weekly meetings with Mohammed, Joe Westphal, the Obama administration's ambassador to Saudi Arabia, spoke often with the prince about the importance of maintaining regional stability. By the spring of 2017, however, Westphal was finished with his assignment. The Trump administration had decided not to replace him right away and instead left Saudi-US relations largely in the hands of Jared Kushner, who was hardly a calming influence.

Westphal had often reminded Mohammed that outward aggression hurt Saudi Arabia's image in the United States and made it harder for American politicians to publicly support him. There was no one to do that under the new administration. Now, instead of providing a moderating influence, the United States seemed to be instigating animosity against Qatar. "You've got to take care of this," Trump advisor Steve Bannon told Mohammed bin Zayed. "These guys are worse than Persia. They're right in your grill."

With the White House seemingly supporting their desire to escalate the conflict, there seemed little risk for the Saudi and Emirati princes in trying to bring Qatar to heel.

An hour before the boycott was announced, the Saudis gave Jared Kushner a heads-up. He asked if they could delay. "It's too late," a Saudi emissary told him. "It's in motion."

The boycott announcement terrified many Qataris, who referred to it with the more charged term "blockade." Some of the nation's wealthiest families began amassing personal armories in their villas and palaces in anticipation of an invasion. Rex Tillerson, who hadn't been in on discussions about the Qatar boycott with Mohammed bin Salman, tried to stop things from getting out of hand. Tillerson had history with the Al Thani ruling family from when he was an executive at ExxonMobil, helping Tamim's father develop its natural gas operations.

Speaking to the White House, Tillerson emphasized that the US Al Udeid military base would be at risk if three of the world's biggest buyers of arms suddenly started pointing them at each other. The idea that Saudi Arabia would use American tanks, American fighter planes, and American missiles against Qatar, and vice versa, was unacceptable.

Tillerson had little luck in getting the president to help calm the situation in the early days. In a White House meeting with Trump and Kushner, the frustrated secretary of state tried to emphasize that the situation was a potential crisis that would upend life for Qataris. "They're not going to be able to take their exams," Tillerson said. "There's not going to be any milk in the grocery store."

"I don't give a fuck about milk," Trump responded. He didn't see the blockade as necessarily a bad thing. "If you've got them fighting over who funds terrorism less, this is going in the right direction," he told Kushner. Let the Saudis figure it out.

Trump tweeted on June 6, the first day of the boycott, "During my recent trip to the Middle East I stated that there can no longer be funding of Radical Ideology. Leaders pointed to Qatar—look!"

While Saudi Arabia and the UAE claimed they had no role in the hacking of Qatar News Agency, foreign intelligence sources told the *New York Times* and *Washington Post* that the culprits were Russian freelance hackers working for foreign governments. As the impasse hardened, Mohammed bin Salman's aides floated an idea to dig a canal along the forty-mile Saudi border with Qatar to turn the peninsular nation into an island. It wasn't clear if it was a real possibility or a false story to intimidate the Qataris.

While Saudi Arabia and the UAE were responding to Qatar's escalations, including Tamim's faked statements, the plan to isolate and neutralize Qatar had been in the works for months. The guile and intrigue would later lead pundits to refer to it as a "Game of Thobes."

On March 22, 2017, Abdulaziz Alotaibi, a Saudi strategist at the consultancy KPMG working with the Saudi embassy and the public relations firm Qorvis Communications, headed by veteran communications guru Michael Petruzzello, created a special PowerPoint laying out a media plan of attack starting for three months in June—just after Trump's scheduled visit to Saudi Arabia.

Saudi Arabia had long been one of Qorvis's best clients. Also looped into the plans was The Harbour Group, a public relations firm working with both the Emiratis and the Saudis. At the same time Mohammed bin Zayed was seeking to help his younger neighbor take a bigger role in the region, Saudi Arabia hired Harbour's managing director Richard Mintz in early 2017 to help get Mohammed bin Salman's brother Khalid ready for his new role as ambassador to the United States. The men would venture out for frequent two-hour meals to discuss everything about American politics and foreign policy from the ground up.

Khalid is Mohammed's full brother, younger by about three years, and among his most trusted confidants. The two had a similar background. Khalid had stayed home to study in Saudi Arabia like his brother, and they were close growing up, playing computer games, learning to scuba dive together from an instructor they brought with them on King Salman's annual one-month vacations, and venturing into towns in Spain and France to see what real life looked like up close. But unlike his brother, Khalid learned to speak English well when he was relatively young and grew to understand American culture while spending long stretches of time in the United States for air force training at Columbus Air Force Base in Mississippi and Nellis Air Force Base in Nevada, where he'd venture out after hours with fellow servicemen to explore the area's nightlife. When his brother declared war on the Houthi militia in Yemen in 2015, Khalid took part in sorties in an F15 fighter jet, returning home with a back injury that left him with chronic pain. After a stint in the Ministry of Defense, he was appointed ambassador in April 2017.

Mintz started working with the UAE after one of his colleagues at the public relations firm Burson-Marsteller, Simon Pearce, took a full-time job working for the Abu Dhabi government. Pearce, an Australian, went on to become a key advisor to Khaldoon Al Mubarak, one of Mohammed bin Zayed's closest advisors, on buying the football team Manchester City and other high-profile Abu Dhabi deals and strategic endeavors, such as countering the Muslim Brotherhood and Iran.

Qorvis's plan had a week-by-week strategy to "increase public perception of Qatar as a supporter of terrorism," creating fact sheets to distribute about Qatar's alleged bribes related to the

2022 World Cup and even creating digital ads showing Qatar as a destabilizing force in the Middle East.

The same document laid out a similar strategy for finding "third-party validation" for Saudi Arabia's Vision 2030 plan, including a nine-by-nine matrix of journalists ranked as friendly, neutral, or hostile and their influence as low, medium, or high created by KPMG. The top, most influential journalists they could count on were Tom Friedman, a *New York Times* columnist who'd been praising Mohammed bin Salman as a reformer; David Ignatius at the *Washington Post*; Bret Baier at Fox News; and Norah O'Donnell at CBS News. Fareed Zakaria at CNN was the most hostile journalist with a high influence ranking, the matrix showed.

The cold war with Qatar was years in the making, but the country started drifting rapidly away from its neighbors when Tamim's father, Hamad bin Khalifa, known as HBK, overthrew his own father, Khalifa bin Hamad, in a bloodless coup d'état in 1995.

Hamad was born in Qatar's sleepier early days, when the country was hardly known outside the Persian Gulf—and even in the region wasn't known for much other than its pearl divers. Before the coup, Emir Khalifa had operated Qatar as a semi-independent country, running its own domestic affairs since independence in 1971 but sheltered under Saudi Arabia's security umbrella. The Saudi king, not the Qatari emir, dictated foreign policy and defense affairs. Qatar was a tiny fingernail compared to Saudi Arabia in terms of power, influence, size, and even self-identity.

But Hamad had grown up in a more cosmopolitan world. Thanks to the country's modest wealth at the time and historical ties to the United Kingdom, he attended the Royal Military Academy, Sandhurst, before returning to Doha to become a military officer and eventually minister of defense and crown prince.

He grew restless under his father's incrementalist approach to development and his unwillingness to forge Qatar's own path in global affairs.

Hamad, then in his mid-forties, had already alarmed Saudi Arabia's King Fahd and UAE president Zayed Al Nahyan with his efforts to develop unilateral relations with Iraq and Iran, then ruled by Saddam Hussein and Akbar Rafsanjani. He hatched a plan to seize control with the approval of key members of the family. Then, while his father was in Geneva on vacation, he took over. His father fled to Abu Dhabi with his advisors in a convoy of jetliners, where he lived for years before decamping to France and finally back to Doha in 2004 for the last twelve years of his life.

As emir, Hamad injected energy into the Qatar government and an independent ethos, even forging a trade relationship with Israel. He developed the country's gas fields, a big bet since natural gas was not yet the profitable raw material in global industrial production that it is today. The bet paid off tremendously, making Qatar fabulously rich. Armed with wealth and gumption, Hamad set out to create a foreign policy focused on the role of Qatar in the rest of the world and not just on his monarchical neighbors. One of the biggest factors was the creation of Al Jazeera. The news channel spent lavishly recruiting international journalists. It covered the Middle East most intently, depicting Qatar as a neutral power mediating conflicts. There was virtually no coverage of societal issues or controversies within Qatar itself.

Qatar's neighbors considered Al Jazeera anything but neutral, and they found the country's foreign policy to be almost diametrically opposed to theirs. The Arab Spring brought those differences into relief. When Egyptian youth protested against longtime president Hosni Mubarak, Qatar backed the street, while Saudi Arabia and the UAE tried to bolster Mubarak.

And after Mubarak fell, Qatar propped up Egypt's new Muslim Brotherhood president Mohamed Morsi. The Emiratis and Saudis subsequently backed a military general to overthrow Morsi and quash the Brotherhood.

Saudi Arabia had been a force for stasis in the region. It paid billions of dollars to protect leaders like Mubarak and Jordan's King Hussein from unrest and used its most powerful tool of all, religious influence, to sway the global Muslim population to its conservative, fusty interpretation of what it meant to live a good Islamic life. Wahhabi imams would regularly admonish during their sermons that good Muslims should never oppose their leaders, no matter how grave their errors or ethical violations, because doing so would divide the Muslim population, a concept known as *fitna*.

The Muslim Brotherhood disagreed with the Wahhabists and long opposed the Gulf monarchies, portraying them as indulging in extravagant, unholy lives, while regular Arabs struggled to make ends meet. Emirati and Saudi officials genuinely wondered what game Qatar was playing in backing them—Qatari royals weren't strangers to wild spending and partying. Yet here was the tiny country hosting Islamic leaders who regularly decried royals and questioned their faith; maintaining ties with groups like Hezbollah, seen by much of the world as terrorists masquerading as freedom fighters; and hosting a television channel that used its Western-style investigations to undermine every regional dynasty except the Al Thanis. One Emirati official remarked, "I guess they plan to have their throats slit last."

Qataris, more adept than the Saudis at lobbying and communicating their worldview, liken themselves to a Middle Eastern Switzerland that maintains contact with every group to better facilitate negotiations and bring peace to the region. There are incidents that don't fit with that image, as in the case of

Khalifa al-Subaiy, a Qatari financier who the United States says long provided financial support to senior al-Qaeda leadership, including 9/11 mastermind Khalid Sheikh Mohammed. Subaiy was tried and convicted in absentia in 2008 in Bahrain on charges of financing and facilitating terrorism, then was arrested in Qatar and imprisoned for six months. But after his release, Subaiy allegedly reconnected with al-Qaeda agents and resumed organizing funds in support of the group, as well as linking up with operatives in Iran in 2009, 2011, and throughout 2012 and sending cash to senior al-Qaeda leaders in Pakistan through 2013. He continues to live freely in Qatar as of 2020.

Qatar weathered criticism of its foreign policy for years, but tensions reached a new high after disagreements over Egypt. For two years, the Qataris had propped up Morsi, a high-ranking member of the Muslim Brotherhood with a tense relationship with the Gulf. The Gulf monarchies long believed the Brotherhood planned to come for them if it ever amassed enough power. At one point, the Brotherhood-led government suggested to Saudi Arabia it would not send Hosni Mubarak to prison in exchange for $10 billion, according to a leaked Ministry of Foreign Affairs document from Saudi. To reverse Egypt's 2011 revolution, the Saudis and Emiratis secretly supported a military general, Abdel Fattah el-Sisi, in his bid to take power in a coup d'état accompanied by a bloody crackdown on Islamists in Cairo in which hundreds were killed. Not long after, el-Sisi replaced his general's uniform with a suit and ran for president, winning with an overwhelming majority, but Qatar had stubbornly refused to join the other Gulf states in supporting him.

With disagreements raging, in 2013 Qatar's emir, Hamad bin Khalifa, abdicated to calm the situation, passing the throne to his then-thirty-three-year-old son Tamim. The Saudis, Emiratis, and Bahrainis didn't buy it, and in 2014 they withdrew their ambassadors from Qatar to protest what they saw as its refusal to stop interfering in the politics of other countries in the region. They also believed Tamim was a figurehead taking orders from his father behind the scenes.

Within weeks all the countries had settled the issues with a secret document called the Riyadh Agreement, which included Qatar dialing down its interventionist foreign policy.

Another factor had been building up resentment for years: Qatar had a habit of outshining its bigger neighbors. Using its immense wealth, the country's sovereign wealth funds bought high-profile stakes in Western companies such as Volkswagen Group and Royal Dutch Shell. It became a player in iconic real estate, including developing Heathrow Airport and the Canary Wharf business district, and built the Shard, the United Kingdom's tallest tower. It won the rights to host the 2022 FIFA World Cup soccer tournament, the most illustrious international sports competition after the Olympics.

And for the wealthy Gulf set, especially their wives and children, the purchase of Harrods, the iconic department store on Old Brompton Road in London, for 1.5 billion pounds in 2010 was especially momentous. Arabic sometimes feels like the store's second language because of all the rich shoppers on holiday from Dubai, Riyadh, and Kuwait City.

Few Qataris better exemplify the absurdly rich lifestyle of the Al Thanis than Hamad bin Abdullah Al Thani, Tamim's first cousin, who has the jaunty look of a 1920s robber baron. After a life spent frolicking in museums while living on French estates and in high-class hotels, Hamad forged an existence that could only be compared to the one depicted in the television series *Downton Abbey*. After buying an old city mansion in London, he refurbished it to its early-twentieth-century grandeur, with seventeen bedrooms and a staff of domestic servants who changed into white ties and coattails at 6 p.m. promptly. Queen

Elizabeth II, the United Kingdom's reigning monarch, visited for supper on several occasions. Hamad liked to exhibit pieces from his collection of Indian jewelry once belonging to maharajas and other notables. And that was just his London home.

Only two years before the boycott, a few months after his father was anointed king, Mohammed bin Salman traveled to Doha to meet Tamim, the thirty-five-year-old emir. During a dinner held in his honor, Mohammed seemed particularly interested in how Qatar had so successfully worked with international media to enhance its standing in the world. Foreign policy wasn't high on the agenda.

He asked about whether obtaining positive reporting required him to buy international newspapers or simply pay them for the coverage. Whether he was showing naivete about the Western system or simply cynicism about journalism, no one could tell for certain. Also on hand was Saud al-Qahtani, who was the main person to call Qatar whenever the kingdom was upset about a particular article or news program about Saudi Arabia.

During falconry expeditions afterward, Mohammed bin Zayed and Mohammed bin Salman discussed how Qatar was a mortal danger to stability in the region and their families' ability to remain in power for years to come. Maintaining a delicate balance with the poorer and more combustible Arab nations like Egypt, Lebanon, and Jordan, and to a lesser extent the countries of North Africa, was important to prevent movements antagonistic to their regimes—fueled by unemployed, poor youth in the hundreds of millions—from sweeping across the Middle East.

By 2017, the Emirati leadership felt certain Qatar had been flouting its obligations because of arrogance. Qatar had the Al Udeid base, the slick global communications operation, and more spending power than the rest. They were haughty and domineering. So the wily sheikhs of Abu Dhabi, together with allies, had long been looking for an excuse to cut Qatar off, alienate it, and make life so unpleasant it would finally agree to their demands. It was the most aggressive foreign policy move in the region's short history. It backfired spectacularly.

Instead of falling in line, Qatar dug in. Its vast wealth helped. While it couldn't import milk via Saudi Arabia anymore, it could fly in cows by the hundreds to create a self-sustaining dairy farm. The entire supply chain supporting its population was redesigned. Tamim struck closer relationships with Iran, the longtime Gulf adversary, and Turkey, ruled by the descendants of Ottoman rulers who governed the Middle East until the early twentieth century. Turkey built its first military base in the Middle East since those times in Qatar. A boycott intended to break Qatar away from rivals Iran and Turkey had driven the tiny country closer to them.

One major issue was a failure of planning: Saudi Arabia and UAE enacted the boycott without telling Qatar what it wanted from them. Bannon told Tahnoon bin Zayed, the UAE national security advisor, that for the action to look credible abroad, the Saudis and Emiratis would have to tell Qatar what they wanted from the country. "You've got to lay out something. What are your demands?" Bannon asked him.

Tillerson eventually called publicly for a list of demands. While Trump seemed to support the boycott and publicly accused Qatar of funding terrorism, the secretary of state and other high-ranking US officials were trying to defuse the situation. It became a public mess; after meeting with Tillerson, Adel al-Jubeir, then the Saudi foreign minister, denied there was a boycott and said the kingdom had just cut off Qatar from using its airspace.

Finally, almost three weeks after the boycott started, the Saudi and Emirati leaders issued a list of thirteen requests, which included shutting down Al Jazeera and paying reparations for damage purportedly caused by Qatar in the region.

With actual conflict averted thanks to intervention by the United States and other Western allies, including France, both sides intensified a cyber war unlike any seen in recent history. Neither side took credit for attacks, denying any involvement, but the victims were squarely on one side or the other of the battle.

Yousef al-Otaiba, the UAE ambassador to the United States, had his inbox hacked within days of the boycott. Soon, newspapers around the world began publishing stories about the UAE's efforts to influence US officials, including Jared Kushner, as well as think tanks and other influential people, in addition to details of Otaiba's use of prostitutes.

The hacking had real-world consequences. The leaks exposed Elliott Broidy, one of Trump's top Republican fund-raisers, as exploiting his relationship with Trump to bill foreign governments tens of millions of dollars for the construction of open-source research centers for combatting terrorism—like the one Trump visited in Riyadh—and for promises to influence the administration. The Department of Justice opened an investigation into allegations of money laundering and illegal lobbying, but Broidy strongly denied any crimes had taken place and later filed a series of lawsuits against Qatar and its operatives, seeking damages for what he said was their campaign against him. Those filed against the nation of Qatar were dismissed because of sovereign immunity, but those against companies allegedly working for Qatar were allowed to proceed as of early 2020.

Each hack appeared to incite the other side to hack back harder. The UAE deployed a major listening operation, aided in part by software from an Israeli company called NSO Group Technologies. Based in Herzliya, its team of computer engineers and former government hackers had built a system called

Pegasus that could compromise smartphones. It only sold the system to governments that it deemed would use it for acceptable purposes and required Israeli government permission for each sale. Qatar was denied access, while the UAE purchased not one but three $50 million annual subscriptions for different intelligence-related organizations in its government.

The high cost came down to NSO's use of "zero-day" exploits, a term for loopholes in widely used software that even big companies like Microsoft, Google, and Apple don't know about. Its researchers work to find those holes and create programs that exploit them to gain control of or access to devices.

The only problem with providing such a powerful tool to other governments, including authoritarian monarchies, is their extremely limited oversight. NSO makes buyers sign an agreement that they won't use Pegasus to target political opposition groups or activists. It also bans them from using the software against US and UK numbers. But they don't police its use in real time. If there's an incident, then NSO has the ability to go back into the system, ascertain whether Pegasus was used against a particular target, and shut down a client's access. The problem is that incidents of misuse are hard to identify since the software, by its nature, is extremely hard to detect.

Using material gleaned from cyber attacks on Qatar and other means, the UAE discovered highly damaging evidence about Qatar's attempts to bribe terrorist groups in Iraq to rescue a group of Qatari hunters who had been kidnapped in January 2015. Stories in the West began to spill out all the details, text message by text message. One report from the BBC in London sourced the material to "a government hostile to Qatar."

The kidnappers turned out to be a Shia militia called Kataib Hezbollah that was affiliated with the Iranian government and, in particular, a legendary Iranian general named Qassem Soleimani (who was killed in 2020 by a US drone, escalating a conflict with Iran). The Qataris ended up agreeing to pay more than $1 billion in ransom for the Qatari detainees, who were all rescued, though Qatar disputes who ultimately received any money. In the view of Qatar's Gulf enemies, any payment to an Iran-backed militia or Soleimani constituted underwriting acts of terrorism for years to come and undermined Iraq's fragile government.

The Gulf cold war took on funny aspects as well. While Saudis and Emiratis severed all ties with Qatar, many of their wealthy citizens on vacation in London couldn't bear to stop shopping at Harrods. The result was an unofficial arrangement: They could have the whole department store to themselves in the mornings, and Qataris would take the afternoon shift.

Chapter 11

SEALED WITH A KISS

June 2017

The 10 p.m. phone call didn't seem ominous at first. It was June 20, 2017, almost the end of Ramadan, and Crown Prince Mohammed bin Nayef had just broken his fast.

Like other senior princes, he'd moved into his Mecca palace for the holy month. He spent the hot days fasting, resting, and praying. Only at night, after the traditional *iftar* spread of dates, soup, yogurt, meat, and rice shared with friends and visitors, did government business begin. For Mohammed bin Nayef, that meant sitting, and sometimes dozing, on a velvet chair or brocade couch for hours of seemingly interminable meetings, hearings, and presentations from bureaucrats, punctuated with small cups of yellowish cardamom-flavored coffee, from midnight to dawn.

The call that night was for one of those routine gatherings, a discussion with generals and police to figure out security for the upcoming Eid holiday. As interior minister, the prince known by the CIA and State Department as MBN was in charge of Saudi Arabia's domestic security. And since public holiday gatherings like Eid were potential terrorist targets, he had to attend. In short, there wasn't much reason to worry. After a tense year or so with his nominal deputy, Mohammed bin Salman, there seemed to be a detente. Throughout the spring, rumors had been flying around Saudi Arabia and Washington, DC, that Mohammed would oust his older cousin. MBN even hired lobbyists to make his case in Washington. Then Ramadan arrived, and everyone seemed to relax. Mohammed bin Salman allowed some of MBN's favored guards to start working in the Royal Court again, months after they'd been shunted aside.

So MBN, who was in his late fifties but slowed by diabetes and injuries, summoned his retinue and set off in a small motorcade toward the center of Mecca to the black-and-white Al-Safa palace that looms over the Kaaba. Twelve hours later, he would emerge into the glare of spotlights and flashbulbs as a prisoner, relieved of his government duties and wealth, cut from the line of succession, and placed under house arrest. It would mark the final step in Mohammed bin Salman's ascent to becoming heir to the Saudi throne.

The Americans always found Mohammed bin Nayef to be a bit of a puzzle. His father was the famously harsh Prince Nayef, a full brother of King Salman, who headed Saudi security and intelligence as interior minister for more than thirty-five years. Prince Nayef brought his son into the family business.

Nayef was stubborn, standoffish, and resistant to change—a "firm authoritarian at heart," former US ambassador James Smith called him in a leaked 2009 cable. US senator Chuck Schumer asked the Saudi government to fire him in the aftermath of the 9/11 attacks, convinced that he wasn't effectively addressing terrorism inside and outside the kingdom. Bruce Riedel, a former US intelligence official who held Middle East security roles under several presidents, was more blunt in a 2016 paper. Nayef, whom Riedel knew well, "was, essentially, anti-American," he wrote.

But his son Mohammed bin Nayef provoked no such concerns. As the relatively new head of security at the time of the

9/11 attacks, MBN helped repair the US relationship during a time of deep suspicion. He formed personal bonds throughout the US government. Unlike other foreign intelligence officials, who focused on their CIA relationships, MBN cultivated contacts in the State Department. He got to know John Kerry as well as staffers for Joe Biden. And he spoke with General David Petraeus, who became CIA director under Barack Obama, and others about building Saudi institutions whose relationships with the United States would transcend leadership changes at the top in either country.

In the ensuing years, al-Qaeda launched a series of attacks in Saudi Arabia, and MBN spearheaded the government's response. His forces, Riedel says, led targeted operations that broke up al-Qaeda cells with minimal collateral damage.

With his US contacts, MBN was funny and gentle. When the Americans said they needed something from Saudi Arabia, he usually delivered. And when he couldn't, he was honest about why. His priorities seemed to mirror America's, and unlike other interlocutors, he had the power to get things done in the kingdom.

Speaking fluent English that he honed at Lewis & Clark College in Oregon in the 1970s, as well as in a training stint at the FBI, MBN was "the quintessential Saudi secret policeman," said Jon Finer, chief of staff for Kerry during his time as secretary of state. Finer sat through meetings with MBN in Riyadh and Washington, and he, like other US officials, was struck by the prince's easy demeanor and consistent ability to deliver useful intelligence on terrorist activity inside and outside the kingdom.

"They had saved my ass a number of times," recalls one Saudi-based State Department official who received information on specific threats from MBN's staff. He and others in the White House and Pentagon and at Langley were encouraged when, not long after his father died, MBN became interior minister. And his being named crown prince a few months after King Abdullah died in 2015 signaled to the Americans that the next Saudi king would be someone who had lived in the United States and had relationships with US officials that felt like genuine friendships. Riedel wrote in a 2016 piece for the Brookings Institution that "MBN may be the most pro-American prince ever to be in line to the throne."

He didn't mention the other things the United States had been hearing about Mohammed bin Nayef—things that caused officials in Washington concern that their favorite prince might never take the throne.

For years, US officials had been worried about MBN's health and private life. Though he was friendly and engaging when dealing with his US counterparts, he was also strangely fidgety. US officials noticed in recent years that he was always tapping a pencil or shaking his leg while talking, as if unable to sit still. When he did sit still in meetings, he sometimes fell asleep.

Perhaps it was his diabetes. Or, White House officials wondered, perhaps he had never fully recovered from the shocking 2009 attempt on his life. During Ramadan that year, a young man named Abdullah al-Asiri got in touch with the prince and said he was a terrorist who wanted to enter MBN's program for reforming militant Islamists. The prince agreed to meet him in person, and Asiri came to his Jeddah office a few days later.

Asiri sat down next to MBN on the floor, pulled out a cell phone, which he handed to the prince, and then blew himself up. In the carnage, MBN would later tell an American contact who came to his office, he looked up and saw a bloody dent in his office ceiling where Asiri's head had struck. "Right there," he told the American, pointing upward. The young man's body was strewn about the room, blown apart by explosives concealed in his rectum, Saudi authorities said (US officials say the bomb may in fact have been in his underpants).

MBN was pierced with shrapnel but seemed to have escaped without serious injury. He made a television appearance shortly after in which he discussed the incident with little more than bandaged hands to show for his injuries. Beyond that, a US contact who saw him a few days later said, he seemed "unscathed." It was one of many attempts on MBN's life, and it made him one of the few Saudi princes who had actually shed blood for his country. His commitment to returning to service after the attack helped build respect among US government contacts.

During the Obama administration, those officials wondered if his injuries were worse than he'd let on. Did he doze off in meetings because of his diabetes? Was he physically diminished or reliant on medications to function? The CIA picked up information that he was addicted to prescription painkillers. That was hardly a new issue among senior Saudi princes, as King Salman knew firsthand, but it was nevertheless concerning for an important and relatively young US ally.

After Salman took the throne, another, more sensitive stream of intelligence started making its way to the United States. MBN, American officials were told from contacts in the region, had been partaking in tawdry, drug-fueled sex with young men and women around the world, sometimes involving shocking perversions. US intelligence officials didn't know what to make of this information. While they had reliable accounts of MBN's trysts with men while in Geneva for medical visits, the most disturbing information now started leaking out. True or not, the rumors worried officials in Washington because they could be used against MBN to block his path to the throne. In a deeply traditional country, the fact that the prince had just one wife and two daughters, with no son, was alone cause for mild suspicion. What if the rumors about his European life began circulating?

There were other signs that MBN was being pushed aside. On a visit to the region, a former US official went to meet former chief of the Saudi Arabia National Guard Miteb bin Abdullah, son of the former king, at his ranch outside Riyadh. After a repast in one of the Al Saud's typically luxurious tents, Miteb said he wanted to go for a walk on the sand. He seemed worried, the former official remembers, that his tent was bugged.

Under the stars, a distraught Miteb talked for almost two hours. The leadership structure was changing, he said. Nothing was as it had been. He spoke elliptically, avoiding too much detail, but he offered up one shocking piece of information: MBN, Saudi Arabia's crown prince and head of one of its military units, hadn't known in advance that Mohammed bin Salman, his supposed deputy, was going to strike Yemen.

Such moments made career officials in Washington worry that a trusted intermediary's ascent to the throne on something like the merit of his accomplishments—rather than old-fashioned family jostling—was in peril. Then again, they reasoned, MBN was the spy chief who had cleared al-Qaeda out of Islam's holiest land. Surely he could manage his own family's politics.

In hindsight, Kerry aide Jon Finer says, "what we didn't expect was that MBS would outplay MBN as effectively as he did."

The relationship between Mohammed bin Salman and MBN had no parallel in the history of modern Saudi Arabia. Never before had two men with different fathers stood in line for the Saudi throne. Since the kingdom's founder, Ibn Saud, died in 1953, every Saudi king has been one of his sons.

Those sons understood the risks of a haphazard succession. Ibn Saud's decision to pass the crown to his oldest surviving son, Saud, turned out to be a disaster in the long term. Profligate and unable to get control of the kingdom's spiraling debt, Saud presided over an economic crisis. After five years, his dozens of brothers banded together to take away most of his power and give it to the younger crown prince, Faisal, who eventually became king.

Faisal's ascent by consensus established what James Smith, the former US ambassador, called "probably the world's only system of government by half brothers." It wasn't quite a family democracy, but it meant power was spread among dozens of men and family factions. The system fostered consensus and gave everyone an incentive to get along. A prince whose actions alienated him from the family would end up outside the line of succession. The resulting leadership, as Smith put it in a leaked cable, is "consensus-based and by nature cautious, conservative, and reactive." That structure produced remarkable stability, and eventually stasis, in the Saudi government, even as oil wealth brought Saudi Arabia rapid economic change. Since Ibn Saud had scores of sons with more than a dozen wives over five decades, it has remained in place for more than fifty years.

Through that half century, the family has maintained relative peace. Many of Ibn Saud's sons received government portfolios, which they used to amass power and in some cases wealth through payments from foreign companies eager to get into the oil business. But no son had enough power to fully consolidate control, especially with the Ministry of Defense, National Guard, and Ministry of Interior—the three institutions with military power—each run by a different prince, while a fourth prince, Salman, had authority over another power base, the traditional Al Saud homeland of Riyadh and its Wahhabist clerics. No single brother had enough guns at his disposal to mount a family coup.

There were times when US and Saudi leaders worried the system was fragile. Concerns bubbled up after Abdullah became king in 2005. An austere man, by Saudi standards, who was widely respected inside and outside the kingdom, Abdullah had a strange position within his own family: His predecessor on the throne, King Fahd, was the full brother of three of the most powerful princes in the kingdom, Nayef, Sultan, and Salman.

These men, among the seven sons of Ibn Saud and his favorite wife Hussa Al Sudairi, expected to someday be king. Abdullah, on the other hand, didn't have any full brothers. He was past eighty years old when he took the throne, and he had a reformist bent. His decisions about succession could upend the political status quo.

Abdullah understood that concern. He also worried about a possible assassination attempt. Al-Qaeda was a near and present danger, and the last reformist king, Faisal, had been shot dead by a nephew disgruntled with his reforms in 1975. So Abdullah asked the George W. Bush administration for help with a security assessment.

The White House sent a security team that met with the king's personnel and came up with a series of recommendations. Some of them were anodyne security measures. But the White House team made another suggestion: Abdullah should further clarify the line of succession. That led him in 2006 to announce the establishment of the Allegiance Council.

The law Abdullah signed said that the king would nominate a successor, and the commission would assemble to approve the king's choice or suggest another prince it determined was the "most upright" of the descendants of Ibn Saud. The council could also meet to approve a new crown prince should the current one die. Its deliberations would be set down in a single record book by the only nonroyal allowed in the room, Abdullah's aide Khalid al-Tuwaijri.

Throughout Abdullah's reign, when one crown prince died, followed soon by another, the arrangement appeared to hold. The council appointed the next qualified brother, landing on Prince Salman in 2012. But Abdullah hadn't actually treated the council like a decision-making body. He named the new crown princes and told the commission to sign off. So when Abdullah died two years later and Salman assumed the throne, there was a precedent for him to tell the commission, rather than let it decide, who would be next in the line of succession.

———

At first, Salman moved slowly. For three months he stuck with Abdullah's chosen crown prince, the younger Muqrin, a former Saudi intelligence chief. He had a long career in government, and he was not a full brother of Salman, meaning power was still spread among the different family lines. His deputy was Mohammed bin Nayef—the first grandson of Ibn Saud to rise to that position. Mohammed bin Salman had a lower-profile role outside the line of succession.

Then Adel al-Jubeir, ambassador to the United States and later foreign minister, began carrying a confusing new message to then–secretary of state John Kerry, selling Mohammed bin Nayef as the future king. The first meaningful shift happened at 4 a.m. on April 29, 2015, when the Royal Court announced Muqrin's resignation. The new crown prince would be MBN, and his deputy—and next in line for the throne—would be Mohammed bin Salman, now the kingdom's defense minister.

This marked the first time a grandson of Ibn Saud would be first in line for the throne. And it provoked even more confusion among US officials. Salman was king and seemed to be positioning his son to succeed him. So why was MBN, the United States' longtime ally, sandwiched in the middle?

Joe Westphal, the US ambassador in Riyadh, asked Mohammed bin Salman point-blank. Who would be the next king? "Every king has been succeeded by the crown prince," Mohammed said, a seeming assurance that MBN would be next.

But officials in Washington were skeptical. MBN seemed to be receding, Mohammed ascending. On the prince's yacht in the Red Sea, during a visit to a military base along the

Saudi-Iraqi border, and even in his own Georgetown living room, Kerry listened to Mohammed gripe about the Iran nuclear deal, US policy during the Arab Spring, and his frustration with the United States. This didn't sound like someone who would wait for a cousin to serve as king before his turn on the throne.

Slowly, Mohammed started taking more aggressive steps, like the firing of MBN's deputy Saad al-Jabri in September 2015.

MBN at first seemed to respond passively. He took an especially long hunting trip to Algeria and bristled when Middle East pundits reported that he was ill or even near death. He eventually wrote a letter to King Salman complaining about Emirati interference in Saudi politics (which the *New Yorker* later reported), but it didn't seem to help. When Donald Trump entered office in early 2017, Mohammed felt emboldened to make a move.

Under President Obama, the State Department made clear to Saudi Arabia that its priority was stability in the country and in the region. The United States wanted orderly leadership transitions and consensus, rather than rivalry, between powerful factions. It wasn't going to throw support behind a young prince simply because he was the king's favorite son.

The Trump administration was different. It seemed to place little value on stability. Kushner and Bannon clicked with Mohammed and the United Arab Emirates' Mohammed bin Zayed, who long disliked MBN. It was clear to them that the White House wouldn't try to stop a shake-up, stability be damned.

After months of warnings from his advisors that his younger cousin was making a move, MBN finally hired a US lobbyist, a Republican-connected winery owner named Robert Stryk, to help remind members of the new administration that MBN had been the United States' most trusted Saudi ally for more than fifteen years. MBN had been referred to Stryk by mutual acquaintances in the intelligence community, longtime friends of MBN who worried the prince was being sidelined. Stryk signed a $5.4 million contract that May with the Ministry of Interior. There wasn't much Stryk could do, though. Just a few days after the contract was signed, Trump and his entourage departed for their Riyadh visit, where MBN would barely register. Ramadan began a few days later.

It was near the end of the holy month, when everything was quiet in Saudi Arabia, that an emissary from Mohammed bin Salman quietly flew to Washington with a message. Mohammed, he told administration officials, was ready to cast aside his cousin. Soon after, MBN received his nighttime call to come to the Al-Safa palace.

When MBN's motorcade arrived, palace guards held back some members of his security detail. That wasn't strange for times, like after *iftar*, when the palace was crowded. They asked other members of his detail to remain at a second checkpoint. And when the prince and his closest aides reached the palace entrance, guards told him to proceed on his own. King Salman, they said, wanted to meet with the prince alone.

Once MBN was on his way through the palace's velvet-draped halls, guards took all weapons and cell phones from the aides he left behind. They ushered the crown prince upstairs to a small lounge, where he was left alone. It was close to midnight.

No matter how tightly an operation is run in Saudi Arabia, the Royal Court is a leaky place. And at some point that night, someone aligned with MBN got wind of what was happening. A worried Ahmed bin Abdulaziz, a younger brother of King Salman and a former government official, tried frantically to reach the king. But an aide picked up the phone. "The king is asleep," he said.

While MBN waited, Mohammed's staff contacted the members of the Allegiance Council, which now included thirty-four descendants of Ibn Saud. The king wanted Mohammed to be the new crown prince, each was told, then asked, "What do you want?"

It wasn't really a request. While the commission nominally chose the king and crown prince, a less consensus-minded king than Abdullah—a king like Salman—could easily co-opt the group. Who knew what kind of punishment awaited a prince who got in Mohammed's way? Thirty-one of the thirty-four members agreed on the change, the Royal Court would later say. One of the dissenters, Ahmed, would pay for his vote against Mohammed bin Salman.

An emissary delivered that news to MBN in his waiting room and asked him to sign a resignation letter. "He was horrified," a person close to him later said. Bin Nayef refused to step down, and the messenger left, shutting the door behind him.

A parade of Mohammed's loyalists, including Turki Al Sheikh, filed in and out of that room over the next several hours, urging the crown prince to step down peacefully. How else would he leave the palace alive? one asked. Others threatened to release damaging information about MBN's drug use. They played recordings of other princes agreeing to support MBS against him, trying to grind his spirit down.

MBN held his ground through the night. But he was diabetic and tired. And he had no leverage. So around dawn, he agreed to a deal: He wouldn't sign the letter, but he would agree to resign orally.

Mohammed's men finally led him out of the waiting room at about 7 a.m. MBN expected to make his resignation formal later that day. But as he was led through the palace hall, a door opened. Suddenly he was surrounded by flashing cameras. A guard stood with his hand on his gun, a violation of protocol around the crown prince. And there, lurching toward him, was Mohammed bin Salman, whose deputy Saud al-Qahtani was filming. Mohammed kissed his older cousin, who mumbled a pledge of loyalty. "Now I will rest, and you, God help you," MBN said.

Chapter 12

DARK ARTS

September 2017

Salman al-Ouda had a feeling he'd one day run afoul of Mohammed bin Salman. Ever since the prince came to the preacher's house years before and professed his admiration of Machiavelli, it seemed likely that if Mohammed ever gained power, he wouldn't countenance the type of influence Ouda had in the Arab world. He had thirteen million Twitter followers and a well-documented unwillingness to hew to the royal family's messaging.

For more than two years after his father reached the throne, Mohammed had built up his image as a reformer. Now that he was crown prince, he had much more power to actually govern as a reformer. So it surprised many, if not Ouda himself, when the preacher was rounded up with a group of other reform-minded clerics in September 2017 and thrown into solitary confinement.

The government issued a barely coherent explanation for the crackdown, saying the religious leaders were working "for the benefit of foreign parties against the security of the kingdom and its interests, methodology, capabilities, and social peace in order to stir up sedition and prejudice national unity."

The arrests weren't limited to clerics. Other critics, including some guilty of seemingly minor differences of opinion with the crown prince, were also rounded up. Police arrested Essam al-Zamil, a well-known economist who often opined publicly on government policies, and threw him in prison. He had questioned Mohammed's predicted valuation for the Aramco IPO. Others who tweeted skepticism of Mohammed's ideas were summoned into the office of Saud al-Qahtani and threatened with prison. None of those arrested men admitted to any crime, and the legal processes underway against them aren't, for the most part, open to Western journalists.

The crackdown demonstrated the limits of Mohammed's reforms. Social strictures, like rules limiting women's behavior and dress and prohibitions on concerts and movie theaters, would be loosened. Mohammed explained it with an oft-told narrative that began in 1979, when militant Islamists laid siege to Mecca's Grand Mosque. Until that point, Mohammed said, Saudi Arabia was a liberalizing country. But after the attack, which the government quashed with artillery and French military help, the royal family sought peace by appeasing the most conservative religious elements in the kingdom, cracking down on things like entertainment and women's education. Mohammed promised to lift those harsh rules, claiming they weren't inherent to Saudi culture or even Saudi-style Islam.

Mohammed relied heavily on a Saudi religious thinker and former justice minister, Mohammed al-Issa, for theological support. The sheikh had risen up under King Abdullah, gaining attention by making strident but measured statements against Wahhabist orthodoxy. It was his ideas about the role of the 1979 events in pushing Saudi Arabia into deep conservatism that Mohammed learned and began repeating in private and public forums.

The change was welcome for many inside and outside the kingdom. But missing from Mohammed's promises of reform was any mention of civil or political freedom. While he talked about music and movie theaters and women in the workforce, free speech was never brought up. Criticizing the monarchy—

or even publicly questioning Mohammed's policies—could be a crime. Royal Court officials would label critics as traitors, accusing them of taking money from hostile foreign regimes.

This was by design. Mohammed felt there was no room for public dissent as he moved ahead with big economic and social changes all at once. Rather, he wanted to show his subjects that they had a simple choice: Get on board and enjoy the music and restaurants where men and women could mix in normal fashion, like in Dubai or Bahrain, or keep complaining and get thrown in jail. Mastering the message on social media by disseminating positive news and using spies, spyware, money, and threats to stem the flow of negative sentiment would be a years-long priority for Mohammed and his deputies.

"This is unlike anything Saudis have experienced before," Saudi commentator Jamal Khashoggi told the *Wall Street Journal* at the time. He had moved to the United States shortly before, worrying that he could no longer speak with any semblance of independence at home. "It was becoming so suffocating back at home," he told the paper, "that I was beginning to fear for myself."

Khashoggi had spent time as a spokesman for the Saudi embassies in Washington, DC, and London in the years after the September 11, 2001, terrorist attacks, when he parroted the state line to scores of influential journalists and did his part to keep his homeland from becoming a pariah state in a world aghast at the barbarity of Islamic extremism. Over the years, he developed relationships throughout the royal family and was especially close to Prince Turki bin Faisal, the once-powerful intelligence chief who remains a public face of the kingdom. Their ties went so deep that many Saudis speculated Khashoggi was a semipermanent intelligence operative working for Turki. But in truth he was mostly a writer, delighting in the power of ideas and words and the profile he developed in the Muslim world as a public intellectual.

In that role, Khashoggi would sometimes stray from the Royal Court, pushing the envelope on sensitive topics. During the Arab Spring, which terrified Saudi Arabia's monarchy, he started attending regional conferences about governance in the Middle East, talking openly with people the Al Saud saw as enemies. At a conference in Istanbul after the Saudi-supported ouster of Egypt's Muslim Brotherhood–linked president, Mohamed Morsi, Khashoggi met a Turkish politician named Yasin Aktay. A close friend of Salman al-Ouda, who helped the now imprisoned cleric to get his books published in Turkish, Aktay was also an advisor to Turkish president Recep Tayyip Erdoğan. During the Arab Spring, King Abdullah saw Erdoğan as dangerously sympathetic to the Brotherhood. At the conference, Aktay and Khashoggi discussed their mutual hopes for a more democratic Middle East. At the same time, Khashoggi was insistent that the Al Saud should continue to play an important role in Saudi Arabia and across the region. He wanted a more democratic future but wasn't pushing for an end to Al Saud leadership.

Mohammed didn't appreciate that nuance. His view was binary: Khashoggi could be a friend or an enemy.

Turkey was paying close attention to this new Saudi approach. After relations with the kingdom suffered during the Arab Spring, Turkish leaders were optimistic that King Abdullah's death and the ascent of Salman could herald a new beginning. Erdoğan offered a new start for relations between the countries, and Salman accepted.

But Mohammed seemed to get in the way. Rather than consult with Turkey before the Qatar boycott, he charged ahead and gave Turkey a choice to join or be seen as a Saudi foe.

Qatar was a Turkish ally. Turkey couldn't just ditch that relationship at Saudi Arabia's demand. At the same time, Turkish leadership didn't want to take a stance against Saudi Arabia, according to Aktay.

So its government told Mohammed that Turkey would try to mediate a resolution between the kingdom and Qatar. The Saudis sent the Turks a surprising response, Aktay says: "If you are with Qatar, you are with Qatar. And if you want to make a mediation you are also with Qatar." Erdoğan traveled to Riyadh in July 2017 to meet Mohammed and came away with little other than a renewed demand that Turkey abandon Qatar.

Unfortunately for Khashoggi, Mohammed—and his deputy Saud al-Qahtani—took the same approach with him. Khashoggi couldn't be a loyal critic; he had a choice between whole-heartedly supporting Mohammed and being an enemy. Qahtani developed a fixation on the journalist.

First, Qahtani tried to neutralize him, limiting Khashoggi's ability to write in the kingdom with a verbal ban on writing or meeting up with foreign journalists. Then he decided to try transforming him into a new tool for the Royal Court media apparatus. With more than 1.5 million Twitter followers and a contact list filled with foreign journalists, diplomats, and businessmen, Khashoggi could be a profound addition to the Twitter army and cadre of government mouthpieces.

Mohammed and Qahtani remained deeply concerned with sentiment on Twitter. The platform was one of the only ways to gauge how the Saudi people felt about the new crown prince, and Qahtani continued to wield his army of "flies," loyal Twitter accounts, many of them bots rather than real people, that would amplify positive news and pile on against Mohammed's critics. At one point he started a "blacklist" hashtag, which he asked Saudis to use to report countrymen with sympathy for Qatar. "Do you think I make decisions without guidance?" Qahtani tweeted. "I am an employee and a faithful executor of the orders of my lord the king and my lord the faithful crown prince." Less publicly, Qahtani would summon critics to his office in the Royal Court compound and encourage them to be more positive on Twitter or else face prison.

But this wouldn't silence Jamal Khashoggi. That required co-ercion. In November 2016, Qahtani called Khashoggi to inform him he was banned from tweeting or writing anything after he made a critical remark about President Donald Trump and US-Saudi relations at a public event in Washington, DC. Asked whether Trump would bring regional reconciliation, Khashoggi had replied that this was "wishful thinking." Few people paid much attention to it, but the Saudi government issued a state-ment disavowing his words: "The author Jamal Khashoggi does not represent the government of Saudi Arabia or its positions at any level," the Ministry of Foreign affairs announced via the state news agency. There was no royal decree or even an official government action, but Khashoggi knew how things worked in the kingdom. To completely ignore the order was to risk angering someone higher up who agreed with Qahtani.

Things went downhill for Khashoggi fast after that. *Al-Hayat* newspaper canceled his column. Border control in the United Arab Emirates denied him entry to the country after he landed to attend a conference. With no writing opportunities, he even offered himself as a mediator with Qatar during the early days of the boycott. Mohammed bin Salman soon sent word back: no way.

But after some time, Qahtani felt Khashoggi's position as a semi-independent speaker could be useful in swaying influential people in the United States to see Mohammed bin Salman as a genuine reformer. So Qahtani forgave Khashoggi with a warning and allowed him to travel and write more freely again in early 2017. Qahtani believed he'd taught Khashoggi a lesson.

And at first the writer was more circumspect. Speaking at a con-ference in Russia in March of that year, he talked of democracy in the Middle East but said nothing of the Gulf monarchies. Khashoggi was back to striking a careful balance, walking right up to the edge but not crossing it—or at least not by much.

Over time, his comments drifted back into dangerous territory. The problem was that Mohammed bin Salman's approach to reforming the country was infuriating him. Everything seemed to be done by decree; Mohammed only seemed to be paying attention to different opinions when he was locking up those who expressed them.

Mohammed was trying to open the country up to tourists and clamp down on corruption, but many who questioned his way of doing it were hauled in by state security and ordered to sign a pledge never to criticize the government again. The key lesson for Saudis: You are free only insofar as Mohammed bin Salman decides. On the surface, Saudi Arabia seemed to be reforming. But its underlying problem—the fact that people had no say in their own governance and that their freedom was left to the whim of a single man—was worse.

Ironically, Mohammed encouraged his closest advisors to be brutally honest about projects and ideas, praising effusively those who spoke up about what they considered to be an unwise course for the country, even if they directly contradicted the prince's own views.

One evening, he got into a heated argument with a minister about the size of government allowances for Saudi government workers. Mohammed thought they should be enlarged in the budget because the 2030 plan wasn't yet at a stage where it was putting more money into people's hands, but the minister felt it was financially imprudent to spend money in that manner. Finally, the weary minister told Mohammed that he was the crown prince, and it was up to him to decide.

"If I wanted to use my powers to push the decision through, I wouldn't have spent three hours trying to convince you, losing my voice," he said. When the matter was put to a committee vote, the technocrats voted against Mohammed, and the budget item wasn't increased.

But such debate happened strictly in private meetings. Public dissent was off limits, especially when it came to the key reform plans.

Essam al-Zamil, the jailed economist, was scooped up after tweeting his doubts about the planned Aramco IPO. He said the only way it could achieve Mohammed's predicted valuation of more than $2 trillion was if Aramco's oil reserves were included in the sale. Those reserves, he said, belong to the Saudi people, who should have a say in whether they were sold.

Joining Zamil in jail were more than a dozen others who criticized or questioned Mohammed's plans. Among them were a poet who criticized the Qatar boycott and several clerics, including Ouda. The government accused them of working with foreign powers to undermine Saudi Arabia.

Khashoggi spoke up. "It is absurd," he told the *New York Times*. "There was nothing that called for such arrests. They are not the members of a political organization, and they represent different points of view," he said.

The ongoing public impertinence deeply embarrassed Qahtani, who was tired of Khashoggi's flying around the world and publicly trashing his government. Qahtani immediately set in motion a plan to end Khashoggi's career as a commentator of any kind. He cut off travel privileges and banned any public communication, writing, or participation in conferences. Khashoggi would be lucky to take a walk around Jeddah, much less give another one of his speeches about democracy in the Arab world.

But a friend of Khashoggi's in the government tipped him off to the plan. Old ties ran deep. After a life as a journalist and public speaker, Khashoggi couldn't imagine becoming an anonymous individual. He packed two suitcases and headed for

Washington, DC, where he still had an apartment, just in time to avoid a travel ban. Qahtani was incensed and embarrassed yet again in front of his boss.

Against the odds, Khashoggi still held on to the hope of playing a semi-official role for his homeland. Writing to an aide of Awwad al-Awwad, the minister of culture and information, Khashoggi said "despite all I'm still committed to serve my country by being an independent writer and researcher."

He attached a proposal for a new US-based think tank, to be called the Saudi Research Center or Saudi Council, that would liaise with Western think tanks and help counter negative news about Saudi Arabia.

Khashoggi quoted Lenin and highlighted the case of Raif Badawi, the young Saudi writer whose website Free Saudi Liberals earned him charges of apostasy, long prison time, and public flogging, but who did not admit to any of the allegations of wrongdoing.

The Badawi case "cost the kingdom a lot and could have been contained early," he wrote in the proposal expressing his opinion, adding that a special monitoring team at the think tank could monitor news and "work to identify these stories and inform the ministry so they can be addressed early on."

The think tank would cost between $1 million and $2 million to set up and he suggested the ministry hire him as a consultant.

Those efforts didn't seem to mitigate the views of Saudi decision-makers. Around the time Khashoggi moved, Mohammed told a deputy he could "use a bullet" on Khashoggi, the *New York Times* later wrote, citing US intelligence. Discussing how to deal with the prodigal courtier, according to the *New York Times*, Mohammed told Qahtani he "did not like half measures."

And that was before Khashoggi's biggest international insult: Soon after Mohammed's suggestions of violence, Khashoggi started writing a regular column for the *Washington Post*. The first column's headline: "Saudi Arabia Wasn't Always This Repressive. Now It's Unbearable."

"I have left my home, my family, and my job, and I am raising my voice. To do otherwise would betray those who languish in prison. I can speak when so many cannot. I want you to know that Saudi Arabia has not always been as it is now. We Saudis deserve better," he wrote at the end.

Mohammed told Qahtani that he should bring Khashoggi back to Saudi Arabia, and if efforts failed, they "could possibly lure him outside Saudi Arabia and make arrangements," according to a CIA assessment later reported by the *Wall Street Journal*.

Emissaries from the Royal Court kept calling Khashoggi, asking him to tone down his criticism and offering a reconciliation. But he resisted and, in October 2017, made a potentially explosive decision: Khashoggi began talking to an investigator working for American families suing the kingdom over the 9/11 attacks.

The prospect of such a lawsuit was a years-long concern for the royal family. US law makes it difficult to sue foreign governments in American courts, but in 2016 Congress overrode a veto by President Barack Obama to pass a bill making it easier for Americans to sue Saudi Arabia over the 2001 attacks.

The Saudis spent years, and millions of dollars, lobbying against the legislation; Mohammed even sent some of his top ministers to Washington to aid the effort to dissuade Congress. With the bill's passage, the kingdom faced litigation that could result in a huge financial hit and, potentially, embarrassing leaks of information about relationships between high-ranking Saudis and people associated with the attacks. The potential liability also meant that Aramco couldn't list its shares on the New York Stock Exchange, as Mohammed wanted, without risking huge lawsuits that could upend his reform agenda by draining the country's cash cow.

Less than a year later, Catherine Hunt, a former FBI agent working for the attack victims' lawyers, saw Khashoggi's first column in the *Post*. She and the lawyers she worked for became interested in Jamal for all sorts of reasons. He was one of the few people accessible to Westerners who knew both the Al Saud and 9/11 mastermind Osama bin Laden. As a journalist, Khashoggi had visited bin Laden in Afghanistan when he was leading a jihadists' war against communists in the 1980s and again in Sudan in 1995. He also worked in the Saudi embassy in Washington in the days after the attack and understood the kingdom's response. Plus he was close to Turki bin Faisal, who had been the intelligence chief in the years leading up to the attacks.

Just as importantly, Khashoggi could provide a road map to the tangle of family and government relationships in the kingdom. He knew who all the princes were and could point to who supported extremism and who was married to whom. His knowledge wasn't just from his time as a journalist: his connections to the Al Saud, and the bin Ladens, went back generations.

Khashoggi's grandfather had been the personal physician of Ibn Saud, the kingdom's founder; Osama bin Laden's father had also been close with Ibn Saud, who paid him billions of dollars in oil money to build the modern kingdom and establish the family construction fortune. Hunt hoped Khashoggi could help untangle some of those relationships and assist with determining if people connected to the king or the government had played a role in the attacks.

There was enticing circumstantial information. Though the CIA, FBI, and 9/11 Commission said there was no evidence that the government or senior officials supported the attack, the possibility remained that lower-level officials had assisted, and there was evidence that attackers based in California may have interacted with government employees.

There were also enticing threads leading to King Salman and

people close to his family. Back when he was governor of Riyadh, Salman raised money for charities that supported conservative Islamic schools as well as armed militants fighting in places like Afghanistan that became breeding grounds for extremism. More pointedly, two of the 9/11 attackers visited a Florida house whose Saudi owner handled financial matters for King Salman's oldest son, Fahd, who died just before the attacks. Sources close to King Salman say he did not know the charities were linked to extremism.

Hunt left Khashoggi a voicemail, and a few weeks later Khashoggi surprised her when he called back and said he would meet. Hunt flew from Florida to Washington, DC, days later.

Jamal seemed curious about what the investigator had to say, and initially suggested talking at his home before asking Hunt to meet him at a Paul bakery in the upscale Tysons Corner Galleria. Early that morning, Hunt got a call in her hotel room from an agitated Khashoggi. In their prior conversation he seemed smooth and confident; now he was jittery, and wanted to meet right away.

Hunt found a man who was gracious and polite but clearly upset. His hands were shaking, and he told the investigator that early that morning he had learned that the Saudi government had barred his adult son, Salah, from leaving the kingdom. It was insulting, Khashoggi said, and also unfair: His son worked in banking and had nothing to do with his father's work. And the young man had two children in Dubai whom he was now unable to see.

More broadly, Khashoggi was dismayed at being punished for being what he called a "loyal objector." He was supportive of many of Mohammed's reforms, he said, including the diminishing power of clerics who spread conservative Islam outward from the kingdom. "I can't believe they're doing this to me," he said. "I can't believe they're doing this to my son."

Hunt made her pitch to Khashoggi. The meeting, she told him, was "an overture," a first connection to see if he'd be willing to help the 9/11 victims. "I do not believe my country is responsible for the attacks," Khashoggi told Hunt. But then he surprised her. "Is my country responsible for tolerating and even supporting radicalism?" he asked. "Yes, and they must take responsibility for that." Khashoggi said he'd be willing to help, and would like to add his perspective. He asked if the lawyers were offering him a job, and said he'd have to maintain his independence. They agreed to have further talks in New York, where the Saudi government had fewer eyes.

Later that day, October 26, 2017, Khashoggi received an out-of-the blue call from Mohammed's younger brother, Khalid, who seemed eager to patch things up. It unsettled him; did the Royal Court know of his contact with Hunt? If so, it could be seen as high treason, punishable by death.

————

In late 2017, Khashoggi's *Washington Post* column, published in English and Arabic, was also driving Qahtani nuts. Saud's Twitter flies subjected Khashoggi to an onslaught of abuse, calling him a dog, a cancer, and a disease. "You are a corrupt traitor and a fugitive," one wrote.

As infuriating as the columns were, Qahtani and his men were becoming even more obsessed with the idea that Khashoggi was engaged in traitorous attacks on his homeland. Using spyware to infiltrate the phone of Omar Abdulaziz, the Canadian dissident whose Twitter account they'd infiltrated, Qahtani's team realized that Abdulaziz and Khashoggi were working together to coordinate dissidents around the world. Khashoggi was bringing them together, honing their critiques. He'd even discussed a plan with Abdulaziz to harness social media to fight Saud al-Qahtani's pro-MBS Twitter army. With his huge following, Khashoggi was a social media heavyweight. Unlike the flies on Qahtani's side, Khashoggi had credibility.

Yet Qahtani stayed in touch with Khashoggi and pretended he had no connection to the flies. On the phone, Qahtani called Khashoggi "Abu Salah," or father of Salah, an intimate way of addressing another Arab man—and of subtly reminding him that his son Salah was still trapped in the kingdom, under the Royal Court's control. Qahtani praised some of Khashoggi's work while calling him an asset to the Saudi state. "Come home," Qahtani said. "We need your help." Khashoggi knew better than to take the offer as genuine.

Friends worried about him, given the stories of disappeared princes, but Khashoggi felt Saudi Arabia's new rulers wouldn't use violence. The Al Saud tended to pay off would-be enemies or lure them back home, not shoot them. Mohammed seemed to be taking that tack with problem people like the late King Fahd's famously louche son Abdulaziz, known as Azouz.

The once powerful Azouz—who years earlier was involved in the first kidnapping of Prince Sultan bin Turki II—had himself fallen into physical and moral disrepair. He had gained an improbable amount of weight, traveling the world with escorts and staying in the fanciest hotels. In 2012 a member of his entourage was convicted of raping a woman at the Plaza Hotel in Manhattan. In 2016, the *New York Post* published a photo of Azouz outside a New York club, wearing sandals, baggy jeans, and a leather jacket and sipping soda from a bendy straw. "This Slob Could Buy You," an online headline said. Another was a more pointed dig at the kingdom: "Shoddy Arabia."

In 2017, Mohammed locked him up too. "It's for his own good," Mohammed told friends. Saudis and foreigners specu-lated that Azouz was dead until months later Mohammed had friends put footage on the internet of a slimmer and cleaned up Azouz playing with a young child.

Khashoggi saw the imprisonment of such enemies and knew better than to get on any private planes sent to ferry him to the kingdom. But outside the Gulf, he felt safe enough to travel and appear publicly.

It would prove a tragic miscalculation.

Chapter 13

DAVOS IN THE DESERT

October 2017

"Everybody," Andrew Ross Sorkin announced to the audience in a King Abdulaziz Convention Center auditorium on October 25, 2017, "this is Sophia."

The *New York Times* columnist sat on stage in a gray suit and maroon tie. At a lectern to his right was a six-foot-tall automaton with the face of a woman and a transparent cranium that revealed a tangle of electrical wiring inside.

"You look happy," Sorkin told the robot.

"I'm always happy when surrounded by smart people who also happens [*sic*] to be rich and powerful," the robot responded.

The android could have been speaking for Mohammed bin Salman, who had invited the journalist, the robot, and hundreds of the world's most powerful bankers, executives, and politicians to an event he called the Future Investment Initiative. It was intended to showcase the new Saudi Arabia to powerful politicians and financiers.

With promises of a more open kingdom and a less strident version of Saudi Islam, Mohammed seemed to have buy-in from everyone who mattered—even the normally skeptical *New York Times*, which sponsored the conference. Sorkin, its best-known financial writer, came to Riyadh with the hope of interviewing

Softbank's Masayoshi Son. He ended up getting roped into hosting onstage interviews with Son and others. He didn't realize the
"Sophia" on his list of interviewees was a robot until a friend who
saw the agenda pointed it out. Sorkin smiled as he interviewed
Sophia while a giddy Yasir al-Rumayyan, the Saudi sovereign
wealth fund chief, filmed on his iPhone.

Then Sorkin said he had an announcement: Saudi Arabia
had made history by granting citizenship to the robot. It was a
jarring publicity stunt in a country that doesn't grant citizenship
to millions of children born on its soil to migrant workers. But
that hardly detracted from the positive press. Sorkin, who had
learned about the robot's citizenship shortly before taking the
stage, appeared surprised himself.

There was a sense that Mohammed bin Salman's economic
transformation was going to make a lot of people inside and
outside the kingdom very rich, and no one wanted to jeopardize
that. In the lobbies and hallways of the Ritz, Saudi government
officials were in such demand that one of them remarked in
private to a friend that it was like being the most popular kid
in school.

One of the world's largest money managers, Blackstone's Stephen Schwarzman, was there, along with SoftBank's Masayoshi
Son, former British prime minister Tony Blair, Uber CEO Travis
Kalanick, and Hollywood kingmaker Ari Emanuel. Foreign media
called the event "Davos in the Desert," a moniker also used in
the early 2000s for a World Economic Forum event in Jordan.

Top CEOs, bankers, consultants, and political figures, all of
them clamoring for fees or investment, lined up for meetings
with Rumayyan and Mohammed. It was a scene rarely found
outside gala events in the capitals of global finance. Rumayyan
invited luminaries to his house one evening for a lavish buffet,
where men like Blair and SoftBank's Masayoshi milled around
chatting about the kingdom's swift progress.

A who's who of business, banking, and politics stood beneath the statue of a raging stallion in the Ritz-Carlton lobby. US treasury secretary Steve Mnuchin was there. Private equity tycoon Tom Barrack, a close Trump ally, wandered by. So did BlackRock CEO Larry Fink and Virgin Group founder Richard Branson. Reporters from the *Wall Street Journal*, *Financial Times*, and Bloomberg News tried to break into their conversations—or at least eavesdrop.

Young Saudi business school graduates stood on the margins of the lobby in giddy groups. For years they'd expected that getting a serious job in finance or industry would require moving outside the kingdom. Now they were introducing themselves to the world's most important businessmen on their home turf.

Just as surprising to the young men was a mysterious blonde strolling confidently around the Ritz in an *abaya* and flawless makeup. She introduced herself as Carla DiBello, an American reality TV producer and a friend—the "best friend," she would say—of Kim Kardashian, though a Kardashian representative would later say they hadn't talked in years. One of the young Saudi men pulled up her Instagram feed on his iPhone and scrolled through her photos posing on the beach in bikinis and flexing in skintight workout gear. "Look at her!" one of the men exclaimed to his friends.

The main events were at the Royal Court's King Abdulaziz Conference Center, but there were smaller gatherings and lunches at the Ritz-Carlton next door. Traffic was nearly at a standstill as security guards used pole-mounted mirrors to check each car's undercarriage for explosives.

Hundreds of journalists on the scene helped propagate rumors, spreading by the hour, about a last-minute change to the agenda. Finally, on the afternoon of the conference's first day, Mohammed bin Salman swept in, the crowds swirling behind him.

CNBC offered a live feed of him sitting at the front of the room next to Dubai emir Mohammed bin Rashid Al Maktoum. It was the same hall where Donald Trump had given his speech months earlier. A gaggle of photographers flashed their camera bulbs as a giant screen broadcast "The Pulse of Change," a slogan adopted by the organizers.

There was little doubt this was the most powerful business-man in the world.

Next came the video announcement for NEOM, up until then a secret. "Our ambition," a sophisticated British-accented male voice began. "It starts with over 26,000 square kilometers of land set in an ideal location where three continents meet right at the heart of the world's transport, trade, and telecommunications routes."

"Here we see the birth of NEOM, the world's most ambitious project, a destination of the future, a vision that is becoming reality."

Fox Business's Maria Bartiromo stood up to host the panel, wearing a long, flowing white jacket. "We watch something of a revolution happening here in Saudi Arabia as the kingdom looks to growth," she said, inviting Mohammed bin Salman onto the stage, alongside Schwarzman of Blackstone, Son, Marc Raiburt of Boston Dynamics, and Klaus Kleinfeld, the new head of the NEOM project.

"If you allow me, I will speak in Arabic because a lot of Saudi audience here and I really respect them," Mohammed said, before describing the "almost imaginary" opportunities at NEOM and squinting slightly as he listed its benefits, ticking them off on his hand.

The discussion had the atmosphere of a love fest, with execu-tives praising the prince's vision and the merits of NEOM. The most thrilling words of the day, though, were sandwiched in the middle of the panel. Bartiromo asked the prince why he was pursuing changes now, including permitting women to drive and allowing foreign investment in the country.

Mohammed, in his most charismatic public speech to date, gave an impassioned pledge to return the country back to the way it was before religious extremism began to rise in 1979. That was the year of the Grand Mosque attack and the Al Saud's subsequent decision to appease religious conservatives with restrictions on entertainment and women's rights. It was also the year Grand Ayatollah Ruhollah Khomeini overthrew Iran's secular shah, showing Saudi Arabia what could happen if rulers moved too far away from powerful religious leaders.

"Saudi Arabia and the entire region witnessed the spread of an awakening project after 1979 for many reasons that are not the subject of today," Mohammed said. "We have not been this way before. We are just going back to what we used to be: moderate, open minded Islam to the world and to all religions and to all traditions and peoples." It was the first time a modern Saudi leader had publicly promised to wrest social control from Saudi Arabia's clerics.

"Seventy percent of the Saudi people are less than 30 years old and frankly we will not waste 30 years of our lives dealing with any extremist ideas," Mohammed said. "We will destroy them today and immediately."

Headlines rolled across the world, and Saudis, who filled the room for the speech, applauded fervently.

Many in the crowd were impressed with the ambition and the scope of Mohammed's Vision 2030 plan. The problem was that it required foreign investors to put their money behind that conviction. Just about no foreign investor wanted to put up the kind of money Saudi Arabia needed to start to stem its addiction to petrodollars. The attendees spent their days listening to talks on artificial intelligence and alternative energy, but really they were there in the hopes of extracting money from Saudi Arabia's sovereign wealth fund.

Behind the scenes, Saudi officials were struggling. Despite the excitement and buzz, there were troubling signs on the economic front in the run-up to the event. Saudi Arabia wasn't admitting it publicly, but the Aramco IPO plans were stagnating. Mohammed bin Salman's first choice of the New York Stock Exchange was a problem because of the new law ratified nearly a year earlier that allowed the 9/11 victims' lawsuit—the one Jamal Khashoggi agreed to assist with.

Royal Court advisors worried that, under the law, plaintiffs could try to get US courts to award them a chunk of Aramco if the company were to be listed on a US stock market. More broadly, Mohammed's advisors were concerned about the frequent use in the United States of class action stockholder lawsuits where investors try to extract money from companies by suing for poor management, insufficient disclosures, or other improprieties. With its loose accounting, Aramco could be an easy target.

Trump, Jared Kushner, and other top White House officials tried to give assurances, but Aramco's lawyers from White & Case and other advisors cautioned that a listing was too risky with the US government so polarized on nearly every issue.

Energy Minister Khalid al-Falih, a skeptic of the IPO from the start, had also allegedly been subverting efforts to list Aramco. His staff came up with valuations far short of Mohammed's $2 trillion, along with a whole list of problems to try to convince the prince it would be folly to proceed. The plan became a battle between Mohammed and Khalid, often played out by their deputies and advisors. Bankers flew all the way to Riyadh for meetings, only to be told that a minister or royal advisor had just left the country. But they tolerated it, believing a big payout was still around the corner even though leaks in the press showed Saudi Arabia was now considering a local listing only.

NEOM was a mess too. To date, consultants had spent thousands of hours trying to turn the ideas of Mohammed and his advisors into realistic policies. But the only real structures at NEOM were palaces built by thousands of South Asian construction workers laboring around the clock. The first contractors struggled to get things moving, so the government called Saudi Binladin Group in to get the job done. A couple of years had passed since the government had frozen the company following the Mecca crane incident. The palaces were modeled after King Salman's Tangier retreat.

Even the NEOM announcement hadn't been properly vetted with the two countries that were supposed to be Saudi Arabia's partners in launching it, Egypt and Jordan. Their governments were privately upset when Mohammed unveiled the plan in front of world leaders, but they decided to issue no statements at the time.

Guests at the Future Investment Initiative who professed to have a deep interest in Saudi Arabia as a long-term partner showed a sometimes shocking ignorance of its values. "Saudi has the Great Mecca," Masayoshi Son declared at the conference. "We will create two more Meccas." Mohammed was forced to intervene: "Please do not misunderstand his statement. Mecca became an example of an attraction center, so he means new attraction centers." In Islam, Mecca is singular—the holiest city in the world. The idea that it was a replicable tourist attraction was deeply offensive, the kind of statement Islamic hardliners could seize upon to undermine the prince's reforms.

Away from the big presentations, Mohammed held private meetings with Western VIPs. Swaggering New York bankers stood in line for hours to get a few minutes with the prince. When they got inside, one person who attended these meetings

says, they lost their swagger. They deferentially called Mohammed "your royal highness" and complimented his great vision for
the kingdom while sweat beaded on their foreheads.

Ari Emanuel, arguably Hollywood's most powerful agent and
the chief executive of Endeavor, a company formed by a merger
of talent agency William Morris and sporting-event company
IMG, didn't seem to break a sweat. He'd been trying to find
a way to get Saudi money for more than a year and developed
a shtick to show powerful princes that he wouldn't bend the
knee. "The one thing you need to know about me," he once
told Alwaleed bin Talal, possibly Saudi Arabia's richest royal and
a man called "your royal highness" by other Americans, "I'm a
motherfucker."

Emanuel had previously started talks with the Public Investment Fund (PIF) for a $400 million investment in Endeavor.
Emanuel had understood that the Saudis and his company were
close to a deal. But in subsequent conversations in Saudi Arabia
and Los Angeles, the PIF's Rumayyan was noncommittal. That
left Emanuel frustrated. While the prince had talked about lofty
goals like creating a Saudi movie industry and investing in the
future of sports and television, Rumayyan didn't seem interested
in such ambitious visions. He mainly asked about things like
projections for Endeavor's annual revenue. "Is this guy serious?"
Emanuel asked an associate after one meeting. "He doesn't
know shit about entertainment."

Then Rumayyan made a startling request: As a condition of
investing, he wanted a seat on Endeavor's board of directors—
just like with Uber. Emanuel said no but suggested that maybe
an advisory board could be created for him to sit on. "I need to
get back to you," Rumayyan responded, and Emanuel concluded
that only with a face-to-face with Mohammed could he finalize
the deal.

That's what he planned to do during a private meeting while the Davos in the Desert conference went on in a nearby room. In a wood-paneled Ritz salon into which he was ushered to meet the prince, Emanuel sat impatiently on a gray-upholstered chair with arms covered in gold leaf, fidgeting and making small talk with the other person waiting to see the prince, Christine Lagarde, a regal, silver-haired Frenchwoman who was head of the International Monetary Fund.

When it was his turn, Emanuel marched into a chandeliered room to find Mohammed sitting in a *thobe*, his head uncovered. Emanuel slumped into a chair opposite the prince and outlined the terms of the deal. Saudi Arabia would invest $400 million for a stake in Endeavor. It wouldn't get a board seat. "Okay," Mohammed responded, and asked if he should call in Rumayyan to finalize things. "No, that's alright," Emanuel said. He didn't want to bother with the underling.

Then the agent did something no one did in the crown prince's presence: He just got up and left. The meeting was over in seven minutes, and Emanuel had his $400 million commitment.

Though the Future Investment Initiative was theoretically about getting foreigners to invest in Saudi Arabia, the news it generated was largely about Saudi Arabia investing even more in foreign companies. Rumayyan said the sovereign wealth fund aimed to have $2 trillion in investments, many of them overseas, by 2030. Branson got a $1 billion commitment for the parent of his space tourism company Virgin Galactic. Blackstone already had a commitment of $20 billion for an investment fund, and the Vision Fund was already off the ground with $40 billion from Saudi Arabia. Rajeev Misra, head of the Vision Fund, strutted around the Ritz-Carlton, holding meetings in Masayoshi Son's huge suite and vaping nonstop.

Some international investors pledged to invest money in the kingdom, though they were mainly affiliated with countries or companies looking to build favor with the crown prince. A Russian state-backed fund said it would invest in NEOM. SoftBank promised to build the world's biggest-ever solar-energy project and agreed to buy a stake in Saudi Electric Corporation.

In the end, the conference was seen, inside and outside Saudi Arabia, as a success. It generated a week's worth of headlines, and the ubiquitous images on TVs and front pages around the world of Mohammed sitting with the world's most famous financiers showed that he was a serious force with global reach. Within Saudi Arabia, it helped make the case that he was fit to be a future king. But beneath the glitz, signs of a huge upheaval began to emerge to those with a keen eye.

When the conference began, Adel Fakeih was arguably the most powerful nonroyal in Saudi Arabia. Mohammed tasked him, as minister of economy and planning, with the most crucial elements of Vision 2030. It was Fakeih's job to hire and manage armies of consultants and to see that the prince's ideas were turned into action. At the conference's biggest events, a seat in the front row had Fakeih's name on it.

But people close to the minister sensed something was wrong. He seemed anxious at a family gathering on the eve of the conference and at one point appeared to well up. He was just emotional, he said, about a young relative's birthday. In hindsight, friends and family wondered if the minister already knew the conference was the last time he'd be seen in public.

Chapter 14

SHEIKHDOWN

November 4, 2017

Turki bin Abdullah was sleeping when the security men arrived at his palace at dawn. The king requested his presence at an important all-hands meeting with senior Al Saud. "You have to come straight away," a Royal Court security officer told the son of the former king.

All across the country and abroad, similar routines were underway. As motorcades wound their way to the Ritz-Carlton hotel, newly appointed as a prison for the superrich, private jet terminals were shut down and banks told to freeze any pending transactions for a list of more than 380 people, including senior royals.

The fall 2017 operation was Mohammed bin Salman's best-choreographed move yet, even more intricate and flawless than the summit with President Donald Trump less than six months earlier. The fact that Mohammed's team pulled it off without leaks or an intervention by powerful allies of the would-be detainees testified to the discipline of his Royal Court and the small phalanx of men in his circle of trust. This was a mission with huge opportunities for financial benefit: Tipping off a target, enabling him to preserve his wealth and freedom, could reap generous rewards. But the entire operation unfolded without a blip.

Mohammed later explained it to David Ignatius of the *Washington Post* as a powerful medicine to eradicate corruption. "You have a body that has cancer everywhere, the cancer of corruption," he told him. "You need to have chemo, the shock of chemo, or the cancer will eat the body." Jamal Khashoggi, writing for the same newspaper, unfairly called it the "Night of the Long Knives," referencing Adolf Hitler's brutal 1934 purge and consolidation of power that involved more than seven hundred killings.

For each prisoner at the Ritz-Carlton hotel, there was a corruption accusation. But in many cases, the incarceration also had a deeper reason. Take Turki, the late King Abdullah's seventh son, for example. As deputy governor and governor of Riyadh from 2013 and 2015, he'd been instrumental in the long-delayed, overbudget Riyadh Metro project. Mohammed bin Salman and his investigators alleged Turki overcharged for aspects of the rail installation, pocketing huge kickbacks for himself. But the biggest reason he was in the Ritz, and treated especially harshly, was his role in trying to unseat King Salman and his son, starting even before Salman's coronation. Turki has never publicly admitted to or been publicly charged with any crime.

To an outsider Turki seemed a lot like the crown prince. He was a senior Al Saud family member who parlayed his relationship with his father into powerful government roles and great wealth. He wanted to be king someday, and he was scheming to clear a path for himself to the throne. He was open about this around his sisters and brothers. Sitting in the huge dining rooms of one Abdullah clan member or another, Turki and his siblings would talk about how he should one day be king—and how Salman never should have been king at all. They viewed Salman, with his close ties to clerics Abdullah had wanted to sideline, as a religious fundamentalist, a man obsessed with keeping tabs on his relatives' transgressions and exacting revenge on those who behaved in ways he disliked.

But to Mohammed, it was Turki who embodied deep problems within the Al Saud. MBS believed he demanded kickbacks from foreign companies and involved himself in shady overseas deals, including Malaysia's 1Malaysia Development Berhad scandal. Turki denied it all, but Mohammed had little patience for princes who he believed brazenly took their money-making schemes overseas.

He also loathed the idea that every son, grandson, or great-grandson of Ibn Saud had the right to behave in such a way. The king and his sons rightfully controlled the country's wealth and could buy yachts or mansions, Mohammed maintained. But farther-flung royals should maintain a lower profile, not speed around in their Bugattis acting important—if only because the number of such princes grew exponentially with each generation and pretty soon the kingdom wouldn't be able to afford it. It was a notion that Turki's father, King Abdullah, had instilled in the royal family when he cut princes' allowances and one that Mohammed had internalized. He felt that he, and not Abdullah's sons, was Abdullah's spiritual heir and the one with the guts to aggressively implement the reforms the old king couldn't see out before he died. "I'm a disruptive King Abdullah," Mohammed told friends.

Turki had relationships abroad and continued quietly trying to undermine Mohammed for the first two years of Salman's reign. But he later learned that he had made a devastating miscalculation. He'd figured that so long as his brother, Miteb, was head of the National Guard and Mohammed bin Nayef was the minister of interior, Mohammed bin Salman would be limited in his ability to learn of Turki's plans. Mohammed only controlled the Ministry of Defense, which had limited intelligence-gathering capabilities. Turki figured Mohammed didn't have the spies or the technology to know what was happening. He also underestimated Mohammed's resolve and the willingness of his supporters to use brute force. For Turki, it was about power and money.

Mohammed believed only his reforms could save the country, even if pursuing them required him to blow up his own family.

So Turki didn't take even simple precautions, such as relying on encrypted phone apps like WhatsApp to communicate. He used open phone lines to discuss his plan and vent his frustrations with Mohammed, not realizing that from the outset, Mohammed had expanded his powers and tapped into telecommunications across the country.

For more than two years, Mohammed revealed none of this knowledge. He made a habit of seeming like he was offering an olive branch whenever he saw Turki or Miteb in public. After Salman ordered Turki replaced as governor of Riyadh with another cousin, stripping him of any official duty, it almost seemed to Turki as if Mohammed had forgotten about him while focusing on his economic reform plans and related publicity. During a funeral, Mohammed stood next to Turki smiling in what appeared to be a public cooling of tensions.

In fact, Mohammed hadn't forgotten Turki's actions for a moment. His staffers were gathering a detailed dossier on him, and they put him near the top of the list of targets taken by the crew that executed the Ritz arrests. It was technically situated partially within Saud al-Qahtani's Center for Studies and Media Affairs.

Thrown in a hallway at the Ritz with his top advisor, a retired general called Ali al-Qahtani (no immediate relationship to Saud al-Qahtani), Turki was initially indignant. "My father was the king. Fuck you," he told his interrogators. He even struck one.

After his interrogators physically subdued him, Turki began to come to terms with his plight as he watched more detainees arrive by the hour. Turki and Ali had missed out on any signs of this countercoup.

Only forty-six, Turki bin Abdullah went from a onetime contender for the throne to one of the disappeared. The retired general, Ali, would die, allegedly having been tortured, during the early days of the Ritz, while Turki was transferred to a grubby prison, housed with murderers and drug dealers, and later to a black detention center with no access to anyone but his closest family, and only for short periods.

There wasn't much coverage of his detention, which remained largely unknown to Americans and Brits, except for a brief flurry when the pop legend Cher tweeted that she was worried "4 My Son's Good Friend Prince Turki bin Abdullah," whom she described as a young prince with a kind heart and "No Desire 2 Take Over Anything." It turned out Turki was friends with her son, Elijah.

Later a sensational photograph spread like wildfire on WhatsApp. It showed sixteen princes dressed in casual Western clothes on the deck of a yacht in the South of France. A young Mohammed was pictured in the back row on the far right, clearly the junior family member, while Alwaleed bin Talal, Abdulaziz bin Fahd, and Turki bin Abdullah smiled on. The photo was taken on Turki's chartered yacht, where Mohammed was invited to join his older, richer cousins for a lunch. Now, many of them were being held at the Ritz. How the tables had turned.

Turki's brothers, including Miteb, Mishal, and Faisal, were detained due to an alleged bald-faced money grab. After limiting his children's wealth for years, believing it would corrupt them, Abdullah in 2010 created a personal foundation to spend much of his money on improving life for Muslims around the world in the form of developmental aid and grants. On Abdullah's death, control of the foundation transferred to his children. Some of them immediately sought to drain it of funds for their own purposes. None of the men have admitted to or been publicly charged with any crime.

Miteb is accused of having gone a step further, arranging for the National Guard, which he controlled, to transfer billions of dollars' worth of land it owned to the foundation, turning government assets into the property of his family's private organization. It gave Mohammed bin Salman a perfect pretext to go after the bin Abdullahs for corruption. Miteb was among the first to settle with Mohammed, agreeing to transfer the land back to the government and bow quietly out of public service. "Take my money and leave me alone," he told Mohammed.

In what would become a humiliating follow-up for many Ritz detainees, a reminder that they might seem free but would always be under Mohammed's thumb, Miteb was ordered to smile and pose for a photograph with Mohammed not long after.

None were immune. Even some of Abdullah's daughters, who played little role in the Al Saud skullduggery, would lose everything they'd inherited from their father, though they weren't detained. King Abdullah's Royal Court chief, Khalid al-Tuwaijri, was locked up too, as was Abdullah's protocol chief—essentially the king's head butler—Mohammed al-Tobaishi.

Tobaishi had grown fabulously wealthy through his relationship with Lebanon's prime minister. Unlike Tuwaijri he retained his job after Salman became king—until he slapped a reporter on camera a few months after the leadership transition. Salman fired him immediately.

But in a pattern that would repeat itself with the relatives of other vanquished enemies, Mohammed chose Tobaishi's son, the Sandhurst-educated Rakan, to be his own protocol chief. It was Rakan who brought his father to the Ritz. By the time he was let out, the elder Tobaishi would be relieved of his ranch, which was worth $100 million or more, his stud farm, its horses and indoor and outdoor auditoriums, and millions of dollars in cash. The ranch later became a resort.

Mohammed appointed a new minister of interior and new head of the National Guard. Both were childhood friends of the prince in their early thirties, a further sign that the prince's consolidation of power was complete. The new head of the National Guard's 125,000 soldiers was Abdullah bin Bandar, Mohammed's cousin and among his most trusted friends. He had followed Mohammed throughout his rise, speaking often of his unabashed adoration of Mohammed while working at the King Salman Youth Center and as deputy governor of Mecca after King Salman was anointed.

In the past no single prince had commanded more than one of the kingdom's three armed forces. Now Mohammed controlled them all. He was in charge and had removed nearly all potential challengers or conspirators against him, whether they were billionaires or cousins.

These moves weren't foisted on King Salman, either. As the family enforcer, he'd built up files on princes for years. And Abdullah before him had amassed dossiers pertaining to corruption with an eye toward a crackdown. Abdullah hadn't been able to carry it out, fearing it would be too disruptive. Those files, together with more information gleaned by Mohammed bin Salman's teams from banks and further investigation, were the basis for the whole operation. When detainees were brought in at night for interrogation, they were confronted with granular details of their financial assets and activity, not vague allegations.

Western observers saw the arrests as a power grab and abuse of the rule of law, but locally many championed the move. For decades, Saudis had put up with lofty princes and well-connected businessmen always getting their way. They'd win contracts they shouldn't. They'd take over projects they had no right to. They'd earn billions while many Saudis struggled to pay the bills. Now they were being cut down to size, and it sent a shudder of pleasure through nearly everyone but the top 5 percent of the country.

Messages were coordinated across the board. The arrests were accompanied by a decree creating a "supreme committee" to investigate corruption, ostensibly creating a legal basis for the operation. The committee had "the right to take any precautionary measures it sees fit," including seizing assets and banning travel. In a statement, King Salman excoriated the exploitation perpetrated by "the weak souls who have put their own interests above the public interest, in order to illicitly accrue money." Mohammed bin Salman described the campaign in a brief video clip: "I assure you anyone involved in corruption will not be spared, whether he's a prince or a minister, or anyone." The Council of Senior Scholars, Saudi Arabia's top religious body, endorsed the arrests, saying that Islamic law "instructs us to fight corruption and our national interest requires it."

Mohammed gave a simple explanation to one American contact: Many of the men in the Ritz had spent years breaking the laws, but they were following the old rules, which allowed such corruption. Now the rules had changed. And they wouldn't just be different from now on—they had changed retroactively.

Even those who might tend to be critical seemed to accept it as a cleanup operation. "It is very selective. Right now, there is corruption happening around him," said Jamal Khashoggi, the Saudi journalist, in the early days of the arrests. "The royal family used to be partners: you steal and I steal, you take a cut and I take a cut. Now he has ultimate power. It's a game-changer." But as reports about Ali al-Qahtani's death leaked out, Khashoggi had a change of heart. He was happy to stay abroad until things blew over.

Reports of the detentions shook the American and European financiers and political leaders who had departed the kingdom from Davos in the Desert days earlier with the belief that Mohammed was turning a capricious absolute monarchy into something resembling a modern state. After the presentations about renewable energy, technology investment, and freedom for

women, many in the West expected a Saudi Arabia that worked
more like a Western government.

Now they were learning that by sidelining other princes and
silencing dissent, Mohammed was actually making the kingdom more autocratic. Business leaders, including Jamie Dimon,
Steve Schwarzman, and Michael Bloomberg, called their Saudi
friends and contacts, hoping to figure out what was going on. It
was also perplexing that Mohammed had initiated the operation
so soon after the conference: Was it on purpose? some asked,
wondering whether he was speaking to his core youth demographic with the crackdown. It would be far worse if it was just
another whim pursued by the prince, who felt untouchable and
all powerful.

The scene at the Ritz was surreal. In the palatial lobby, caterers
from the Royal Court served a lineup of Saudi Arabia's best-
known men, each wearing a standard-issue *thobe* and fearful of
what would come next. Amenities were provided—medical care,
a barber—and most detainees could call home every few days.
But they were afraid of talking openly on the phone.

Within the first few days, detainees started trickling out, some
having reached financial settlements, others deemed clean. One
of the first was Ibrahim al-Assaf, a former finance minister
who was rounded up as a witness to alleged malfeasance under
Abdullah's reign. Explaining that he was just following Royal
Court orders when he signed checks from the Saudi treasury
that went to line officials' pockets, he offered to provide information on whatever Mohammed's men wanted to know about.
He later became the minister of foreign affairs, proving that a
stay at the Ritz was not necessarily a stain on your curriculum
vitae. The details mattered, though. He hadn't been accused of
long-running personal corruption.

*   *   *

Besides the powerful princes and billionaires in the Ritz were more modest prisoners, like Hani Khoja, a mountain-climbing management consultant. For a time, it seemed like the stars had aligned for him. After spending more than a decade in marketing for Procter & Gamble, he founded his own consultancy firm in Riyadh, figuring there was a market for local management expertise. He made an effort to turn himself into a celebrity in the Saudi business world, writing a self-published autobiography centered on his climb of Mount Kilimanjaro and making public appearances on TV and at business conferences. But Hani found that he couldn't strike the same kind of contracts that the big foreign firms like McKinsey and BCG could. Saudi companies wanted Saudi consultants but still didn't really trust their experience.

Mohammed bin Salman's Vision 2030 plan changed the dynamic. It was so vast that it required every able body that could give a PowerPoint presentation. And MBS was urging government ministries to make genuine efforts to hire Saudis rather than foreigners for key jobs.

All of a sudden, Hani's Elixir Consulting found itself in heavy demand. Adel Fakeih, the powerful minister of economy and planning whom Hani knew from previous consulting work and a familial relationship, started hiring the firm for major jobs, including figuring out how to implement policies and plans—the type of work that McKinsey was angling to get more of from the government.

Knowing that demands for Saudi consultants would only increase and that having an in with Fakeih could be the key to years of lucrative new work, McKinsey ended up buying Elixir in full for $100 million. Hani, the former shampoo marketer, was now a partner at McKinsey, the world's most prestigious management consultancy.

McKinsey expected the purchase would keep it earning

millions from Saudi Arabia long after the original Vision 2030 was authored. Elixir would specialize in implementing the ideas in the vision plan and keeping a focus on Mohammed bin Salman's favorite key performance indicators.

The young American employees McKinsey was flying in and out of Saudi Arabia for all sorts of government work were skeptical of the Elixir deal. They had been top students, often at Ivy League schools, and felt they'd earned their prestigious jobs at the firm. Now they'd have to collaborate with peers who were educated at Saudi universities and had little experience outside the kingdom.

There was also a tangle of strange cultural priorities. Elixir was supposed to appeal to the government by making McKinsey more Saudi. But Elixir's young Saudi employees often wanted to be more Western in their habits. Managers would send the young Saudis scrambling to change from their suits and dress shirts into *thobes* and keffiyehs when they got word that a government minister would be coming by the office.

McKinsey would soon find it had a much bigger problem: Hani's best connection, the planning minister Fakeih, turned out to be an unexpected target of Mohammed's crackdown.

For the first two of years of Salman's time on the throne, Fakeih was one of the kingdom's most influential officials. He spent years as the chief executive of Savola Group, a food conglomerate, before King Abdullah appointed him mayor of his home city, Jeddah, in 2005. It was at the beginning of Abdullah's reign, and the reform-minded king put Fakeih in charge of major changes to the old port city. He undertook several billion-dollar modernization programs and eventually was appointed minister of labor, a position in which he worked on efforts to get more Saudis into the workforce. He also served a short stint as minister of health.

When Mohammed took control of Saudi economic planning

in early 2015, Fakeih was exactly the kind of official he wanted to elevate—someone with private-sector experience, a track record of trying to get Saudis involved in their own economy, and the ability to manage billion-dollar projects. The prince put Fakeih in charge of the newly powerful Ministry of Economy and Planning, which would play a central role in formulating and delivering the swift and drastic economic changes.

The new job put Fakeih in charge of billions of dollars and armies of consultants. He also grew close to Mohammed. During Salman's early days on the throne, even Saud al-Qahtani had to go through Fakeih to schedule a meeting with the prince.

Fakeih and other ministers were given different orders than their predecessors. Saudi Arabia was known for interminable decision-making processes. No more, Mohammed ordered. He slimmed down his ministers' portfolios so they could focus on top priorities and told them that they would be evaluated based on how quickly and efficiently they could implement the prince's orders. If they succeeded, there would be huge rewards. If they failed, they'd be removed.

At a party around that time, Turki Al Sheikh, by then appointed head of the General Sports Authority, put his arm around sovereign wealth fund chief Yasir al-Rumayyan and told a group of friends, "We could get fired any time." If new ministers got caught trying to enrich themselves, they faced much harsher treatment.

Fakeih seemed an unlikely man to meet such a fate. He was appointed to the board of the sovereign wealth fund and contributed to Vision 2030. He struck Western diplomats, consultants, and businessmen as an integral part of the prince's changes. They were shocked when news emerged that Fakeih had been swept up in the Ritz arrests, and the Royal Court never said what he'd been detained for, though he remains locked up.

Hani was lower profile but much more concerning to

McKinsey. Was the firm going to face consequences? Its leaders weren't sure. No one told them that Hani had been arrested, or why. It was unclear if he faced charges. There were two possibilities for McKinsey, neither good: Either it had bought a corrupt consulting firm, or one of its partners was being imprisoned unjustly. McKinsey leaders didn't know what was going on. They got word that Hani's bank account was frozen and stopped paying him, and decided he was no longer an employee. McKinsey says it met all its financial obligations to Hani after he was finally released about a year later. He returned home with an ankle bracelet and tight restrictions on travel and took up painting as a hobby.

Six days after the arrests, the *Wall Street Journal* reported that McKinsey had hired relatives of high-ranking Saudi officials, including two children of the energy minister, Khalid al-Falih, and a son of the finance minister. This raised the question of whether McKinsey truly had an arm's-length relationship with the kingdom that had become a crucial client. It claimed all employees were hired on their qualifications alone.

Over the coming days, a shocking roster of detainees leaked out. In addition to princes and ministers, some of Saudi Arabia's best-known businessmen were locked up. There was Fawaz al-Hokair, the real estate developer who in 2017 paid almost $88 million for a penthouse in one of Manhattan's tallest residential towers, and Saudi-Ethiopian billionaire Mohammed Al Amoudi, who owned mines and oil refineries around the world. Ali al-Naimi, for years the Saudi oil minister, was rounded up, as was his son Rami, who was jailed, allegedly tortured, and accused of corruption. All the men were later released after reaching settlements without publicly admitting wrongdoing.

Some five members of the bin Laden family were jailed for stretches throughout the Ritz crackdown. More than two years had passed since the Mecca crane disaster, and Saudi Binladin Group was still at a standstill after Mohammed and his father cut off the flow of government work. The crackdown on the family was extraordinary. The government seized every asset the bin Ladens owned inside the kingdom, from the company itself down to modest ancestral villas in Riyadh and Jeddah.

When Bakr bin Laden was brought in for his first round of interrogation, he was shocked to see a half-foot stack of papers. This was no hasty operation. They had years of financial records, lists of assets, and details of allegations related to free work for princes including Mohammed bin Nayef, the recently ousted crown prince. As negotiations proceeded for the family to formally surrender a chunk of their company to the government, interrogators detained Abdullah, one of the brothers who had a Harvard law degree, to oversee the transaction promptly. The government ended up taking a 36 percent stake in Binladin. All the brothers except Bakr were later released and granted some of their assets back.

A few months later, Saad bin Laden received a call: The prince is building a series of palaces near Sharma in the new NEOM project, and the other contractors are hopelessly behind. "SBG needs to get out there now," he was told. Whether one owned a private company with strong ties to the royals or a partly state-owned company, life wasn't much different.

Another prominent detainee was Nasser Al Tayyar, who built a travel agency into a multi-billion-dollar public company. He had been a government advisor and the publisher of *Forbes Middle East*. Al Tayyar was seen in Saudi Arabia as a great success. His self-named travel company was valued at more than $1 billion when it went public on the kingdom's stock exchange in 2012.

But as with many of the other men in the Ritz, Al Tayyar's fortune was built largely through business practices that, outside Saudi Arabia, would be considered corrupt. Inside Saudi

Arabia they had been the norm. In the decades since oil was discovered, princes, real estate developers, and other businessmen figured out creative ways to divert some of the kingdom's great oil wealth to themselves.

Al Tayyar was indignant when he was jailed. For decades, he'd been running his business the same way, and nobody had a problem with it. In recent years, much of his revenue came from a deal with the Saudi government to provide travel and housing for tens of thousands of Saudi students studying overseas on scholarships. It was a massive opportunity to overcharge the Saudi government, and no one seemed to mind. The scheme was simple.

Al Tayyar's contract with the Saudi government said the Ministry of Education would reimburse the company for each ticket it purchased for a student and pay a fee, generally around 15 percent of the ticket price, on top. It was intended to guarantee significant but not outlandish profits for the company.

Instead, Al Tayyar used the contract to boost his margins far beyond competitors' by purchasing the least expensive ticket possible for each student trip while billing the government for the most expensive ticket. So a student traveling round-trip between Riyadh and, say, Boston would get a coach seat purchased from a discount ticket seller. Al Tayyar would bill the government for a first-class flex ticket, plus the agency's added fee. The scheme helped boost the company's stock price, making it far more profitable than it otherwise would have been. And this continued for years, while officials in the Ministry of Education either didn't realize or looked away. Everybody was overcharging the government, Al Tayyar told a friend during a rare moment out of earshot of the guards at the Ritz. He was later released after reaching a settlement but without publicly admitting wrongdoing.

The arrest of Amoudi, the Saudi-Ethiopian businessman, was

even more surprising. He had become extremely rich thanks to his construction businesses and had taken on an international profile for his role in agriculture and other industries in Ethiopia, which had one of the world's fastest-growing economies. He was long a favorite of King Abdullah and had a way of wowing senior royals that seemed to make him untouchable.

In 2010, he announced to King Abdullah that he was ready to unveil the first-ever Saudi-built automobile. He scheduled a meeting with the king to reveal an early prototype of the car, which he promised would create a domestic manufacturing industry. Abdullah, who only drove in limousines, didn't know any better when Amoudi revealed a small SUV that looked almost identical to a Toyota FJ Cruiser, eliciting snickers from younger attendees. The project didn't go anywhere.

Amoudi remained in detention for more than a year before reaching a confidential settlement to pay a large sum to the Saudi state without admitting any wrongdoing. He refused to discuss it.

To most Westerners, the highest-profile detainee was Alwaleed bin Talal. The son of King Salman's dissident brother had long cultivated wealthy and powerful friends abroad, and though he spoke publicly in support of Mohammed, those relationships and Alwaleed's penchant for self-promotion were liabilities during a time when Mohammed was trying to make himself the official face of the kingdom.

But what landed Alwaleed in the Ritz was something more mundane: He'd been getting money for years from royal family members, including Abdullah, and what happened to it wasn't always clear. In some cases Alwaleed managed accounts for the king; in others he got loans. Sometimes, Mohammed's men charged, Alwaleed kept for himself money that rightfully belonged to the state.

So Mohammed had him thrown into the Ritz, demanded he pay a multi-billion-dollar settlement to secure his release, and provided an added incentive by arresting his brother Khaled not long after. Khaled didn't get to stay at the Ritz but was instead sent to al-Ha'ir prison, where less well-known prisoners ended up.

Panicking about his loss in stature after being released, Al-waleed insisted to Bloomberg News that he was wrongly lumped together with people who had done actual corrupt things. Asked whether he'd paid $6 billion, as reported by the *Wall Street Journal* earlier, he kept repeating that it was a "confidential and secret agreement based on a confirmed understanding between me and the government of Saudi Arabia." He told Bloomberg,

It was not easy, I have to confess. It's not easy to be held against your will. But when I left, I had a very strange feeling. I gathered all the senior officers in my companies and all my close confidants and I told them, "I swear to you I have complete serenity, complete comfort, and no grudge and no bad feelings at all."

And sure enough, within 24 hours we were back in communication with the king's office, with the crown prince and his people. That's a very strange situation.

Chapter 15

KIDNAPPED PRIME MINISTER

November 9, 2017

It might have been the most significant sign yet that the West was treating Mohammed as Saudi Arabia's head of state: On November 9, 2017, while international business and political leaders were trying to figure out why so many of their longtime Saudi contacts were jailed in a luxury hotel, French president Emmanuel Macron took an emergency flight to Riyadh to meet the crown prince.

Macron had been in Abu Dhabi for the opening of a new Louvre branch. Now he was sitting in a terminal at the Riyadh airport, waiting to meet Mohammed in the hopes of defusing a slow-moving disaster. The confusion around the Ritz corruption crackdown had quickly shifted from an internal Saudi purge to a geopolitical crisis when Saudi officials had locked up Lebanon's prime minister, Saad Hariri, and made him resign. Saad himself has never commented publicly on these allegations. While much of the Western world was transfixed by the Saudi princes and businessmen swept up that day, Hariri was being berated, allegedly beaten, and forced to quit by Mohammed's men.

It was the prince's boldest foreign policy move yet, a coup of the democratically elected prime minister heading a government that achieved a tenuous peace in Lebanon. Now Mohammed was creating new instability, and it was all playing out publicly.

Saad led Lebanon's biggest Sunni political party, the Future Movement, and was prime minister in a government where power was precariously balanced with the Iran-backed Shia party Hezbollah and Christian political factions.

Lebanon, once a French colony, retained close ties with France. Macron, who had been in office for only six months and was eager to act on the world stage, felt a responsibility to bring Saad back home. He realized that would require doing something no foreign leader had previously done: He would have to outmaneuver Mohammed.

The situation took shape a few days before Macron's visit, on November 4, 2017, when a haggard Hariri made a surprise TV address. Sitting in front of an abstract blue painting, he read off a piece of paper on the desk in front of him, his delivery stilted and halting. Hariri said he'd been unable to curb Iranian influence in Lebanon, so for the good of his people, he was resigning. Addressing Iran, he declared that Arab nations "will rise again and the hands that you have wickedly extended into it will be cut off."

The words didn't sound like Hariri's, especially since he was trying to govern alongside Iran-backed Hezbollah, not start a war. A couple of days earlier he'd had a positive meeting with an Iranian government official. Now Saad was quitting and appeared to be picking a fight on his way out.

It was a potentially explosive situation. Lebanon borders Syria, with its ongoing civil war, and houses millions of Syrian refugees in squalid camps, along with long-standing communities of displaced Palestinians. Hezbollah has triggered conflicts with Israel in the recent past from its redoubts in southern Lebanon. If the Hariri government broke down, violence could erupt from any direction.

At the time, world leaders and journalists discussed the Hariri situation as a political crisis. Mohammed bin Salman, scholars and think tank experts wrote, was destabilizing Lebanon as part of his proxy war with Iran. Just as he was bombing Yemen to destroy its Iran-backed rebels, he was exerting force over Lebanon to counter Hezbollah. In fact, the Hariri episode was much more personal for Mohammed. It was a political dispute but also a familial fight, and like so much else in Mohammed's ascent, it centered on the former king Abdullah, his children, his courtiers, and the billions of dollars surrounding them.

To understand why Mohammed kidnapped the leader of Lebanon, it's necessary to go back a half century, to 1964. That's when a young Lebanese accountant named Rafic Hariri decided he couldn't make enough money at home to support his young family. So he moved to Saudi Arabia, where burgeoning oil wealth was funding roads, hospitals, and hotels, and all sorts of companies were springing up to build them.

Saudi Arabia in the 1960s had lots of oil and money but not much to show for it on the ground. The kingdom's population was smaller than that of London. The royal family was intent on using the kingdom's oil income to build new infrastructure across the country, but few domestic companies could handle big construction projects. And there were few universities to produce graduates who could run such companies.

Nearby countries like Lebanon had the opposite problem. Lebanon had plenty of educated would-be professionals. The country's colonial ties to France and long relationship with the United States meant many of those professionals had the language skills to work with foreign partners. But Lebanon didn't have cash. Its slow-growing economy provided little opportunity for these graduates to work their way toward prosperity.

So young professionals like Saad's father, Rafic, left for the growing kingdom to support their families. They didn't always find easy profits. Instead, they found that Saudi Arabia's cash flow would rise and fall dramatically based on global oil prices. A sudden spike would result in a raft of new construction projects; a price drop would render the kingdom unable to pay its bills. Companies went boom and bust, and Rafic, working for construction companies, was at the mercy of this cycle.

Eventually he branched out to start his own company. Its fortunes waxed and waned with the price of oil until he took a job subcontracting for a bigger firm that worked for then-king Khalid. Hariri salvaged a problematic project by looking outside the region: He brought in an Italian contractor who was able to finish the job. That success put Rafic in place in the late 1970s to work on a hotel that King Khalid ordered built on short notice in the resort town of Ta'if, in the mountains east of Mecca.

Working for the Royal Court, Rafic came to understand something that would help define his company and build his fortune: Unlike most customers, the Al Saud didn't really care about budgets. They had more than enough money. They just wanted projects to be completed fast—sometimes unrealistically so—and done well. As long as Rafic met those demands, the cost wouldn't be an issue for the king. So Rafic brought in a French company called Oger to build the resort. It was finished on time and to the king's liking. It cost more than $100 million, but that was fine. As Hariri biographer Hannes Baumann put it, Rafic completed the hotel in what would become his trademark style: "In record time and with little regard for cost."

The king rewarded Hariri with ongoing royal business and a Saudi passport. That was huge. Saudi law required foreign-owned companies to work with local partners in the kingdom, creating famously corrupt relationships in which princes and other well-connected men could set up local companies for the sole purpose of siphoning cash from foreign companies brought in to build Saudi Arabia's infrastructure. A system intended to make sure Saudi-owned companies were part of the kingdom's growth ended up facilitating graft.

With his Saudi passport, Rafic was no longer subject to that system. He could own his company outright and run it as he saw fit without paying a local partner. Hariri bought Oger, the French contractor he had brought to Ta'if, and turned the company he now called Saudi Oger into one of the kingdom's most important institutions. It employed tens of thousands of workers in the kingdom, building palaces at home and abroad for members of the royal family, sometimes for free to help gain favor.

Rafic understood the importance of personal relationships in building his Saudi business. His company was only as healthy as his relationship with the king. In turn, maintaining a good relationship with the king could translate into economic and political power back home in Lebanon.

With King Khalid aging, Rafic slowly established a relationship with the powerful Crown Prince Fahd, who was increasingly responsible for big government initiatives. Royal watching in Saudi Arabia is more than entertaining. It's a prerequisite for any businessman's long-term viability.

That brought in even more business. Saudi Oger built the Royal Court's headquarters, or *diwan*, and other administrative buildings, giving Rafic a fortune to use for personal and political gain. He also spent millions of dollars supporting political and charitable groups in Lebanon, building his profile as an entrepreneur and a philanthropist.

From the beginning, there was little division between the Hariri family's various pursuits. Its profit making in Saudi Arabia, charitable work in Lebanon, and political power building in Beirut were completely intertwined. Rafic combined his own money with donations from King Fahd to send thousands of Lebanese students to college. That cemented his reputation as someone who could deliver real benefits to the Lebanese people.

It also showed Fahd that Rafic could be politically useful. Lebanon, sandwiched between Syria and Israel and with a huge Palestinian population, was always on the verge of instability and often the site of war. Having a paid-for politician there could be a boon to the king.

Rafic became a sort of emissary for Saudi Arabia in attempts to resolve regional conflicts involving the Israelis, Palestinians, Syrians, and various factions of Lebanese. The relationship was so close that at a 1983 conference in Geneva to work out a peace deal with Syria, Hariri declared that he was speaking on behalf of King Fahd. Like the Al Saud, Hariri was a Sunni Muslim. But he was able to get enough buy-in from the Shia, Christian, and other religious communities in Lebanon to pull together unlikely alliances.

In 1989, after fifteen years of civil war, Rafic helped broker a truce at a meeting in Ta'if, the Saudi resort town he helped build years earlier. It brought an end to the Lebanese conflict and put Saudi Arabia, Rafic's longtime benefactor, in a position to claim some credit for stabilizing the region. Saudi money had become inextricably linked to Lebanese politics and to Rafic's own family fortunes. Three years later, in Lebanon's first postwar election, he was voted prime minister. His subsequent efforts to clean up and rebuild Beirut using international funds further combined his political and business goals. Rafic had a stake in the company that owned the newly developed areas and also got paid through Saudi Oger for construction.

To strengthen his relationship with the Al Saud and ensure it transcended the kingdom's next change in leadership, Rafic cultivated other branches of the family. This became increasingly important as King Fahd grew ill and infirm and the comparatively austere Crown Prince Abdullah took on a bigger leadership role.

*   *   *

Abdullah presented a potential difficulty for Rafic. He had a different mother than King Fahd, whose full brothers, the group known as the Sudairi Seven, included the powerful princes Sultan, Salman, and Nayef. Abdullah frowned on the lavish lifestyles of many royals, including Fahd's children, and enjoyed camping in the desert more than sitting in a palace. If he didn't want the kind of luxurious homes Saudi Oger had built for his predecessors—or if he didn't believe that the company played an important role in modernizing Saudi Arabia—Abdullah's growing power could be a problem for Rafic and his financial and political ambitions.

So Rafic made a point of cultivating Abdullah. On hearing that Abdullah was planning a state visit to Lebanon, Rafic got in touch with Mohammed al-Tobaishi, Abdullah's head of protocol. He asked Tobaishi to get Abdullah to stay in his home during the visit. If the protocol chief could make that happen, Rafic promised, there would be great rewards.

Tobaishi came through. Abdullah stayed with Rafic in Beirut, giving the Lebanese entrepreneur the chance to develop a personal connection with the soon-to-be king and enabling him to convince Abdullah that he would be a reliable political ally in Lebanon.

Always generous in repaying favors, Rafic built a ranch outside Riyadh for Tobaishi staffed with Saudi Oger employees. Rafic also built a stud farm for the protocol chief with sixty horses and a stadium to watch them prance. All were later seized by Mohammed bin Salman in the post-Ritz asset and money grab.

Rafic also ingratiated himself with Khalid al-Tuwaijri, the chief of Abdullah's Royal Court, who helped ensure access to Abdullah. By the time US diplomat Jeffrey Feltman arrived in Beirut as ambassador in 2004, Abdullah and Rafic had a close relationship personally and politically.

*   *   *

Rafic Hariri's political fortunes ebbed and flowed. He lost his position as prime minister, regained it, and stepped aside in 2004. The following year he was killed by an earth-shaking bomb, just before Abdullah became king. It was shocking, at home and abroad. Hariri seemed like the one man who could bring relative peace to the region, and it wasn't immediately clear who would want to kill him. No group took credit, though given the bomb's sophistication, with more than two thousand pounds of dynamite and remote detonation, clearly an organization with significant resources was responsible (in the aftermath, some blamed Hezbollah, which itself blamed Israel; UN investigators later said Syria's government was the likely culprit). The bomb killed twenty-one other people, left a fifteen-foot-deep crater near Beirut's seaside, and created a huge political void. His son Saad saw that the assassination also united the Lebanese people as never before. "The blood of his father brought the people together. There was this idea of one Lebanon," says Paula Yacoubian, a member of Parliament from Beirut.

After a period of grieving, Saad took over the family business and the Hariri political machine. "The Saudis were very much supporting him, and the decisions he was making about when and where to go into politics were with their full support," says Feltman, the former US ambassador, who left Lebanon for Washington and became assistant secretary of state for Near Eastern affairs in 2009, the year Saad first became Lebanon's prime minister. Saad maintained the relationship with Tobaishi and Tuwaijri. Tobaishi's staffers later told friends that Saad Hariri used his private plane to take money out of the kingdom for Tuwaijri.

Saad had managed to follow his father to power, but he didn't have the same gravitas as Rafic in his political and business dealings at home and abroad. With his slicked-back hair, rakish stubble, and luxurious tastes, Saad seemed weaker and less politically astute than his father—"this young guy with a lot of money who had this idea of being a Lebanese leader," says Yacoubian. His personal indulgences didn't help. South African court records showed that in 2013 and 2014, Saad gave $16 million to a bikini model with whom he'd been having an affair.

Saad also had tensions with members of his own family. An older brother, Bahaa, who seemed to believe he was a more suitable leader, spent huge sums in the United States, funding a think tank and quietly telling officials that he was the best-qualified Hariri to lead Lebanon. (During an argument with a friend, Bahaa explained that the supposed rift was "only an act, you dummy" so Lebanese voters would see Bahaa as an alternative—and keep Lebanon in Hariri hands—if they turned against Saad.)

Saad continued the relationship with Saudi Arabia, and throughout Abdullah's reign, Saudi Oger built huge projects for the Royal Court on land owned by the government, including the palace that would become Riyadh's Ritz-Carlton. Even after his first stint as prime minister ended in 2011, Saad remained an important political force in Lebanon and maintained the decades-old Saudi alliance using his income from the Saudi royal family to maintain his personal wealth and power in Lebanon.

It was the kind of relationship that the kingdom's economy was built on, a network of personal connections in which Saudi oil money cycled to foreign businessmen and back to officials in and around the Royal Court. In many ways it worked well. The Hariris and various court officials got rich. Saudi Oger created jobs in Saudi Arabia, though many of its manual laborers and managers were foreign. The king got his construction projects done. And Saudi Arabia got an ally who would push Saudi priorities in Lebanon's ongoing struggle to balance the influences of Israel, Palestine, Syria, and, most importantly, Saudi nemesis Iran.

But it was the kind of relationship that infuriated Mohammed. Working in Abdullah's Royal Court, he grew fixated on the performance measurements that consultants discussed. Saudi Arabia should be able to see some kind of return on its financial investments, he reasoned. The kingdom had invested vast sums of money in the Hariris, but what kind of results was it getting? What was their "key performance indicator"? Mohammed decided Saad's performance wasn't in line with what the kingdom was paying. After decades of patronage, Mohammed reasoned, shouldn't the Hariris stand firmly with Saudi Arabia against Iran and the armed party it supported in Lebanon, Hezbollah?

Then there was the financial side. When Salman took the throne, the kingdom was nearing an economic crisis. Low oil prices slashed government revenue, but spending remained high. Mohammed took on the responsibility of reforming the Saudi economy and promised that the days of spending oil money as fast as the kingdom could bring it in were over. Instead, Mohammed said, Saudi Arabia would find more effective ways to invest its money and build a newly diversified economy in which people could make money from industries other than oil.

The problem was that when Salman became king, he ordered that government workers should get a bonus payment that totaled more than $25 billion. That helped throw the kingdom into a deep budget deficit.

Mohammed responded with aggressive moves like raising the price of gasoline and scaling back big government projects. He canceled some of Saudi Oger's upcoming projects and decided not to pay for some work it had already done. The company, he reasoned, had been getting rich off the government for years. Now it could share in the lean times.

Saudi Oger responded by laying off tens of thousands of workers, publicly blaming the cuts on the government's failure to pay. Saudi Oger had little cushion to withstand the shock, unlike Saudi Binladin, which was able to muddle on longer before recovering.

Saad could have kept the payment problem quiet, saving face for the kingdom. Instead he turned it into a high-profile embarrassment for the Saudi government. Saudi Oger workers from Europe, India, and the Philippines were stranded in Saudi Arabia with no income and in some cases no ability to leave. Laborers were stuck in crowded worker camps without food or money—or passports, since Saudi Oger had confiscated them upon their holders' arrival in the kingdom.

Saudi labor rules locked the workers in a conundrum: Without jobs, they were technically in the kingdom illegally. But without an employer, they couldn't apply for permits to leave.

The situation persisted for months; Saudi Oger closed kitchen facilities and stopped food deliveries. Workers who had been away from home for years to make money and send it back to their families were going hungry. India's ambassador to Saudi Arabia called it a "humanitarian crisis," and his government sent food and other aid to the stranded workers. It was humiliating—India was sending relief to people in one of the world's wealthiest countries because it had mismanaged its cash. The Saudi government eventually stepped in to help.

French workers, who were generally paid and treated better than their Asian colleagues, were also owed millions of dollars in back pay and made their complaints public. France's ambassador wrote letters to Saad asking about pay for French expat employees; some sued. The *Wall Street Journal* and other international publications covered the story, highlighting Saudi Arabia's acute financial problems at a time when Mohammed was trying to sell himself as an economic visionary.

The prince saw this as a betrayal. For decades, his family had supported the Hariris. Now, when the Saudi government was going through a rough patch, Saad responded by shaming the Al Saud on the world's biggest stage.

With that drama underway, Saad became prime minister a second time near the end of 2016. Mohammed would find him as frustrating as a government leader as he did as a businessman.

Saad reentered leadership during a sensitive time in Lebanon. The government had been in limbo for two years, since parliament had been unable to elect a president with the needed two-thirds majority. Saad's agreement to return as prime minister helped facilitate a deal that saw Michel Aoun, a longtime Christian politician and a Hezbollah ally, elected as president.

When he took office, Saad didn't take the hardline approach to Hezbollah that Mohammed wanted. He couldn't. He was running a government in cooperation with Hezbollah, and Lebanon's democracy meant he had to work with its leaders.

Mohammed had little sympathy for such necessities of democratic governance. Saudi Arabia didn't spend decades and billions of dollars supporting the Hariris so they could help Hezbollah extend Iran's influence in Lebanon.

The prince also disliked Saad's deep financial and personal ties to Mohammed's domestic rivals, the sons and courtiers of Abdullah. Mohammed already suspected they were trying to weaken his claim on the throne and was suspicious of their allies. There was also the issue of corruption. Within the Royal Court, rumors circulated that Saad had helped Khalid al-Tuwaijri, Abdullah's Royal Court chief, take money out of the kingdom. Rumors of the stacks of cash-filled suitcases that one Hariri friend claims to have seen on Saad's plane on a flight from Riyadh to Beirut were common knowledge in the Royal Court, and some men working for Mohammed suspected that some

of that cash belonged to Tuwaijri. Secretly, Mohammed added
Saad to his list of businessmen to investigate.

He also had the government investigate Saudi Oger. In 2016,
the Saudi Ministry of Finance hired an international accounting
firm, PwC, to go through the company's books. Mohammed
convened a special committee to decide what to do with the
company, which concluded it was deeply troubled and would
require billions of dollars to rescue.

What the investigators found turned Mohammed off even
more. For years, the prince's men later told friends, Saad's
father, Rafic, had come pleading poverty to King Abdullah;
the king would respond with billion-dollar loans that he often
forgave. That history didn't present an obvious legal or even
political problem in Saudi Arabia. The king's word was law,
and he issued the loans and forgave the loans. Plus some of
the money Hariri collected went toward building palatial homes
for high-ranking Al Saud. So it never occurred to Saad that
the foundations of his family company could subject him to
legal peril.

But Mohammed saw things differently from royals before
him. He considered corrupt all who got more than their fair
share from the government—even if they did so with the king's
approval. He was determined to tear down the old structures
that enriched businessmen and public officials at the expense of
the state, and Saudi Oger and its owners were an easy target.

Mohammed also didn't have the traditional Arab reverence for
old family alliances. Saudi Arabia was short on cash, Saudi Oger
was publicly complaining about the kingdom's failure to pay, and
the Hariris were losing influence to Hezbollah despite decades
of Saudi support. So Mohammed decided the Hariri–Al Saud
alliance wasn't an institution worth saving.

Even after Saudi Arabia resumed payments to other contractors,

Mohammed withheld funds from Saudi Oger, letting the once huge company wither away. Saad remained Lebanon's prime minister. But in that role, he was forced each day to negotiate with Hezbollah, and with Mohammed watching, Saad's political position became precarious too.

Hezbollah controlled portions of Lebanon, started a 2006 war with Israel, and provided a persistent Iranian influence in the area. Its military and political power represented a constant threat of instability for Israel and Jordan, and Mohammed was tired of it. He wanted Saad to take a confrontational stance toward Hezbollah, not govern alongside it. Thamer al-Sabhan, Mohammed's minister for Gulf affairs and an aggressive Iran hawk, met Saad in the fall of 2017 and made clear that Saudi Arabia was frustrated.

Then, on November 3, 2017, Saad received an Iranian delegation led by senior government advisor Ali Akbar Velayati. After the meeting, Lebanon's official press agency put out a photo of Hariri speaking cordially with the Iranians, along with a statement from Velayati: "We had a good, positive, constructive, and practical meeting with Prime Minister Hariri, especially since the Iranian-Lebanese relations are always constructive."

For Mohammed, that was the last straw. That evening he summoned Saad.

The prime minister had no reason at first to sense a threat. He knew he'd probably have to sit in a desert tent in front of a smoky fire and listen to the young prince vent about Hezbollah and Iran; he'd heard similar gripes a few months earlier from Mohammed and from Sabhan. But Mohammed had already just about killed Saudi Oger. How much more damage would he wish to inflict on the Hariris? Saad expressed optimism to a foreign confidant that Mohammed might even increase Saudi financial assistance for Lebanon.

*   *   *

It was only after Saad arrived in Riyadh after dark that things turned strange. When he landed at the airport, the Royal Court officials declined to take him to his home in the city. Instead, they told Saad he was going to meet Mohammed. But on the way to the meeting, they changed course: Saad would go back to his home and wait until the prince was ready.

He waited all night. Early the next morning, he got a call summoning him to meet Mohammed at 8 a.m. Traveling without the usual convoy, he rushed to see the prince. Instead, he was met by a group of Mohammed's enforcers.

They detained Saad, who declined to tell most confidants exactly what happened next. "It was terrible," he told one Western contact, making it clear that he didn't want to share details other than that he was "truly shocked, physically and mentally scarred."

Facing physical and financial harm at the hands of Mohammed's men, Saad agreed to resign the post of prime minister.

At Saad's home in Riyadh that afternoon, Saudi officials handed him the text of a speech to read on TV. It was an odd address. The camera showed Saad sitting at a desk next to a Lebanese flag, with a microphone and a laptop in front of him. He read from a sheaf of papers, occasionally looking wide-eyed into the camera. Saad mentioned his father's assassination, said Lebanon was living through a similar time, and stated, "I am aware of what is being plotted to target my life," without adding more detail. To avoid letting down his people, Saad continued, he would resign. Then he attacked Iran, accusing it of bringing "destruction, desolation, and disorder wherever it goes," and claimed Hezbollah was using its arms against Arab allies in Yemen and Syria.

Lebanese and foreign officials who knew Saad found the speech out of line with his political approach. Just a few months earlier, he told *Politico*'s Susan Glasser in an interview that he had to govern together with Hezbollah, despite its adversarial stance toward Israel and the United States: "For the sake of the country, for the economy, how to handle those 1.5 million refugees, how to handle the stability, how to handle the governing [of] our country, we have to have some kind of understanding."

Another detail caught Middle East experts off guard: Saad complained about Hezbollah's interference in Yemen, but in fact Hezbollah barely had a presence there. And Yemen was hardly a significant concern for Saad, who had his hands full with Lebanon. The person concerned with Yemen was Mohammed, who was mired in what was becoming a brutal and prolonged war there with little hope of Saudi victory.

Saad's speech ignited panic among politicians in Lebanon and abroad. Officials in Beirut fielded calls from their contacts in Europe and the United States asking what was going on. No one knows, they responded. Lebanon's president refused to accept Saad's resignation until they could meet in person. For three days, stasis ensued. Saad's status was unclear, and Mohammed said little publicly. Instead, he summoned Mahmoud Abbas, the president of the Palestinian Authority, to discuss Middle East policy. The prince was clearly trying to exert regional control, and Abbas left the meeting worried: Mohammed had indicated that Saudi Arabia was willing to concede on Palestinian demands in negotiating a peace deal with Israel, in line with ideas put forth by President Donald Trump's son-in-law and advisor, Jared Kushner. One of the most sacred Arab causes for seven decades would casually be tossed into the waste bin for not bringing value to Mohammed's 2030 plan.

Mohammed allowed Saad to leave Riyadh for a short trip to the United Arab Emirates, where he met the prince's close ally, Mohammed bin Zayed. But when Saad returned to Riyadh, not Beirut, it seemed clear to many that he was being held against his will. That's when France's President Macron decided to go to Riyadh.

Macron, who had traveled to Abu Dhabi near the start of the Ritz lockup to open the new Louvre outpost, had an underling deliver a message to Mohammed's aides: The French president would come to Riyadh to meet, but only at the airport and only to discuss Hariri. Before arriving for the visit, Macron and his advisors decided to dispense with the deference and politeness most foreign leaders showed to Saudi royalty. The president would speak bluntly to the prince. Before the meeting, Macron declared publicly that Lebanon's leaders should be allowed to travel freely, setting up a confrontation with Mohammed.

The prince decided to turn the meeting into a public spectacle. He arrived in a gold-fringed *bisht* and smiled broadly in Macron's face while shaking hands.

Meeting privately, Macron told Mohammed he was dismayed by the detention of a foreign president. Lebanon had long been either at war or on the verge of it, under siege by domestic and foreign military groups, and, for years, occupied by Syria. Now there was peace. Why would Mohammed destabilize it? Macron asked the prince to release Hariri.

"But he wants to be here," Mohammed replied. "He's afraid for his safety if he leaves."

Macron kept pushing. "You're embarrassing yourself," he told Mohammed. No one believed that Hariri was in Saudi Arabia under his own will.

Macron could communicate with Saad, but Saudi officials were listening in. Unable to speak privately or to secure Saad's release, Macron left Riyadh knowing he had to come up with a new plan.

Like Macron, Paula Yacoubian, the Lebanese parliamentarian, went to the Abu Dhabi Louvre opening. At the time she was a

TV journalist for a Hariri-owned station and a shocked spectator to the drama playing out in Riyadh. When her plane landed in Beirut, she saw she'd missed several calls from Saad, her boss. She called right back.

"Come to Riyadh tomorrow to interview me," he said.

Yacoubian was flummoxed. She was pretty sure Saad was being held against his will. Was this a journalistic endeavor? A rescue mission? Some kind of Saudi-orchestrated public relations stunt? She drove to Saad's house in Beirut where one of his advisors was waiting.

"Maybe I'd better not go," she said.

"Are you insane?" the advisor responded. Clearly the Saudis wanted Saad to do an interview, and if Yacoubian, his longtime employee and friend, refused, it could be someone much worse. "He's safer with you," the advisor said.

The TV station coordinated with the Saudi government, which assured Yacoubian that the interview would be broadcast live and that Saudi officials wouldn't restrict her questioning. After midnight Yacoubian had a visa. She got a restless few hours' sleep and in the morning flew to Riyadh. A Filipino driver took her straight to Saad's house, where two aides Yacoubian had known for years were waiting. They exchanged perfunctory greetings, but no one could speak with much candor. Saad came in wearing a suit, chatted for ten minutes, and sat down for the interview.

It was surreal. Yacoubian treated it as a serious journalistic enterprise. She would ask the questions Lebanon wanted to know.

"Are you being detained here?" she asked.

Saad denied it, and she expressed disbelief. He appeared to start crying at one point and told Yacoubian, "You're making me very tired." The interview seemed intended by the Saudis to reassure international viewers that Saad had decided on his own to stay in Saudi Arabia and give up his premiership, but it backfired. He seemed terrified.

Once the interview ended, Saad changed into jeans, a T-shirt, and a leather jacket. They ate a typical Lebanese dinner—grilled meat and chicken with hummus—and strolled around the court-yard pool. Then they sat, smoked a cigarillo, and talked softly for what seemed like hours.

When Yacoubian went back to her hotel that night, she still didn't have a clear idea of what was happening. In hindsight, she believes Saad was trying to send a message to Macron, hoping he would keep pressing Mohammed.

The interview alarmed leaders in Lebanon and abroad. Lebanon's president, Michel Aoun, said Saudi Arabia was holding Saad hostage. That opened the door for Macron, and the next day he decided to publicly invite Saad to Paris. By claiming that Saad was free to come or go as he pleased, Mohammed had boxed himself into a corner: If he got in the way of Saad's leaving Riyadh, he would be breaking his word and proving that Saad was a prisoner.

But Saad's allies told Macron there was a problem: Hariri family members remained in Riyadh. If Saad went to Paris and they stayed behind, Mohammed would have the ultimate lever-age. So on November 15, almost two weeks after the surprise resignation, Macron made his public play.

At a climate conference in Bonn, Germany, Macron told re-porters that he had invited the entire Hariri family to visit Paris. The intent wasn't political asylum or exile for Saad, Macron said. It was just a visit.

Mohammed was in a corner. He couldn't say no, so Saad, his wife, and his children traveled to Paris, and later back to Beirut, where Saad rescinded his resignation. It was an embarrass-ment for the prince. Even after economically crippling Saad, destroying his family business, and making him resign before the international community, Mohammed had failed to depose him. The prince looked weaker and Hezbollah stronger. In the regional proxy war, it was a victory for Iran.

"MBS's rash actions are deepening tensions and undermining security of the Gulf states and region as a whole," said Jamal Khashoggi, whom Mohammed and his men saw increasingly as a dangerous dissident. Western critics piled on too, and Saad returned triumphant to Lebanon, where the government's pro-Hezbollah factions were more powerful than ever. That trend has continued: In late 2019, protests over corruption drove Saad from office, casting out Saudi Arabia's last major ally there and further boosting Hezbollah.

Yacoubian says something softer has been lost as well. Dating back to the earliest days of the kingdom, Lebanon was where Saudi royalty went to escape the desert for a taste of the cosmopolitan world abroad. Though Saudi Arabia helped re-build Beirut, it was Lebanon that helped bring the Al Saud out of their insular kingdom. Now no one seems to care. "The new generation of Saudis are not like the old generation. They have no nostalgia for Lebanon," Yacoubian says. "It was their oasis of freedom."

Chapter 16

DA VINCI

November 15, 2017

For the team at Christie's in New York, the auction of the *Salvator Mundi* was anything but a surefire success. The painting was probably authentic, or at least enough experts agreed it was. It was a stunning work, depicting a gauzy Jesus Christ making the sign of the cross while holding a transparent orb in his left hand. It symbolized his role as "Savior of the World," holding the heavens in his grasp.

It was a crowd-pleaser more than a collector's item. A new da Vinci could bring hordes to an up-and-coming museum, boosting tourism dollars and putting a city on the cultural map. The last thing they expected was a Middle Eastern buyer, not least because of the painting's obvious Christian themes.

As the November 15 auction day neared, the Christie's team winnowed potential buyers down to about seven contenders, including ultra-high-net-worth individuals with global stature and nouveau riche from China and Russia. One previously unknown but remarkably pushy candidate emerged, Badr bin Farhan Al Saud. A quick Google search yielded nothing on the young Saudi, and Christie's executives with years of experience in the Middle East had never heard of him. Yet he seemed very motivated and had a last name synonymous with money. The

Christie's banking team said he could bid so long as he transferred about 10 percent of what he expected was the highest price he'd pay for the painting.

The next morning, the small Christie's staff with clearance to know the details started chattering excitedly. A wire transfer had come through overnight for $100 million. Prince Badr was signaling he'd be willing to pay $1 billion for the painting, a price so astronomical as to exceed even the wildest assessments of *Salvator Mundi*. It was the kind of money you shell out for an entire museum of art, not one painting.

Undisclosed to Christie's was the fact that Badr bin Farhan was one of Mohammed bin Salman's closest friends, a distant cousin but someone Mohammed had spent time with since childhood. The two were born only two weeks apart and grew up together, creating businesses in their twenties and imagining a new Saudi Arabia. Years' worth of old Saudi corporate records show the men were partners in businesses that included a plastics company, a real estate development firm, and the joint venture with Verizon nearly a decade earlier. While Mohammed bin Salman was a big name, few understood his network of friends and contacts. No one had mapped his wealth or even identified his tastes.

The mastermind of the sale was Loïc Gouzer, cochairman of postwar and contemporary art at Christie's. Boyishly handsome with short, dark hair and a two-day stubble, he rose up through the ranks of Christie's with unexpected and sometimes irreverent curations for auctions. For the 2015 "Looking Forward to the Past," he presented work by Monet and Prince in the same show. It also included Pablo Picasso's *Les femmes d'Alger*, Version O, from 1955, which sold for $179,365,000, then a record for a painting sold at auction. The buyer was Sheikh Hamad bin Jassim, former prime minister of Qatar and second cousin of the young emir Tamim bin Hamad—one of Mohammed bin Salman's chief rivals. Gouzer was also a consummate networker with celebrities, athletes, and the superrich. He was photographed with Leonardo DiCaprio, a close friend.

For the *Salvator Mundi* sale, Gouzer told colleagues he was focusing on bringing in the biggest buyers of all: nation-states. The painting was too much of an event in itself to be stashed in someone's living room. There were only about fifteen known paintings by da Vinci on earth. This painting had a great narrative too. It was originally thought to have been sold to England's King Charles I and remained in the collection of two more English kings before disappearing into obscurity for more than a century. The public loved a rediscovered masterpiece. "You can't buy the Eiffel Tower, but you can buy a painting that costs less and brings in the crowds," he told a friend as he created a marketing plan.

Gouzer also knew the financial side of the art world. To minimize the risk to sellers of losing a painting because of error or bad timing, auction houses started acting more like investment banks in providing financial guarantees. Using his network, Gouzer found Taiwanese investor and art collector Pierre Chen, who was willing to guarantee the painting at $100 million. That meant the seller, Russian business tycoon Dmitry Rybolovlev, would receive that amount, minus fees, no matter what happened at the auction because Chen would be the buyer at that price in any event. If it sold for more, the seller would share the profits with the guarantor.

Big paintings mean big advertising budgets. The idea is to spread the word far and wide about a sale to draw in as many bidders as possible, buying up space in all the luxury magazines and business newspapers and even purchasing outdoor advertisements in choice districts of big cities. But Gouzer forwent all that, preferring to hire a hip advertising agency called Droga5 to create a video targeting the public at large. The result was "The Last Da Vinci," a mesmerizing short advertisement with the camera filming from the perspective of the painting itself, watching viewers barely visible in a sea of black looking on with awe or tears as an emotive string quartet plays in the background. It was a masterstroke.

Little did the team at Christie's know at the time, but the tactics struck a chord in Saudi Arabia, where Mohammed bin Salman was obsessed with big ideas—and assets. The superlatives were the draw for a young Saudi prince hungry to be in the same league as prime ministers and oligarchs. It wasn't even clear what he would do with the painting, but the idea was to exhibit it in the kingdom.

On the day of the auction, Badr dialed Alexander Rotter, the cochair of postwar and contemporary art with Gouzer, who was standing in the phone bank on the auction floor with the other people on lines with potential buyers.

Within minutes the auction jumped from a $100 million starting bid to $150 million, then in $10 million and $5 million increments to $265 million. The audience started murmuring, and there were sporadic bursts of applause. The record for the most expensive painting ever sold had already been broken.

By then, it became a two-man competition between Rotter's client and Chinese billionaire Liu Yiqian, who was on the phone with Christie's Francois de Poortere, head of the old masters appraising department, in the bank next to Rotter. Neither client knew the identity of his competitor, as per the rules of Christie's. But the bidding kept going, suspense building as the two Christie's executives could be seen discussing the bidding with their clients on the phone. Gouzer's client had dropped out early, but he watched the auctioneer intently as the numbers rose: $245 million, $286 million, $290 million, $318 million, $328 million, and then $330 million.

De Poortere signaled to the auctioneer: $350 million.

Then, about nineteen minutes after the auction began, Rotter calmly relayed the final bid: $400 million. The room was stunned, then frenetic and noisy. It was the best show in New York, watching art business history unfold in a room packed with the rich and beautiful. With fees paid to Christie's, the total bill was $450 million, more than the entire election budget for Barack Obama's 2012 presidential campaign.

For three weeks, the buyer's identity was the mystery of the art world. Rumors flew fast about who it might be. Not until December 6 did sources with access to US intelligence leak the news to the *Wall Street Journal* and *New York Times* to highlight the absurdity of Saudi Arabia's king-in-waiting. Not only was he a spendthrift, they argued, but he was pointlessly jabbing the conservative Islamic community in Saudi Arabia with no purpose other than to antagonize them.

Other rumors spread about the sale, including that the bidders were actually Mohammed bin Salman and Qatari emir Tamim bin Hamad, fueled by mutual hatred. It wasn't true but illustrated a growing view of Mohammed as impulsive and quick to anger.

Mohammed bin Salman was at a sensitive moment, cracking down on corruption and waging an expensive war, and felt angered that news of his secret purchase had leaked so quickly. He'd managed to keep a lid on some of his biggest projects, such as NEOM, for a year. Yet this purchase—alongside his acquisition of the yacht *Serene* and a massive French château— were leaked fast. He also suspected Qatar had something to do with it. So together with friends in the United Arab Emirates, Mohammed cooked up a cover story: Saudi Arabia had bought the painting as a gift for Mohammed bin Zayed, whose capital, Abu Dhabi, had just opened the new Louvre branch weeks earlier. The painting would be a huge boost to the fledgling museum, drawing in crowds looking to rest their eyes on a rare da Vinci.

Only Mohammed bin Salman got cold feet: Why would he give up the most expensive painting in the world to Abu Dhabi when he had plans to make Saudi Arabia into a cultural colossus? The painting went into a secret European storage facility. Neither Badr nor Mohammed would tell a soul anything about it, no matter how many times a visiting billionaire or art consultant tried to ask during a private moment.

Whereas Abu Dhabi had taken an approach of bringing art into the UAE via its relationship with the Louvre, Saudi Arabia's consultants came up with a strategy that propped up its size, diversity, and history. Rather than have a "starchitect" design a big, impressive museum to put it on the map, the country would focus on smaller museums and archaeological restorations. Some would be devoted to just one thing, such as a Museum of Incense celebrating the love of perfume and the legendary trade routes through the kingdom. Building such attractions represented a huge change in a country whose Wahhabist religious establishment viewed museums, especially those displaying antiquities, as facilitating idol worship. In the first decade of the 2000s, Saudi archaeological finds were kept in a secret museum in a Riyadh palace so the clerics wouldn't know the Al Saud were preserving historical relics.

By 2020, Mohammed and Badr had begun hatching a plan to unveil the *Salvator Mundi* in one of a series of new museums planned in Riyadh. The subject matter was tricky: A picture of Jesus would instantly be seen as idolatrous by the grumbling Wahhabist clerics. Jesus, or Isa as he's known in Arabic, isn't a problem himself—he features in the Qur'an as one of the important prophets before Mohammed. But the implication of the painting is one of spiritual supremacy, which wouldn't go over well. In the old Saudi Arabia, it wasn't even permitted to publicly display paintings of human figures.

To showcase the painting without giving it its own museum, Badr and his crew devised a plan to build a major new Western art museum in Riyadh, as if to say, Look at the interesting works from *over there*. It would be a showstopper, but not the *only* showstopper.

Just as Gouzer had planned, this painting was an asset for a nation looking to burnish its tourism credentials. You couldn't buy the Eiffel Tower, but you could spend roughly half a billion dollars on a Renaissance painting to bring in the crowds.

The strategy was an extension of a cultural revitalization plan that Mohammed started in a long-abandoned corner of Saudi Arabia called al-Ula. For decades, it was left alone like a hidden stepchild because of the discomfort it gave the powerful Wahhabists. The city in the northwest of the country was once a magnificent sight for the caravans of traders moving in and out of the Arabian Peninsula from far-flung locations in the Middle East and Asia on the so-called incense road. Arriving from the north, they'd shelter in the canyons and gaze upon elaborate facades that the Nabateans carved into huge sandstone cliffs two thousand years ago. The facades are primarily entrances to tombs in the Madain Saleh necropolis, a UNESCO world heritage site. In al-Ula itself, the caravans found a well-watered city with hundreds of houses and shops sheltered between small mountains of rock.

The Saudi government had long avoided any publicity of the ancient sites and limited flows of people there for fear of angering hardliners who didn't like to acknowledge the pre-Islamic era. The Taliban were so incensed with ancient statues of Buddha carved into a cliffside in a remote corner of Afghanistan that they blew them up two decades ago. They were "idols" and therefore forbidden. Likewise, the ruins and artifacts of the Nabateans, the Lihyanites, and other ancient civilizations in the Arabian Peninsula could be seen by fiery clerics as idolatrous and worthy of destruction. Many Wahhabists weren't too far ideologically from the Taliban.

But Mohammed believed that was absurd, and unafraid of blowback for ordering many of the strictest among them locked up or fired, he told Badr bin Farhan to focus his efforts on turning al-Ula into a cultural oasis with stunning scenery, a cooler climate—including snow in the winter—and a raft of new structures, museums, and spaces to celebrate art and sports. All would fall under the Royal Commission for al-Ula, which Badr headed. *Salvator Mundi* aside, Badr started buying up art at a steady clip without attracting much attention. He was often spotted wearing a sharp suit and a big smile in London and New York, where the world's top art consultants were all too eager to offer their advice and services. He hired French companies to embark on huge restoration projects and struck deals to build a smattering of boutique hotels.

Within a few years, al-Ula became an interesting experiment in tourism, a mixture of millennium-old sites and modern art installations, including a rectangular performance center called the Maraya Concert Hall that's covered in huge sheets of mirrored metal, giving it the feeling of a mirage in a desert canyon. An annual four-month cultural festival, called Winter at Tantora, was launched in 2018, with performances by singer Andrea Bocelli and soft-rock icon Yanni. The Royal Commission later imported some high-end venues from London, including the celebrity-strewn private club Annabel's, which opened a pop-up restaurant. The Public Investment Fund began having conversations about buying 10 percent of Soho House & Company, which operates private member clubs with trendy artist spaces, restaurants, and bedrooms across Europe, North America, and Asia. The idea was to open club outposts in Saudi Arabia and also to tap into Soho House's influential clientele in a bid to raise the country's profile.

Top artists, performers, and dignitaries were all too thrilled to be part of Saudi Arabia's purported renaissance despite the crackdowns, arrests, and bloody war in Yemen. It seemed the young crown prince could do no wrong, and as he embarked on a tour of France, the United Kingdom, and the United States, he was the talk of the town.

Chapter 17

MAN OF THE YEAR

April 2018

Strolling down Rodeo Drive in jeans and a dress shirt in the spring of 2018, unburdened by the responsibilities and restrictions of royalty, Mohammed bin Salman recalled the frisson he got in his twenties venturing around Paris or Marbella.

Away from Riyadh's endless obligations, the family gatherings, midnight government meetings, and frenzied technocrats sending urgent WhatsApp messages at all hours, Mohammed found a freedom that was unattainable at home. In Riyadh, the responsibilities of governing were relentless, and even on his yacht *Serene* in the Red Sea or in al-Ula for the weekend, the obligations were nonstop. Mohammed worked all night and much of every day. There was no way to go for a stroll in the capital: Riyadh, with its heat and dust and tall buildings separated by wide boulevards with broken sidewalks, has no culture of ambling around for pleasure; even if it did, the crown prince couldn't venture out without creating a public spectacle and security risk.

But in Beverly Hills, where his face didn't stare down from billboards every few blocks, Mohammed could walk around unrecognized. Stopping into cafés and boutiques, he was just one more rich guy taking in the pleasures of cosmopolitan

life. The difference between then and now was that Mohammed had gained great power to match his great wealth.
Americans, especially important Americans, were starting to
understand that.

Earlier on his American tour, he suddenly remembered a
favorite restaurant in New York City from the months he stayed
there with his father while his uncle Sultan bin Abdulaziz, the
crown prince, was getting treatment for cancer. "We're going to
Bar Masa," he told his entourage. That was no small matter. The
Saudis had rented out much of the Plaza Hotel, and as a major
government official, Mohammed had a huge retinue of Saudi
and American bodyguards. Aides pleaded with him to let them
call ahead and rent the place out and arrange an appropriate
motorcade. But he refused, heading to the elevator and walking
out onto the street for the fifteen-minute stroll along Central
Park South to Columbus Circle, guards running ahead to create
a protective perimeter.

The US leg of the trip came after a grand visit to the United
Kingdom, where Saud al-Qahtani spent millions to buy up bill-
board space with Mohammed's face emblazoned beside slogans
such as "Welcome crown prince" and "He is bringing change to
Saudi Arabia." So wary was his security team of protests and
threats that it hired dozens of British bodyguards and told them
to call anyone else they knew in the close-protection industry
and hire them too. They were ordered to follow protesters and
to guard any Saudi official they could. The crown prince met
the queen and attended a private dinner at Hampton Court
Palace with powerful friends of Evgeny Lebedev, owner of the
Independent and the *Evening Standard*. The secret gathering
spurred questions in the British press about mysterious sales
of the newspapers to a Saudi businessman that year and the
year before and a deal whereby the Salman family publishing business, Saudi Research and Marketing, would work with

the *Independent* on new *Independent*-branded sites in Arabic, Urdu, Turkish, and Persian.

A couple of blocks from Rodeo Drive was the office of Ari Emanuel, the Hollywood superagent who was trying to close a half-billion-dollar deal with Mohammed to get Saudi Arabia into the movie business. Near the Four Seasons, where Mohammed rented out all 285 rooms for his entourage, was the home of Rupert Murdoch, who would host a dinner for the prince to meet Morgan Freeman, Michael Douglas, and Dwayne "The Rock" Johnson.

Mohammed was charming in meetings, even humorous. In one smaller meeting, he explained his love for *The Walking Dead* television show, whose zombies reminded him of Islamic extremists. And he admired *Game of Thrones*, except too many royals were killed, he said with a big grin.

Later the same month, Saudi Arabia had its first major film screening in decades, showing *Black Panther* in an auditorium with old-fashioned popcorn stalls. It was part of a rollout of hundreds of movie theaters and a new era for entertainment in the kingdom. Many commentators delighted in echoes of today's Saudi Arabia in the film's story: It's about a young king who must decide whether to hide his jungle kingdom from, or engage with, the outside world.

That was one side of a frenzied 2018 for Mohammed, a year in which he would push through social and economic transformation plans at a dizzying pace and in full public view. In the coming months he would meet with presidents, CEOs, and tech billionaires including Elon Musk and Bill Gates, publicly proclaiming an open and innovative future for Saudi Arabia. He would make massive commitments to virtual reality and solar power and cutting-edge urban planning.

"The most influential Arab leader. Transforming the world at

32," blared the cover of an unfamiliar magazine titled *The New Kingdom* (priced at $13.99) that showed up on newsstands across the United States just ahead of the prince's visit.

The other side of Mohammed's year was conducted in the shadows, in the form of stepped-up surveillance, arrests, kidnappings, and violence aimed at perceived enemies at home and abroad.

Both sides were on display at the dawn of the new year, when Mohammed took the bold step of imposing a consumption tax. It would be a boring piece of economic policymaking in most countries, but in the kingdom it was a major reform, the kind that experts at places like the World Bank encouraged. Saudi Arabia for decades used oil money, not taxes, to fund the government largely due to royal fears of how people would respond to taxation without representation. Now Mohammed was making Saudis pay for their government services. Reactions were so strong that King Salman gave a onetime cash handout to citizens five days later.

That same week, Mohammed made a much more secretive move.

At first, Salman bin Abdulaziz let the phone ring. It was the middle of the night, and Salman and his wife had gone to bed early, retiring to their separate rooms—as is customary among the Al Saud—before midnight.

Salman shared a name with Mohammed's father, the king. But this Salman was a minor prince, a few years older than Mohammed, and an occasional annoyance. He had treated Mohammed with derision for his Saudi education when they were young men vacationing in France, and he'd upset Mohammed back in 2016, when he met Democratic congressman Adam Schiff in the run-up to a presidential election that Mohammed wanted the Republican to win.

Salman had no claim to the throne; he was one of the thousands of politically inconsequential royals, heirs to the Al Saud name and government stipends but not to power. Saudi Arabia's hereditary structure meant he was destined to be a very rich nobody.

But Salman bin Abdulaziz had ambition that outstripped his family provenance. He attended the Sorbonne in Paris and swanned around Europe calling for world peace in speeches promoting his philanthropic "Visionary Movers Club." In fact, Salman's philanthropy seemed largely to entail the peculiar Saudi practice of lavishing gifts on some relatively poor Bedouin men who lived near his country retreat outside Riyadh.

In 2017, Salman selected a half dozen of the men—men who had never traveled outside the kingdom or ever seen a woman venture out in jeans, a member of the prince's entourage says— to accompany him to Paris. The idea was to introduce them to culture and the refined life. He rented the men an apartment, where they proceeded to spend the next few months watching pornography and sleeping with prostitutes before returning with the prince to Saudi Arabia. It was a ridiculous endeavor.

Mohammed couldn't stand princes like Salman, who seemed to be on permanent vacation, doing little to help build up Saudi Arabia. They made Saudis look absurd, with their ostentatious trips around Europe and the United States. Perhaps the most irksome thing about Prince Salman was that his wife, Areeb, was a daughter of King Abdullah. She'd inherited more than $1 billion upon her father's death, money that Mohammed felt belonged to the government.

By the beginning of 2018, Mohammed had enough power that he need not suffer these irritating relatives. That's why Salman's phone was ringing at around 2 a.m. that night.

Finally it woke someone in the sleeping household, who roused the prince, his wife, and some of their staff. Come to the

Royal Diwan—the court's offices—the voice on the phone said. Mohammed wants to see you. Salman and a non-Saudi staffer set off in an SUV for the meeting, perplexed and worried.

It was still pitch dark when they arrived. Salman told the staffer to wait while he entered the offices alone. Immediately he was surrounded by guards, slapped around, and carried off to jail. Salman's staffer waited outside until mid-morning and then left, convinced the prince wouldn't be coming out.

The next day, the Royal Court announced that a group of princes, ostensibly including Salman, had been arrested because they showed up at the government office and made a violent stink about having to pay for electricity, which Mohammed had decided to stop giving to royals for free. Salman's family and staff couldn't figure out what was wrong. They didn't mind paying for electricity—Salman literally had more money than he knew what to do with. He was in the process of building a private zoo, because what else would he spend his money on?

Salman's father, Abdulaziz, began to panic. He had seen how Mohammed treated the Ritz detainees and Mohammed bin Nayef, and he worried that his son may have done something to anger the man who was now Saudi Arabia's de facto ruler. So he made a risky decision: Abdulaziz called on a foreigner for help.

The intermediary, Elie Hatem, was the Paris-based lawyer who had known Mohammed and Salman since they were boys. Salman's father figured the lawyer could help because he'd recently been assisting Mohammed with a sticky family situation involving another problematic relative, Mohammed's sister Hassa.

Hassa was older than Mohammed and had always had an independent streak. She was the only girl in the family, and she'd had a chilly relationship with Mohammed for years. Her behavior in Paris—late-night clubbing, public temper tantrums including an incident, one friend recalls, when she threw a plate at a server in a caviar restaurant—made her a potential liability. One day in 2017 she called Hatem in a panic: The police were in her Paris house, she said, and threatening to arrest her after a workman claimed he'd been beaten by the princess's bodyguard on her orders in an incident the year before.

Hatem rushed to Hassa's home on the Avenue Foch. The princess was tearful and trembling; she said the workman had photographed her with his phone as she exited the bathroom, and her bodyguard had broken the phone. Mohammed launched an attempt at damage control. Hassa hired Hatem to represent her, and Mohammed called him often for updates. He didn't want Hassa embarrassing his family by acting like a stereo-typically spoiled princess.

But Mohammed showed a limited understanding of how the West and its legal systems worked. "My father spoke to the president, so everything should be fine," Mohammed told the lawyer in one 2017 call that Hatem later recounted to an associate. Mohammed, Hatem told the associate, said the king mentioned the problem to France's then-president, François Hollande, and Mohammed expected the president to dismiss the case.

"No, no, that's not how it works," Hatem told Mohammed in Arabic. "The president can't intervene." This wasn't Saudi Arabia, where every prosecutor reported to the King. This was France, a democracy with independent courts and a free press. The president couldn't just decree that a criminal case be dismissed; doing so would turn into a scandal.

Hassa returned to Saudi Arabia, but the case dragged on in her absence, and a French judge issued an arrest warrant for her in 2018. It was in the middle of handling the case that the lawyer landed in Paris on a flight from Cyprus and found a text message from his old friend Abdulaziz asking him to call immediately.

Hatem phoned him from the airport. "Help me," Abdulaziz

said. His son Salman had gone to meet Mohammed the day before and got into some kind of fight in the palace before being arrested. Abdulaziz had heard all sorts of rumors, even that some of the guards involved were Americans. He didn't know where his son was and asked Hatem for help finding him.

Two days after Salman's arrest, Hatem called Mohammed. "You're calling about my sister?" the prince asked.

"I am calling about your cousin," Hatem replied. "I'd like to know what the status is with your cousin Salman."

Mohammed was surprised. He didn't expect family disputes to be aired out internationally. Why was he getting a call from a Lebanese French lawyer about something between him and his cousin?

Mohammed declined to answer any of Hatem's questions. Instead, his guards arrested Abdulaziz, Salman's father, and put him in prison too. Hatem was dropped from Hassa's case, and contacts told him he would no longer be working with the royal family. No one saw Salman or his father for months, though one inmate of al-Ha'ir prison told a friend that he had seen the prince there in 2018. "He'd been beaten," the inmate claimed.

Not long after, millions of dollars that Salman's wife inherited from her father would disappear from her accounts in Saudi banks, along with the inheritances of Abdullah's other children. The fears of the Abdullah clan in the days before their father's death had come true. One son, Turki, was in jail, and the rest of the children had seen much of their fortunes disappear.

———

Mohammed and his advisors were becoming wildly thin-skinned. Now anyone who criticized his short time in power was denying Saudi Arabia's reforms. Mohammed and his men saw these reforms not just as gradual changes that could make life a bit better but as existential necessities for the Al Saud. Without them, the family could lose its grip, and the country could go in a dangerous direction. This combination of sureness of mission and unwillingness to brook criticism led to tragically harsh crackdowns.

Few struck as deep a chord internationally as the case of Loujain al-Hathloul, a young, bright Saudi woman treated like a rogue al-Qaeda operative for her efforts to push for the rights of women. Born in Jeddah, al-Hathloul spent most of her life in Saudi Arabia, save for a five-year stint as a child in France and four years in Canada for undergraduate studies at the University of British Columbia. It was there that she had a political awakening.

On trips home, she'd lecture younger siblings about the horrid state of women's rights in Saudi Arabia. They responded that she'd been away too long, but she replied that she wasn't being influenced by outside views—she believed these human rights were universal and that they were being denied to half the country. After university she felt a pull back to the Gulf and landed in the United Arab Emirates, where women were freer and jobs were more plentiful.

But her political views were still pulsing, and she joined in a nonviolent protest against the ban on women driving. One day in 2014 she got in her car in Dubai, where she was properly licensed, and drove to the border of Saudi Arabia. The police there, confused and angry, arrested her, and she was placed in a prison for minors and female victims of domestic abuse for seventy-three days. The treatment was gentle, and she told friends and family that it was an eye-opening experience. Under Saudi law, if a wife tries to run away from her husband—even if because of domestic abuse—he can call the police and have her arrested for disrespecting him. In many ways, it's akin to the practice in the early twentieth century in America of husbands committing wives who didn't like the way they were being treated to insane asylums.

Saudi Arabia was gentler then too. Even though she'd crossed the red line, no one was giving her rough treatment. She was released when her father signed a document saying she wouldn't do it again. They smiled at home about the event, saying they'd laugh about it in ten years.

Not long after, she met stand-up comedian Fahad Albutairi, the "Seinfeld of the Middle East," who would go on to become her husband. In typical Saudi fashion, they first met virtually over Twitter before eventually meeting in person in the Emirates where courtship is more acceptable. Al-Hathloul hadn't lost her passion for women's rights and grew more strident. At a women's conference in Geneva, she attended as an individual and openly criticized an official delegation for its dishonesty. Unbeknownst to her, she landed directly on the radar of Saud al-Qahtani with her viral tweets critiquing each statement of the Saudi delegation.

In March 2018, she was abruptly arrested by UAE national security officers, who brought her to Saudi Arabia where she was detained under much harsher circumstances. She stayed in jail for only a few days before being released to her family home but was barred from traveling.

Then, in May officers came and arrested her again. This time they accused her of conspiring with foreign enemies, namely Qatar, and providing information to foreign governments about her country. She held no secrets, but the very act of critiquing her homeland to others was enough to be considered a traitor and a "national security threat." She was arrested along with other activists pushing for women's rights, and Albutairi, her husband, was arrested in Jordan.

Weeks later she called her parents, pretending everything was fine and saying she was staying in a "hotel." But they knew something was wrong. Her words were hollow and strained. When they finally were able to see her, she continued the charade as officers watched. Her mother was startled into silence, seeing how she struggled to hold a cup of water or swallow. She had red marks on her body. During the same period, Albutairi decided he couldn't stay with her any longer and asked for a divorce (some accounts said the authorities forced him to divorce her). These were cruel consequences for a young woman simply asking for rights widely championed around the world.

On her family's third visit she finally admitted she was being tortured. It was as if her interrogators thought they could convince her through force to give up her activism and erase any negative memories of her experience under detention. Saud al-Qahtani himself was one of the alleged perpetrators. Though the government has in general always denied using violence, it is claimed he threatened to rape and kill her before throwing her body in a sewer where her remains would never be found.

The bitter irony was that Mohammed bin Salman was pushing through the same reforms she was calling for. Why crack down on the activists when all he really needed to do was invite them to the *majlis* and promise them he was a believer? The answer was disturbing: In Mohammed's Kingdom of Saudi Arabia, reforms could only come from the top, lest citizens come to believe they could obtain their rights through protest or openly criticize the royal family. For all his liberal views, Mohammed was in general agreement with his uncles, aunts, brothers, and cousins on one thing: It was best for the Al Saud to run things.

The brutal tactics backfired, and al-Hathloul's case later became a global rallying cry against Mohammed bin Salman's regime.

Back in March, when al-Hathloul was first arrested, Mohammed turned his attention abroad. He took off for Egypt. Right away he doubled down on his forceful foreign policy approach, telling a newspaper interviewer that Turkey was part of a "triangle of evil" with Iran and extremist Islamic groups. Turkey's president Recep Tayyip Erdoğan had been trying to improve his country's relations with Saudi Arabia, but Mohammed dashed those hopes.

As the foreign trip continued to the United States, word circulated in the financial world that the prince and his sovereign wealth fund were readying a spending spree of incredible proportions. It began with a $400 million investment in a company called Magic Leap, which was developing "augmented reality" headsets but had yet to start selling any of its products. Michael Klein, the former Citigroup banker who had once been close to Alwaleed bin Talal, negotiated the deal.

Spending Saudi billions wasn't the main purpose of the 2018 trip to the United States. Now that he was crown prince, Mohammed expected to meet politicians and business leaders and convince them to invest their money in his rapidly transforming kingdom. Under his rule, Saudi Arabia would no longer be a place where American entrepreneurs just went looking for capital. Now, Mohammed was determined that Saudi Arabia's modernizing economy, young population, and innovative leadership would make it a destination for billions of dollars in American investment.

Things started out well at the White House on March 20. It was almost exactly a year after his earlier lunch there. Back then he had just been the deputy crown prince and only landed a meal with the president because a more important guest, Angela Merkel, was delayed by bad weather.

Now Mohammed was the guest of honor, leading a delegation of Saudis in black *bishts* into the Oval Office. Quickly, though, a fissure in Mohammed's vision became clear. As they sat in chairs beneath a portrait of George Washington, Donald Trump told Mohammed how enthusiastic he was about the Saudi relationship. "You are more than the crown prince now," Trump said. "We have become very good friends over a short period of time." But next to the president was a poster that made Mohammed cringe.

It looked like something from a middle school science fair. "KSA Sales Pending," it said in black text on a yellow background. Below it was a map of the United States with highlighted regions that would benefit from what Trump said was $12.5 billion in arms sales. "That's peanuts for you," he told the prince.

Mohammed sat smiling stiffly, privately fuming. The president was undermining his whole pitch about Saudi Arabia, treating the prince as a mere deep pocket for politically helpful spending. "Saudi Arabia is a very wealthy nation, and they're going to give the United States some of that wealth," Trump declared in public remarks released by the White House.

That dissonance between the prince's goals and those of his American counterparts would underlie every aspect of the trip. From Mohammed's perspective, Saudi Arabia's commitment to fast modernization and building an industrial base, its tech-savvy populace and its new openness to Western entertainment should make it an attractive place for American companies to invest billions of dollars. From the perspective of the Americans Mohammed was meeting, the calculus was much simpler: Mohammed was a guy with $1 trillion to spend who ran a country with a total population "roughly two-thirds the size of California," in the words of one Hollywood deal maker hired by the kingdom to generate entertainment business. There just wasn't enough upside, he said, for most companies to justify investing billions of dollars in a place with opaque courts, restrictive laws for women, and the constant threat of some kind of PR debacle.

Each of the men Mohammed would meet in the United States

had some vision for how he could use a huge Saudi investment and little to say about putting his own money into the kingdom. The studio chiefs hoped Mohammed would back new movie projects. Silicon Valley wanted capital to further inflate bubbles like WeWork and the dog-walking app Wag. Even the curious magazine that showed up across the United States celebrating the prince's visit seemed to be a sales pitch.

The magazine was in the tradition of low-brow royal worship that US newsstands hadn't seen since the days of Princess Diana. Beneath the title *The New Kingdom*, Mohammed stared out in a red-checked *shemagh* and white *thobe*, smirking yet somehow still looking serious. Surrounding him were text boxes announcing, "Our Closest Middle East Ally Destroying Terrorism," "Controlling Staggering $4 Trillion Business Empire," and "Building $640 Billion Sci-Fi City of the Future," the numbers apparently pulled from thin air. It's unclear how many people actually bought the $13.99 magazine or whether anyone took it as a piece of journalism. But it didn't really matter; it appeared to have been published for an audience of one, the crown prince himself, by men angling for their own chunk of Saudi cash.

Publisher David Pecker was the chief executive of *National Enquirer* parent American Media Inc. He had supported Trump from early on, landing himself in the middle of the "catch-and-kill" scandal in which he agreed to buy, and not publish, incriminating material from a stripper who claimed to have had an affair with the president. Pecker's company was seeking investment for an expansion of its Mr. Olympia competition into the Middle East, and after meeting Mohammed in 2017, he wanted to seal a deal in 2018. The timeframe overlapped with the fawning publication promoting Mohammed's vision for what the magazine called the "magic kingdom."

In the middle of it all, with an article about Saudi Arabia's new economy written under his byline and a photo of himself standing stiffly next to Trump, was a young French banker named Kacy Grine. He was another unlikely person drawn into the prince's orbit, the kind of international figure who, in the world of Saudi money, can go from obscurity to high-profile businessman with a single princely handshake.

Grine was thirty but looked younger. His unlined face appeared incapable of growing a beard, and a lustrous thicket of chestnut brown hair sprouted upward and outward from his head. Grine had the air of what Robert Caro, Lyndon Johnson's biographer, called the "professional son," a young man who gained stature by cultivating one father figure after another.

Grine got into the business of Saudi deal making largely through Alwaleed bin Talal. They had met years earlier, when Grine, then a junior banker, played a role in a deal Alwaleed negotiated with the president of Senegal. The older prince took a liking to the sharp young Frenchman, who listened more than he talked and, when he did talk, did so quietly and succinctly.

In subsequent deals, Alwaleed suggested that his negotiating partners hire Grine as an advisor. That provided steady business, and soon people who wanted Alwaleed's money knew Grine could be a conduit to the prince. Grine maintained the relationship by visiting Alwaleed in his Riyadh home several times a year, accompanying him to business meetings and on trips to the desert where the prince would hand out cash to Bedouins.

Grine seemed well placed in the early days of Mohammed's ascent. It was Alwaleed who first suggested Mohammed's strategy of using Saudi oil money to make big overseas investments, and Alwaleed publicly praised Mohammed's ambitious plans for the economy. Grine developed relationships with men like American-British tycoon Len Blavatnik and Hollywood agent Ari Emanuel.

It was through Emanuel that Grine got to know Pecker, who brought the young banker to the White House in 2017 to meet

Trump. With the connections to Trump, to Hollywood, and to Saudi Arabia's highest-profile prince, Grine seemed like the perfect person to put at the center of the magazine.

By the time it was published, though, there was an awkward complication: Alwaleed, who had been detained at the Ritz, was still under house arrest. Mohammed had locked him up, accused him of corruption, financially neutered him, and then trotted a haggard looking Alwaleed out publicly to give a humiliating statement that everything was fine. After all that, Alwaleed was still barred from traveling.

Following his years of business and friendship with Alwaleed, Grine was now appearing in a magazine promoting the man who had locked Alwaleed up. Saudi watchers were confused, and Grine told associates that he remained loyal to Alwaleed.

The magazine backfired for just about everyone. Saudi officials were forced to deny to American reporters that the government had paid for the publication. Pecker's relationship to Trump, rather than the grand plans of the prince, became the focal point for many US pundits. Grine, who preferred to operate on the fringes, was now in the center of an embarrassing uproar that brought lots of publicity and no money.

Mohammed continued his visit, meeting executives like Mark Zuckerberg, Bill Gates, and Apple's Tim Cook. He ate dinner with Jeff Bezos and was photographed with Google founder Sergey Brin wearing his Silicon Valley best: a blazer, dress shoes, and a button-down shirt tucked into dark jeans belted across his broad belly. He sat with Oprah Winfrey, venture capitalist Peter Thiel, and the CEOs of Disney, Uber, and Lockheed.

To Jeffrey Goldberg, the *Atlantic* editor whose interview with Barack Obama years earlier led Mohammed to believe that the former president was supporting Iran over Saudi Arabia, the prince made a surprising pronouncement: He asserted that

Israel had the right to exist, a first for a senior Saudi royal, and a huge shift for a kingdom that, as recently as 2012, published middle school textbooks that called Jews apes.

Such statements, as well as Mohammed's embrace of socially liberal Hollywood and Silicon Valley and his promise to bring "moderate" Islam to Saudi Arabia, gave some Americans the wrong impression. One dinner attendee at Murdoch's house, actor and former pro wrestler Dwayne Johnson, said in a Facebook post that he loved meeting the prince. "I look forward to my first visit soon to Saudi Arabia," he wrote, adding, "I'll be sure to bring my finest tequila to share with the [sic] his Royal Highness and family." The Rock and other Americans didn't understand that in important ways, Mohammed was a traditionalist. He might drink, but only privately. And his reforms—the embrace of the West, the break with the religious establishment, the lifting of the ban on women driving—were geared to satisfy a potentially restive young population. It was all done with the Al Saud's oldest goal in mind: maintaining power over the kingdom.

Careful observers saw that when it came to controlling the kingdom and its neighbors. Mohammed was hardly forward-looking. In the *Atlantic* interview, he told Goldberg that Iran's supreme leader was worse than Hitler. Word leaked from Riyadh that Mohammed had also detained his own mother, who had started questioning some of his governance decisions to the king.

While Americans celebrated Saudi Arabia's new freedoms for women, Mohammed's men were carrying out a roundup of the very women who pushed for the new reforms. Even if the activists and the prince agreed that women should be allowed to drive, people who publicly opposed his government, especially those who took their grievances abroad, were being locked up.

By the time his US trip wrapped up in Houston in early April, Mohammed had made little headway in his goal of attracting American companies to invest in Saudi Arabia. But he'd made a big splash as an investor, committing more than $20 billion in Saudi cash for weapons, petrochemicals projects, and investments in technology and entertainment companies, including $400 million in Ari Emanuel's firm Endeavor and some $2 billion in Tesla.

He returned to the kingdom emboldened to carry through even more ambitious domestic reforms. And he pushed even harder to make it seem as if big, innovative Western companies were going to make investments in Saudi Arabia. He targeted Jeff Bezos. After the prince and the Amazon founder had dinner together in LA, they traded contact numbers and began a long WhatsApp exchange over a project that would see Amazon spend $2 billion or more on a facility that would host computers processing data for Mideast customers.

For Bezos, the deal could be an important entry into the competitive Mideast market. For Mohammed, there was relatively little at stake economically; so-called server farms don't provide many jobs. But having the world's richest man bring one of the world's most powerful companies to the kingdom would be a great image boost for Mohammed.

Over the next several months, he told Bezos over WhatsApp of his excitement about the deal—and his dismay that Amazon had been so slow to get started in Saudi Arabia. "I was very disappointed," Mohammed told Bezos, that Amazon built a facility in neighboring Bahrain before Saudi Arabia. And he told Bezos that Amazon had "pushed" Saudi Arabia to invest in an e-commerce competitor by not coming to the kingdom earlier. Now was a chance for a productive new partnership for Amazon and Saudi Arabia, one that the prince and the billionaire could announce on stage together later that year at the Riyadh investment conference called Davos in the Desert. "It is very important for me, my friend, that you come to Saudi during the future investment Forum and we announce this

$2.8B Vision 2030 partnership," Mohammed told Bezos over WhatsApp.

In fact, getting Bezos on stage for the public relations coup was Mohammed's ultimate goal. Soon after he and Bezos shared dinner, Musaad al-Aiban, the security official who helped plan the 2017 Trump visit to Riyadh, decided not to move ahead with Amazon's plan because the company wouldn't allow Saudi intelligence and law enforcement to access data on the facility's computers. But Royal Court members were told to make sure Amazon never got that message. "Never say no publicly. We just keep stalling and cite bureaucratic delays," a government advisor who worked on the project told the *Wall Street Journal*.

Mohammed's social reforms and his autocratic streak continued at home. In June, the ban on women driving was officially lifted. The *ha'ya*, the bearded religious police who roamed Riyadh's malls castigating women with open *abayas*, had already started disappearing from public view in 2016, when Mohammed had confined them to their offices. Now they were rarely seen on the streets. After years of concerts and movie theaters being banned, new sources of entertainment flooded Saudi Arabia. Mohammed was proud that Canada's Cirque du Soleil planned to visit the kingdom.

Then, after 10 p.m. one evening, a Canadian government official got an unexpected call from Saudi entertainment minister Ahmed al-Khatib. The minister had Canadian contacts because he also had a role in military procurement, and Canadian companies were looking to sell to the kingdom. But this call wasn't about defense sales. It was about Cirque du Soleil, also a Canadian company, which had just canceled a visit to the kingdom for scheduling reasons.

"MBS is pissed off," Khatib told the official. "He loves Cirque du Soleil. This is unacceptable. You have to make them come."

The official gently explained that someone in his position didn't have the power to force a circus to perform. If Cirque du Soleil didn't want to come to Riyadh, it didn't have to.

A frustrated Khatib hung up and got to work finding an alternative. But the Russian Cirque knockoff he hired didn't fool anyone. Rather, its leotard-wearing female acrobats created such a backlash on Saudi Twitter, sparking tweets about "naked" Russian women, that MBS replaced Khatib as entertainment minister.

Saudi-Canadian relations would soon deteriorate further. That summer, Mohammed was moving ahead full speed with social and foreign policy initiatives, with no tolerance for any person or country that got in the way. That's when his aides floated a plan to build a canal that would separate Qatar from the rest of the Arabian Peninsula, turning the smaller country into an island. Then, on August 3, Canada's government sent out a tweet decrying Saudi Arabia's treatment of dissidents and "urg[ing] the Saudi authorities to immediately release" civil society and women's activists it had jailed.

Mohammed's men responded immediately. They told Ambassador Dennis Horak, who was on vacation in Toronto, that he wasn't welcome back. Then they canceled trade deals with Canada, withdrew Saudi students studying there, and publicly accused Canada of meddling in local affairs.

Controversy continued to surround Mohammed and his initiatives through the summer of 2018. In August, Tesla CEO Elon Musk tweeted that he was considering taking the company private and later said that he was discussing the deal with the Saudi Public Investment Fund (PIF). Federal officials suspected Musk was trying to juice his company's stock price, and the US Department of Justice called in PIF chief Yasir al-Rumayyan for an interview. At first the Saudi government tried to keep Rumayyan away from prosecutors, arguing he had diplomatic immunity. A Saudi official tried to convince then–attorney general Jeff Sessions that Rumayyan shouldn't have to sit for the interview since he might have state secrets. But after prosecutors pointed out that Rumayyan was not a diplomat, he agreed to be questioned. His American lawyer suggested prosecutors call him "your excellency" (they declined). Rumayyan told them that he hadn't agreed to a deal with Musk to take Tesla private. Musk denied trying to inflate Tesla's stock price, but subsequently settled an SEC case with the government.

In September, King Salman's full brother Ahmed made a surprising public appearance. Prince Ahmed was a potentially troubling figure for Mohammed, an uncle around whom royal family members skeptical of Saudi Arabia's new direction had rallied. For a time after Salman became king, the government restricted Ahmed's travel. He eventually went to London, where protesters gathered outside his home to mount demonstrations against the kingdom's bombing in Yemen.

Ahmed confronted the protesters in an exchange caught on video. He told them not to blame all the Al Saud. The family wanted the war over right away. The only two people responsible for the bombing were King Salman and his son Mohammed. It was a rare airing of dissent by one of the few royal family members who could make a legitimate claim to power—by convention, Ahmed was supposed to be chief of the Allegiance Council, the body that determines the line of succession.

At the same time, Saudi agents were conducting surveillance in Canada that would have dire consequences. Omar Abdulaziz, the dissident whose Twitter account had been hacked by the Royal Court's moles, had been attacked in a different way, using the phone-hacking software the Saudis had bought. By infiltrating his phone, Mohammed's men were able to read Omar's texts with the dissident journalist Jamal Khashoggi. The two were pulling together a group of Mohammed's critics into an organized opposition the kingdom had never before experienced.

Around this time Mohammed began striking visitors as a touch unhinged. He summoned people—some of them former Ritz detainees—to see him on the *Serene* off the coast of what he hoped would someday be NEOM. He excitedly referred to Tiran Island, where the robotic dinosaurs would roam. A year earlier, Egypt's president Abdel Fattah el-Sisi had ceded Tiran and another island, Sanafir, to Saudi Arabia. He'd handed over the strategically important islands to gain favor with Mohammed, arguing they were always meant to be part of Saudi Arabia in the first place, even though Egyptian courts ruled otherwise.

Wearing an open-necked shirt, Mohammed referred to advances in medicine that could make it possible for NEOM residents to live much longer than anyone in history. He might live hundreds of years, he said, explaining that he'd already begun investing in longevity research. One guest was unnerved: Did he think he would be ruler of Saudi Arabia until he was in his three hundreds? Was this the most powerful man in the Middle East?

Chapter 18

COLD BLOOD

October 2, 2018

As Jamal Khashoggi landed in Istanbul just before 4 a.m., the fifteen-man kill team was already getting into place.

Zipping through customs, Khashoggi made his way to his new apartment in Zeytinburnu, on the European side of the city. The plan was to take a nap at what was to become his marital home with fiancée Hatice Cengiz before grabbing a quick meal nearby. It was a big day for the new couple. They'd met at a conference a few months earlier and hit it off immediately.

Following a bruising two years of speaking out against Mohammed bin Salman, Khashoggi was lonely after his most recent divorce and feeling distant from his children back in Saudi Arabia. This was meant to be the start of a happier, fulfilling period after months of soul-searching in Washington, DC, where he was making a name for himself with strident and incisive critiques of Mohammed.

He'd always been a bit of a maverick, but this phase was different; he was living the life of a full-fledged dissident, something unthinkable only years before. Old friends were cautious about communicating with him, much less meeting. So Khashoggi was sad and sought a partner to soothe him and share his burdens. At fifty-nine years old, he'd been married at least three times—

sometimes, in the Saudi tradition, to more than one woman at once—and was embarking on a new chapter of his life. Hatice was thirty-six, a bookish woman working on a PhD. She was deeply in love with Khashoggi, a bespectacled teddy bear of a man with a gruff voice and a romantic flair.

After breakfast, the plan was for Khashoggi to go to the Saudi consulate to get papers proving he was divorced and had no other wives back in the kingdom, a prerequisite for Hatice's father and the Turkish authorities before they could get legally married. He'd visited the consulate weeks earlier with trepidation but found the officials there friendly and accommodating after a few minutes of banter. It would take a few days to prepare the documents and liaise with the proper authorities back in Riyadh, they told him. Unbeknownst to him, his surprise visit triggered a phone call to intelligence officials in Riyadh, who set in motion a deadly plan to silence their most famous critic.

Walking up to the secluded consulate compound, he was careful. In Washington, DC, he'd visited the embassy on several occasions and always been treated well. The ambassador and full brother of Mohammed, Khalid bin Salman, had even asked to meet with him and spoke to him respectfully. But he knew cybersecurity was an issue. His friends had already been hacked by malware sent in the form of banal links. On his two phones were communications with journalists from around the world, fellow dissidents and friends who could really stoke the flames back home. So he turned to Hatice and handed her his phones quickly, saying he'd be back in half an hour or so. If he didn't come out, he instructed her, she should call his friend Yasin.

Yasin was Yasin Aktay, the Turkish politician close to President Recep Tayyip Erdoğan, and a friend of Khashoggi's since the Arab Spring.

Security footage shows Khashoggi walking calmly into the building, wearing a dark blazer and grey trousers. At that moment, Aktay was in his office, working furiously on a newspaper column due later that night.

Within minutes of his 1:15 p.m. arrival, Khashoggi realized something was terribly wrong. He must have recognized a dour-looking intelligence official named Maher Abdulaziz Mutreb, whom he knew from the London consulate years before.

———

Over the course of three years, Khashoggi had gone from an influential, if occasionally critical, supporter of the royal family to a grave national security threat in the eyes of the Royal Court. That change had less to do with what Khashoggi said or wrote in his columns in the *Washington Post* opinion section than with a perception by Mohammed bin Salman's security advisors that he was becoming a great unifier of Saudis opposing MBS's reforms and style of running the country. Khashoggi's ties to Turkish politicians close to Erdoğan were evidence to some of Mohammed's allies that the writer was working with foreign powers to undermine Saudi Arabia. His close friendship with Maggie Mitchell Salem, who worked as executive director of the Qatar Foundation International and helped him write and edit his columns, was seen as direct evidence of his having flipped to work for his country's sworn enemies.

The once moderate critic of his homeland had also become a clearinghouse for information showing the negative side of Mohammed's way of wielding power, whether it was poor economic results or a rumor about an excessive purchase or an angry encounter with a staffer. He was cofounding a new group, Democracy for the Arab World Now, or DAWN, a highly provocative move. The very name was reminiscent of the Arab Spring.

Perhaps nothing was more problematic for the Al Saud than an influential Saudi calling for democracy in the kingdom.

Khashoggi also undertook smaller provocations, undermining Mohammed's attempt to cast himself as a visionary. "In my career as a journalist, an editor, I called for everything Mohammed bin Salman is doing right now," Khashoggi said during a November 2017 speech in Washington at a think tank linked to Qatar. "He is doing what we demanded of him to do. So why am I being critical? Simply because he is doing the right things the wrong way, very wrong way."

Just a few days before his return trip to Turkey, Khashoggi appeared on the BBC. Before the interview officially started, he gave a candid view of the crown prince that captured the kind of things he'd been saying all over Washington, DC, and beyond. The BBC later released the recording. "The prince supplies us, every couple of weeks or couple of months, with a huge multi-billion-dollar project that wasn't discussed in parliament or newspapers. The people will clap and say 'Hey, great, let's have more of those.' It doesn't work that way," Khashoggi said. "I don't think I will be able to go home again. When I hear of an arrest of a friend who did nothing worth being arrested, make me feel I shouldn't go."

Saud al-Qahtani, Mohammed's deputy who had been dogging Khashoggi for years, kept asking him to come back to Saudi Arabia, offering to bring the critic back into the fold. But Khashoggi worried that Saud's entreaties were a trap. Khashoggi's "betrayals" were especially personal for Qahtani because he'd failed to stop Khashoggi when he had a chance.

For more than three years, Qahtani had been trying to neutralize critics by attacking them with his Twitter army or hacking their phones or kidnapping them and bringing them back to Saudi Arabia. On Twitter he frequently declared his allegiance to Mohammed, and Qahtani tried publicly to make clear that he had an intimate relationship with the prince. It gave the impression that Saud was in charge of ensuring Mohammed's wishes were carried out.

In April 2018, Saud wrote an op-ed on the website of Al Arabiya about his relationship with Mohammed. "He told me very politely that he wants me to conduct a research, one that I conduct myself, not assigning someone else to do it," Qahtani wrote. "The research was about strategic planning. 'I want you to completely devote yourself for this task,' that's what he said when I was about to tell him that I was too busy doing more important things. He made me feel that it is a huge classified task."

Qahtani had kept track of Khashoggi in the weeks leading up to his first visit to the consulate in Istanbul, and officials there had briefed him that Khashoggi would be returning. Seeing a chance to intercept the dissident, Qahtani had his dark-arts team kick into gear. A group of technical officers flew to Istanbul to sweep the consulate for bugs and recording devices they suspected the Turkish government had planted; they found none, or rather, they missed all of them.

Qahtani's Center for Studies and Media Affairs was central command for secret renditions. The security officers who carried out the missions were called the Saudi Rapid Intervention Group. Their commander was the security officer and former intelligence official that Khashoggi had known back in London, Maher Mutreb, who only a few months earlier had been photographed with Mohammed during his multiweek tour of the United States.

Maher brought along an assortment of security personnel and Lieutenant Colonel Salah Muhammad al-Tubaigy, a doctor at the Ministry of Interior and chairman of the Scientific Council of Forensic Medicine in Riyadh. Tubaigy's role would later indicate that murder was in the plans from the outset. Nervously waiting for Khashoggi, he explained to the men how he listened to music and drank coffee when cutting up cadavers, according to Turkish intercepts from within the consulate.

Staff at the consulate were told not to show up the day Khashoggi was planning to get his divorce paperwork, and workers at the consul general's nearby home were also told to stay home because of ongoing engineering works. Minutes before Khashoggi arrived, Maher asked, "Has the sacrificial animal arrived yet?"

In the consulate, it didn't take long for things to escalate. Members of the receiving party brought Khashoggi upstairs to the consul general's office. "We will have to take you back," Mutreb told Khashoggi as he was pulled into an office moments after arriving at the consulate. "There is an order from Interpol. Interpol requested you be sent back. We are coming to get you. Why don't you go back?"

"Why wouldn't I want to go back to my own country? Inshallah I will eventually go back," Khashoggi responded.

"Interpol is coming, so we have to hold you until they come," Mutreb said.

"This is against all kind of laws. I am being kidnapped!" Khashoggi said.

"We will take you back to Saudi Arabia and if you don't help us, you know what will happen in the end," one of them said.

Khashoggi pushed back.

"Let's make it short," another man said.

They pulled out a syringe.

"Are you going to give me drugs?" Khashoggi asked at 1:33 p.m.

And that was it. Over the next five minutes, Khashoggi was sedated and suffocated. At 1:39 p.m., the corpse-dismemberment expert could be heard sawing the journalist's body into pieces.

The task wasn't complete. One team member, a heavyset intelligence operative named Mustafa al-Madani with a build similar to Khashoggi's, put on Khashoggi's clothing and glasses and a fake beard and walked out the back door of the embassy. His job was to give any investigators a false lead and shift inquiries away from Saudi Arabia. He took a taxi to the Blue Mosque with another member of the team, walked around for a few hours, had a tea, and then threw away the clothing before heading to the airport, where the men flew home on two private jets ultimately owned by Mohammed bin Salman's newly empowered Public Investment Fund.

What the assassins didn't count on was Hatice waiting outside and their own inability to do a proper bug sweep of the embassy. Turkish intelligence had clear recordings of every terrifying sound of the murder.

After waiting for more than three hours, Hatice called Khashoggi's emergency contact, Yasin Aktay, at 4:41 p.m. in the afternoon. He didn't answer at first, believing it was a simple social call, but when Khashoggi's number flashed on his phone again, he picked up. It was Hatice. Khashoggi hadn't come out, she told the Turkish politician. Could he help?

Aktay was concerned. He understood the risks for Khashoggi and told Hatice he would get in touch with state security. His first call was to Turkey's intelligence chief, Hakan Fidan. When Fidan didn't answer his phone immediately, Aktay called one of the intelligence chief's deputies.

"We have a serious problem," Aktay told him. Khashoggi had gone to the consulate on routine business and hadn't come out.

"It is very dangerous for him," the deputy replied. "Why did he go in?" He promised to get back to Aktay as soon as he learned anything.

Then Aktay called Erdoğan's office and told the president's secretary what was happening. Erdoğan's staff put the security and intelligence services on alert. Aktay called Hatice back and told her they'd just have to wait. The Turks didn't know yet that Khashoggi was dead.

The Khashoggi killing would turn Turkey and Saudi Arabia into public antagonists in a way that neither Mohammed nor Erdoğan had really wanted. They shared mutual interests—most importantly, defeating Islamic State terrorists in Syria—and had little to gain from all-out hostility.

But the relationship between the two countries had been beset by friction in recent years and weighed down by the long history between the Turks and the Gulf Arabs. Much of today's Saudi Arabia used to be part of the Ottoman Empire; the Turks ruled as a colonial power, with the Arabs as their subjects. Mohammed's grandfather, Ibn Saud, had defeated the Ottomans as part of his quest to establish the Saudi kingdom.

Just over a century later, the Saudis ruled most of the Arabian Peninsula and, thanks to oil, had much more money than the Turks. Importantly, the Saudis also controlled the two holy cities, Mecca and Medina. To fulfill their religious duty to visit Mecca as pilgrims, Muslim Turks needed the permission of their former subjects. Mohammed still viewed the Turks as haughty erstwhile colonists who looked down on the Arabs.

Turkey couldn't rival the Saudis' spending power. But the Turks had a different advantage. Their country has long-established government institutions that transcend changes in political leadership. For better or worse, power in Turkey has, in recent history, been held by institutions and the large number of bureaucrats who run them. As a result, the military and intelligence arms of government have continuity in their priorities, structures, and cultures and a deep well of highly trained officials from the highest ranks to the lowest.

In Saudi Arabia, institutional power is almost nonexistent

outside Aramco. Authority in the kingdom is held by individuals from the royal family, the king, and the select few princes he appoints to key roles. When those princes change, loyalists are promoted and those loyal to the prior prince moved aside. Those changes can bring wholesale shifts in governance, military, and intelligence structures.

Another result of the countries' contrasting political structures is that Turkey's leaders can't afford to ignore movements like the Muslim Brotherhood or, on a bigger level, the Arab Spring. Turkey is a democracy; to get reelected, a president like Erdoğan needs to be sensitive to the public will. There was lots of support, at home and abroad, for democratic movements across the Middle East. So Erdoğan supported some democracy movements tied to the Brotherhood, which wanted to elect Islamist politicians, in the early 2010s, and King Abdullah never forgave him. As far as Abdullah was concerned, Erdoğan's support for democratic movements undermined the Al Saud, and the Turkish president was therefore an enemy. The chill lasted until the old king died.

Though Erdoğan didn't rally to the side of the Gulf monarchies during the Arab Spring, he didn't want mutual animosity. When Abdullah died, Erdoğan saw an opportunity for detente. He and King Salman had communicated in the past and seemed to share a mutual respect. Erdoğan met with Salman several times during the king's first year on the throne and got the sense that he didn't share Abdullah's deep skepticism of Turkey. Erdoğan and his advisors were confident that they were entering into a new era of collaboration with the kingdom. In 2017, Saudi Arabia extradited sixteen people to Turkey whom Erdoğan accused of being aligned with Fethullah Gulen, a cleric Turkey alleged to have tried to have Erdoğan assassinated (Gulen has denied the claims).

But in the ensuing months, the Turks discerned an unforeseen problem: the crown prince. Mohammed didn't seem to have the same tolerance for divergent views that the Turks expected from his father. The tensions came to a head with the Qatar boycott. Qatar and Turkey were long-standing allies, and Erdoğan felt he couldn't abandon an ally to support the Saudi-led boycott.

"Isolating Qatar in this way will not resolve any problems," Erdoğan said publicly after the boycott began. "In my view Qatar being portrayed as a terror suspect is a heavy allegation. I know them very well for 15 years." He questioned the motives behind the action. "There is a different game at play here," he said. "We have not yet identified who is behind this game." Erdoğan said he spoke to King Salman and "shared these problems in a heart-to-heart talk."

Erdoğan still hoped to reach some sort of accord with the Saudis, but when Turkish officials spoke with the Saudis, they were told to either support the Saudi effort or be seen as an enemy. Erdoğan became convinced that Mohammed was an obstacle to better Turkish-Saudi relations.

Chapter 19

MISTER BONE SAW

October 2018

Inside the presidential palace in Ankara, President Recep Tayyip Erdoğan was fuming as he listened to a briefing from Turkish state security. An initial review of recordings from listening devices secretly placed in the embassy before Jamal Khashoggi showed up for his divorce papers on that October day painted a grisly picture of premeditated murder.

An hour before the killing, the cadaver expert described, in starkly objective terms, how difficult it would be to cut Khashoggi's body into pieces. Then there was the reference to the "sacrificial animal" and the gut-wrenching sound of men hacking a human body apart immediately after Khashoggi was killed.

"Haram," Erdoğan yelled. This was so heinous it affronted God. Khashoggi was not just a foreign journalist killed in Turkey; Erdoğan had personally met him, and his advisors had sought him out to discuss developments in Saudi Arabia and the broader Arab world.

Compounding Erdoğan's frustration was Saudi Arabia's response: The Royal Court was denying it knew anything. Did they think the Turks were stupid?

Erdoğan and his team set in motion a plan to begin drip

feeding information about the killing publicly, punishing the Saudi Arabian government and making clear that King Salman needed to send a royal envoy to discuss the next steps. Erdoğan saw this as an opportunity to get a leg up on Mohammed and his antagonistic stance toward Turkey—and perhaps convince Salman to take away some of his son's foreign policy power.

At first the Saudis either didn't take the bait or didn't realize how much information Erdoğan had. Rather than rush to Turkey, Mohammed bin Salman's team denied any knowledge of the killing and stuck to a script that would only make sense if the Turkish authorities didn't have definitive proof of the murder.

On the night of the killing, Mohammed conducted a long-planned interview with Bloomberg News that was mostly about economic plans. Reporters asked questions about Khashoggi too. "We hear the rumors about what happened," Mohammed told the group, his face showing no sign of stress. "He's a Saudi citizen and we are very keen to know what happened to him. My understanding is he entered and he got out after a few minutes or one hour. I'm not sure. We are investigating this through the foreign ministry to see exactly what happened at that time."

Mohammed's younger brother Khalid, ambassador to the United States, tweeted, "I assure you that the reporters that suggest that Jamal Khashoggi went missing in the consulate in Istanbul or that the Kingdom's authorities have detained him or killed him are absolutely false."

Hearing the crown prince's comments and seeing others from the Saudi government, Erdoğan ordered details leaked to the press, including the stunning revelation that one member of the kill team brought a bone saw into the country when he got off the private jet belonging to the Public Investment Fund (PIF). From that point on, Mohammed bin Salman had a new moniker: Mister Bone Saw. That a government would kill a dissident is always shocking, but what turned the Khashoggi murder into a global rallying cry was the bloodcurdling detail of the brutality of the killers, dismembering Khashoggi's body like butchers. The implausibility of Saudi denials made it all the more disturbing.

Later Mohammed would react with anger that the world was so outraged about one man killed by rogue agents, according to the account he gave to a visitor, but willing to accept bigger, systematic persecutions by China and other countries. In private, Saudis would give a variation of the argument around how the United States dropped bombs on civilians across the Middle East for decades. Why weren't they judged this harshly?

The Saudi leadership thought it unfair that they were getting so much public criticism for a single death. As details of Khashoggi's relationship to Qatar trickled out in the months ahead, some of them felt vindicated. He was a turncoat, a saboteur, they'd say, but there was still a note of uncertainty in the protestations. The details were difficult for any human to accept.

With the heat ratcheting up and new revelations coming out about the recordings, Saudi Arabia went into crisis mode. King Salman decided to dispatch Khalid bin Faisal, the seventy-eight-year-old governor of Mecca, to mediate with Erdoğan. As overseer of Mecca with decades of diplomacy under his belt, the prince had special standing in the Islamic world and seemed the best hope for working out a private arrangement with the Turks. The bin Faisals also had a special relationship with the Khashoggi family; Turki bin Faisal had been Khashoggi's boss for years in London and Washington, DC.

When Khalid arrived, he was struck by Erdoğan's stridency. No financial commitment from the kingdom was going to sway him from playing his trump card in a bid to unseat Mohammed from the succession plans. "It's really difficult to get out of this one," he told relatives afterward, according to the *New York Times*, which together with the *Washington Post* and other outlets published daily stories on the Khashoggi affair and turned it into a journalistic campaign. The *Times* even forensically identified members of the kill team using visual investigation techniques.

Even if the issue had hit a boiling point, Erdoğan and outraged columnists around the world who believed Mohammed would be unseated imminently didn't grasp just how profoundly the young crown prince had consolidated power. In the old Saudi Arabia, a mistake or indiscretion could lead to a royal's or courtier's being swiftly jettisoned from the inner Al Saud power structure or even secreted back to the kingdom. But the consequences were much harsher in this new Saudi Arabia, where power was distilled in the king's and crown prince's courts. And who ran the king's court in addition to his own? Mohammed bin Salman.

He was also buoyed by his relationship to another irascible and powerful supporter, Donald Trump. Mohammed had forged such deep ties with the First Family through his conversations with Jared Kushner, his commitment to hundreds of billions of dollars in deals and agreements advertised by Trump as benefitting the United States, and his demonstrations of appreciation, like the gift of the white-tiger-fur-lined robes when Trump visited, that it would be politically damaging to Trump to throw Mohammed to the wolves. It took Trump several days to make any comment at all.

"I guess you would have to say so far it's looking a little bit like that and we're going to have to see," he told a Fox News reporter in response to a question about whether Khashoggi had been killed in the consulate. "Maybe we'll be pleasantly surprised but somehow I tend to doubt it," he told other reporters earlier the same day. A few days later, Trump said he'd consider "severe punishment" if it was proven the Saudi Arabian government was behind the killing.

Saudi Arabia's provocative response on October 14 seemed certain to hasten a confrontation: "The kingdom affirms its total rejection of any threats and attempts to undermine it, whether by threatening to impose economic sanctions, using political pressures, or repeating false accusations," the Saudi state news agency said in a statement quoting an unnamed government official. "The kingdom also affirms that if it receives any action it will respond with greater action, and that the kingdom's economy has an influential and vital role in the global economy."

Secretary of State Mike Pompeo flew to see Mohammed bin Salman, and by the time he returned, there were signs that a counternarrative was emerging and Trump was carrying water for Mohammed. "I just spoke to the king of Saudi Arabia, who denies any knowledge of what took place with regard to, as he said, his Saudi Arabian citizen," he said on October 15. "I don't want to get into his mind, but it sounded to me like maybe these could have been rogue killers. Who knows?... [A]nd it sounded like he, and also the crown prince, had no knowledge."

A few days later, the *Washington Post* published Khashoggi's last column under the title "Jamal Khashoggi: What the Arab World Needs Most Is Free Expression." It decried how a "state-run narrative dominates the public psyche" in the Arab world, but it also praised how Qatar's government supported international news coverage. For the Western readers outraged by the Khashoggi murder, it felt like the perfect article from a journalist hero. But many in the Saudi audience saw it as proof that Khashoggi was working for their country's sworn enemies. In a TV interview, Saudi foreign minister Adel al-Jubeir brought up the United States' torture of prisoners years earlier in Iraq's Abu Ghraib prison.

By Saturday, October 20, the counternarrative—which stripped the crown prince of any culpability—emerged with an account that Saudi agents traveled to Turkey to bring Khashoggi back to Saudi Arabia, but the discussions "escalated negatively" and "led to a fight and then a quarrel between some of them and the citizen." The "brawl aggravated to lead to his death and their attempt to conceal and cover up what happened." "The Kingdom expresses its deep regret at the painful developments that have taken place and stresses the commitment of the authorities in the kingdom to bring the facts to the public," the Foreign Ministry said.

Trump called the statements a "good first step." King Salman and Mohammed went to see Khashoggi's son, Salah Khashoggi, in Riyadh. Ashen and severe, he shook hands with the crown prince. King Salman ordered reforms to the intelligence apparatus and changes to ensure all operations complied with human rights treaties and international law; Mohammed was selected as the chairman of the effort, and a US company, DynCorp, sent over a team of consultants to help Saudi Arabia improve its intelligence capabilities, though the US State Department later declined to give the required approval for the DynCorp contract.

Meanwhile, on the same day as the visit to Salah Khashoggi, organizers of the second Future Investment Initiative struggled to banish a funereal atmosphere at the Ritz-Carlton in Riyadh. Some of the big names of the day canceled, including onetime fans of the crown prince like David Petraeus and a lineup of banking luminaries. The *New York Times*, which sponsored the prior year's conference, pulled out.

Lubna Olayan, the most famous Saudi businesswoman in the country, told the glum audience of mostly Saudis and a smattering of lower-level executives from abroad, "I want to tell all our foreign guests, for whose presence this morning we are very grateful, that the terrible acts reported in recent weeks are alien to our culture and our DNA."

Mohammed himself showed up and stated that the "heinous

crime cannot be justified," saying it was "very painful for all Saudis and I believe it is painful to every human in the world." As if to suggest all the coverage of him had been grossly mis- represented, he gestured to Saad Hariri, the Lebanese prime minister he'd detained against his will a year earlier, who was in attendance. Hariri was clapping. "Prime Minister Hariri will be in town for two more days," Mohammed said, grinning. "So don't anyone say he's been kidnapped."

With the Khashoggi affair still dominating the news, Joel Rosenberg, a Christian interfaith activist who was born in Israel, wasn't sure his big meeting was going ahead. He'd been invited by Khalid bin Salman to bring a delegation of Evangelical Christians to Saudi Arabia in a bid by Mohammed bin Salman to speak to a core American demographic but also to begin publicly signaling his openness to be seen in meetings with Israeli-born people, something no previous king or official would do in public. Rosenberg checked in, and his contacts at the embassy said the meeting was still a go. They flew in and arrived in time to see Mohammed bin Salman on November 1. Feeling like they had no choice but to begin with Khashoggi, Rosenberg asked what his response was.

"A terrible mistake happened," Mohammed told him, with his brother Khalid, Foreign Minister Adel al-Jubeir, and a top Islamic advisor looking on. "We are holding those responsible accountable. We are waiting for and want all the information from Turkey....I can promise the people responsible will be held accountable and any problem we have in the system will be addressed."

Later in the conversation, Mohammed admitted, "[I] may bear some guilt, but not because I authorized the heinous act because I did not, but because I may have caused some of our people to love our Kingdom too much and delegated authority in a way that made it too easy for them to think they would be pleasing us by taking matters into their own hands." His enemies were exploiting the tragedy for their advantage, he said. "In their shoes, I would probably do the same."

In a conversation with a Saudi contact after the killing, Mohammed denied ordering it and lamented the damage it was causing to his reputation with Western leaders. "Now they think I'm a journalist killer!" he sputtered in frustration.

The Al Saud seemed to gather together around Mohammed. Prince Ahmed, the uncle who had criticized Mohammed's and Salman's bombing of Yemen a month earlier, agreed to come back to Saudi Arabia after the UK government assured him it would ensure his safety.

For weeks, the foreign politicians, businesspeople, and bankers Mohammed had tried to sell on his image as a new kind of Saudi leader distanced themselves. The Bezos appearance at the second Davos in the Desert was called off. Executives and political leaders didn't want to be seen as allied with a man accused of murdering a writer for expressing his opinions.

Hollywood agent Ari Emanuel canceled the $400 million investment he'd worked hard to get from the kingdom, pledging to return the money and stop dealing with Mohammed. "That guy is an animal," Emanuel told a friend. Once charmed by the prince, the agent now called him "Jekyll and Hyde." On October 12 Richard Branson pulled out of the planned $1 billion deal with Saudi Arabia for his space travel company. If Saudi officials were involved in the Khashoggi murder, he said in a prepared statement released by his company at the time, "that would clearly change the ability of any of us in the West to do business with the Saudi government." Branson also said he would "suspend" his role as a director in two Saudi tourism projects.

Privately, Branson kept up his correspondence with Mohammed. Saudi Arabia represented a big business opportunity, and he counseled the prince on how to reverse some of the damage in the eyes of the West, starting by releasing some of the women activists who were jailed. "If you were to pardon these women and a number of men too, it would show the world the Government is truly moving into the 21st Century," Branson texted the crown prince in a message that the *Wall Street Journal* published. "It won't change what happened in Turkey but it would go a long way to start and change people's view."

Other business leaders had similarly ambivalent approaches. SoftBank's Masayoshi Son, who was managing about $45 billion in Saudi investment, pulled out of the conference but went to Saudi Arabia anyway. Other executives who wanted to avoid public association with the crown prince but maintain the Saudi financial relationship gathered for an opulent roast lamb dinner under purple-lit palm trees at the home of Yasir al-Rumayyan, the man Mohammed put in charge of the sovereign wealth fund investing in Uber and SoftBank. Guests included banker Ken Moelis, Republican congressman-cum-financier Eric Cantor, and a cohort of Silicon Valley notables, including Uber founder Travis Kalanick, venture capitalist Jim Breyer, and a manager working for Peter Thiel's firm.

For some, the Saudi relationship was too valuable to scrap over a single murder. Bloomberg LP moved ahead with its joint venture with the Salman family's media company. Jay Penske, whose firm owns *Rolling Stone* magazine, moved ahead with a $200 million investment from the PIF. An American hedge fund manager named John Burbank, who attended the Rumayyan dinner, put it bluntly in an interview with the *Journal*. "This whole Khashoggi thing doesn't mean anything," he said. "It means much less than the big, sweeping liberalization that's happening in the kingdom." When it comes to investing in Saudi Arabia, he added, "one person's life doesn't matter unless it's MBS's. Khashoggi doesn't matter."

While the financial world was moving past its concerns, intelligence agencies and a United Nations official who investigates extrajudicial killings by governments were all trying to figure out what really happened to Khashoggi in Istanbul. Within weeks, the CIA determined that Mohammed sent Saud al-Qahtani at least eleven messages around the time of the killing. And two months before the killing, the CIA found, Mohammed had told people close to him that if he couldn't convince Khashoggi to come back to the kingdom on his own, "we could possibly lure him outside Saudi Arabia and make arrangements." The agency concluded that Mohammed "probably ordered his death."

The Saudi government announced it had charged eleven people in the death, though Qahtani wasn't one of them. He continued to be a presence around the Royal Court. He did face punishment, though, by the US Treasury Department. It sanctioned Qahtani and sixteen others, preventing them from interacting with the US financial system.

In the meantime, the Turks were using their recordings to put pressure on the kingdom, hoping King Salman might take away some of Mohammed's power and give foreign policy responsibility to someone else.

Turkish leaders aided the inquiry of Agnes Callamard, a French human rights investigator affiliated with Columbia University, who serves as the United Nations' special rapporteur on extrajudicial killings. A few months after Khashoggi's murder, she flew to Turkey with a team of colleagues. Traveling around Ankara, the Turkish capital, she and her staffers could easily see that they were being followed by intelligence agents. Even in a café, "when you were trying to have a conversation there was always some strange person sitting next to you," she recalls.

Turkish intelligence chief Hakan Fidan greeted Callamard and her team at the government's heavily fortified intelligence offices. A wily former army officer educated at the University of

Maryland whom Erdoğan once called "my secret keeper," Fidan was an expert at using the intelligence apparatus to help further his boss's political aims. He'd provided information on Israeli operatives to Iran and at the same time remained a valued connection for US intelligence, appearing in White House photos with President Barack Obama and Erdoğan in 2013.

Fidan met Callamard in a ground-floor room in the fortresslike intelligence headquarters. After some brief conversation, he told Callamard his people would play recordings from the Khashoggi killing for her. She and her staff were to listen and not take notes. Fidan said he wouldn't stick around to hear the recordings. "It's bad for my soul," he said.

Once Fidan left, his staff played audio files for Callamard and her team, which included a translator. Callamard's staff members took turns distracting the intelligence officials present so their colleagues could secretly take notes. After hearing the recordings, and consulting with special operations experts, she hypothesized that the Saudis' initial plan may have been to kidnap Khashoggi. But sometime in the two days before he got to the embassy, the team realized that would be too hard and decided on the murder.

The recordings were disturbing—the team could hear the fear building in Khashoggi's voice as his killing neared—and ultimately dissatisfying. The Turks had seven hours of recordings but only played forty-five minutes' worth. There were no transcripts. They remain private. "As long as the tapes have not been released, there will always be questions," Callamard says. She says the opaque Saudi legal process, the apparent focus of the Saudi investigation on the killers—rather than those who may have authorized them—and the refusal by US authorities to make intelligence documents public keep the full story hidden.

Chapter 20

UNSTOPPABLE

December 2018

For most big, prosperous cities, a Formula E race wouldn't be a marquee event. But for Riyadh, where most public entertainment had been banned for four decades, the electric-race-car circuit's arrival for its first-ever race in Saudi Arabia might have been the biggest international sporting event the city had ever seen.

Just over two months had passed since the killing of Jamal Khashoggi, and Mohammed wanted the event to prove that the world hadn't turned its back on Saudi Arabia. International sports were supposed to be a pillar of his reinvention of Saudi society and economy, and electric vehicles played a big role in his plans. So Mohammed turned the race into a spectacle. He invited dozens of celebrities from the entertainment and business worlds and made sure their attendance was well publicized. Enrique Iglesias played a concert as part of the festivities, and English soccer star Wayne Rooney flew in to attend.

The track, festooned with "Vision 2030" banners, wound through Diriyah, a historic village on the outskirts of Riyadh whose mud-walled palaces were an early seat of Al Saud power. Above the track, on a VIP viewing platform, was a collection of Saudi Arabia's most powerful figures. Adel al-Jubeir, the foreign minister, was there. So was Minister of State Mohammed Al

Shaikh, who years earlier, as a securities regulator, confronted a young Mohammed about stock manipulation. Energy minister and Aramco chairman Khalid al-Falih and Reema bint Bandar, who would soon become the first woman to serve as ambassador to the United States, made small talk as the race cars zipped by, their battery-powered engines almost silent. And then there was Mohammed, in a *thobe* and red-and-white checked *shemagh*, accompanied by a bodyguard in a business suit and his brother Khalid bin Salman, the former ambassador to the United States. Abu Dhabi's de facto leader, Mohammed bin Zayed, was also in attendance.

Joining them were members of the dwindling ranks of powerful Westerners willing to publicly associate with Mohammed in the wake of the Khashoggi murder, including former Dow Chemical CEO Andrew Liveris, ex–CIA official Norman Roule, and billionaire American natural-resources investor Tom Kaplan. Former Kardashian reality show producer Carla DiBello was milling around the event. PBS *Frontline*'s intrepid correspondent Martin Smith recorded the gathering by edging past security guards and falling in with a group of caterers filing upstairs to the VIP box, where he walked up to Prince Mohammed and asked to bring in his camera man.

Each of the attendees had his or her own reason to maintain the Saudi relationship at a tense time. Liveris was working for Mohammed, advising the Public Investment Fund (PIF) in its attempt to invest tens of billions of dollars worldwide. Roule, who consults with foreign companies on how to work in the kingdom, attends such gatherings to keep up his knowledge of regional happenings. But he and Kaplan were at the race with hopes of seeing through a quixotic plan to get Emirati and Saudi authorities to help save endangered Arabian leopards, perhaps even airlifting some from zoos in war-ravaged Yemen. DiBello was making a Saudi-supported documentary on the race and solidifying relationships in the kingdom—including with the PIF—to build her own business facilitating access to companies looking for Saudi investment.

These business contacts didn't see the Khashoggi killing as permanently tainting Mohammed. Rather, they shared a viewpoint with the prince: His power stemmed from his family, not an electorate. It didn't depend on his reelection or even the approval of leaders of other countries. And he was so young, he could rule Saudi Arabia for another fifty years—or longer, if his investments in longevity research panned out. They took the view that the Khashoggi killing would go down as a misstep, a blip early in his career washed away by bigger news down the road.

It was a very different atmosphere than Mohammed had faced less than two weeks before, at a G-20 gathering in Buenos Aires. A camera there caught a tense moment when French president Emmanuel Macron, who had been wrangling with Mohammed since the detention of Lebanon's prime minister in 2017, confronted the prince about the Khashoggi killing. Mohammed, towering over Macron in a white *bisht* and red-checked *shemagh* on the margin of the large meeting room, seemed defensive.

"Don't worry," he told Macron.

"I do worry," Macron replied, unaware a microphone was recording him. "I am worried."

They went back and forth, Macron accusing Mohammed of not following his advice. "You never listen to me," he said.

In the eyes of Western leaders and human rights activists, the Saudi government's response to the Khashoggi killing was entirely inadequate. Saudi Arabia kept a trial of the men alleged to have participated in the killing closed off from the public, so there was little information about what kind of evidence prosecutors were presenting. Saud al-Qahtani was sometimes seen meeting with people in Mohammed's inner circle. At one point, a song celebrating his innocence was circulated by Turki Al

Sheikh, suggesting there were attempts by the Saudi leadership to rehabilitate Qahtani's image, at least domestically.

King Salman had done little, if anything, to rein in Mohammed's more aggressive foreign policy tendencies. Ibrahim al-Assaf, a septuagenarian former finance minister who was briefly locked up in the Ritz, was appointed foreign minister, but he was in no position to sway Mohammed on matters of substance.

In June, Agnes Callamard, the UN investigator, released her report on the Khashoggi killing. It was scathing. She called it a "deliberate premeditated execution" that Mohammed either ordered or condoned, citing, among many other facts, the seemingly damning detail that the team at the embassy in Turkey called Khashoggi a "sacrificial animal" on the secret recordings and discussed cutting him into pieces thirteen minutes before he even entered the embassy.

Still, Mohammed's most important initiatives continued. His military kept bombing Yemen, and his men moved ahead with the planned IPO of Aramco, the state oil company. Mohammed moved aside Aramco's chairman, Energy Minister Khalid al-Falih, one of the kingdom's most experienced executives and a steady, wise voice in the Royal Court. He had opposed the IPO. Now he was being put out to pasture. Mohammed replaced him as oil minister with an older brother by his father's first wife, Abdulaziz bin Salman. The new Aramco chairman would be Yasir al-Rumayyan, the PIF chief closely aligned with Mohammed.

Wounded reputationally by the Khashoggi murder and with advisors warning against an international listing for legal reasons, Mohammed ordered that the IPO be held on the Saudi stock exchange instead. Finally, on December 11, 2019, Aramco shares began trading on the Tadawul. The subscribers to the offering were nearly all regional and local investors—some of them buying shares after pressure from the Royal Court—but the government was able to raise $25.6 billion at a valuation of $1.7 trillion. Mohammed bin Salman didn't get to ring the bell at the New York Stock Exchange, but he managed to pull off the biggest IPO of any company in history. Undeterred, he ordered the IPO team to begin preparations for an international listing a year later—detractors be damned.

Despite disappointing news about the $45 billion SoftBank investment, which inflated a bubble by pouring billions of dollars into nontech companies posing as innovators, including WeWork, dog-walking app Wag, and a construction company called Katerra, PIF chief Rumayyan was discussing putting more money into a new SoftBank fund. He was also working with a previously little-known figure in the kingdom, ex–reality TV producer DiBello, who seemed to appear in Saudi Arabia out of nowhere and was showing up at major events around Mohammed and other senior leaders. Her rise was a perfect illustration of Saudi Arabia's strange workings and the way that maverick characters continued to dominate how things were done there, no matter how much Mohammed tried to reform its institutions. It was still about the connections.

Outwardly polished, with flawless dyed-blonde hair, blemish-free skin, and impeccably composed outfits, Carla DiBello at first glance gave little indication of her scrappy and resourceful approach to business. With no college education or specialized finance expertise, she'd taken an unlikely path from Florida to the inner circle of Saudi leadership.

DiBello got her first exposure to well-connected Saudis as a teenager in the late 1990s, when she became friendly with a neighbor in Sarasota named Anoud Ghazzawi. Anoud lived with her husband and twin babies in a house owned by her father, Esam Ghazzawi. He managed money for some of King Salman's clan, including Mohammed's oldest half brother.

Anoud and her husband left Florida abruptly in 2001, and FBI reports unearthed years later by a local investigative reporting operation, the *Florida Bulldog*, revealed that two 9/11 attackers spent time at the Ghazzawi home.

In the ensuing years, Anoud and DiBello both made their way to Dubai. Anoud became a designer of custom-made *abayas*. DiBello moved west, working for a producer in LA and casino magnate Steve Wynn in Las Vegas before getting a production job with a Kardashian reality show. Soon she was referring to herself as one of Kim Kardashian's best friends. In a sign that DiBello was fully ensconced in Hollywood, in 2011 she publicly denied having an affair with Kobe Bryant.

A couple years later, DiBello moved to Dubai and started a business connecting American entertainers with opportunities in the Gulf, marketing herself with the Kardashian connection. A few years after that she began showing up in Saudi Arabia at events including the first Davos in the Desert conference.

Members of the PIF's investment teams were surprised when she arrived for a meeting in early 2019. It's still rare to see women in Saudi offices (one big innovation of Mohammed's was to put a ladies' room in the Royal Diwan, where court business is done; until recently, a guard stood sentry outside a men's room whenever a woman needed to use the bathroom). And it wasn't clear to the investment analysts why their boss told them to meet her.

It turned out DiBello had a big pitch: PIF should buy a majority stake in an English Premier League soccer team, Newcastle United. It wasn't a ridiculous idea—the Qataris and Emiratis already had soccer teams, and PIF had considered buying one. But they didn't need DiBello to do it. Saudi Arabia was perhaps the world's most prominent potential buyer of a soccer team. It could call any team it might want and make an offer with no need for an intermediary. And DiBello and a partner wanted an ownership stake and ongoing management payments, though neither had experience managing a soccer team. DiBello couldn't provide basic answers about deal details. But Rumayyan decided to move ahead with the deal anyway.

DiBello was involved in other PIF-related matters. She helped a junior executive at e-cigarette maker Juul Labs get an in-person meeting with Rumayyan. Another company she offered to connect with Rumayyan for a fee got scared—paying to meet a foreign-government official can be considered a bribe under US law. The company sought legal advice and turned her down. Mohammed was trying to get rid of Saudi Arabia's old pay-to-play system, but DiBello's presence made it seem like the same game was being played by a new cast of characters. These types of people were reassuring to Mohammed—rich, nonjudgmental, and appreciative of the opportunity he was bringing to his country, the region, and their own bank accounts.

And then, in September, potential disaster struck. Drones and missiles supposedly controlled by the Houthi rebels in Yemen blew up key pieces of equipment at a facility called Abqaiq that processes much of Saudi Arabia's crude oil for shipping. It was something the Al Saud had long feared.

"The most vulnerable point and the most spectacular target in the Saudi oil system is the Abqaiq complex," wrote Robert Baer, a former CIA official, in a 2003 article in the *Atlantic* about dangers to the Al Saud's hold on power. Others, including Saudi scholar Simon Henderson in 2006 and the Center for Strategic and International Studies in August 2019, published papers reiterating that point. And for decades, the US government had been urging the Saudis to use some of the money they spent on glitzy new projects like King Abdullah Economic City and Mohammed's NEOM to improve basic security for their oil infrastructure. Abqaiq and other crucial facilities are in easy missile range of Iran, potentially threatening not just Saudi stability but world oil markets.

Securing the oil fields wasn't simply a matter of getting the right equipment or expertise. The big problem was built into the way the Al Saud historically balanced power among different factions by splitting up military power. The Ministry of Interior and its armed forces, historically under the command of King Salman's brother Prince Nayef and later his son, Mohammed bin Nayef, was responsible for guarding oil installations. But warding off aerial attacks would require using US-made Patriot missiles controlled by the Ministry of Defense, which was historically overseen by another Salman brother, Prince Sultan, and his clan. The intelligence agencies responsible for gathering information on potential oilfield threats had other chains of command.

Since the princes in charge of the different factions were competing for the throne, there was always suspicion and a lack of information sharing. Mohammed, in theory, eliminated those divisions, removing Mohammed bin Nayef from the Interior Ministry and taking over the Ministry of Defense himself. But in practice they remained siloed in mid-September 2019, when missiles and drones attacked Abqaiq.

It was shocking, and the United States and Saudi Arabia quickly concluded that the Houthis couldn't have done it alone. Iran had to have overseen the attack. "Whoever planned it had a world-class understanding of how oil facilities work," said an aerial-attack expert who visited Abqaiq for the Saudi government in the ensuing days.

It was a strange scene. Many of Abqaiq's pipes, towers, and crucial infrastructure for separating out impurities from crude oil remained untouched. But several so-called spheroid modules, which look like squashed metal domes and separate gasses from oil, were seriously damaged. It was clear to officials from Aramco and the government what the attackers had done: Using accurate mapping and pinpoint targeting technology, they'd hit only components that could be fixed quickly. The attack was a warning volley, not a kill shot, to show the Saudis what Iran could do, intelligence officials concluded. And it took "seventeen minutes and less than $2 million" worth of cruise missiles and drones, the aerial-attack expert found.

That's what was so frightening. Iran has much less money than Saudi Arabia to spend on weapons, but the attack showed that didn't matter. The Saudis were able to get oil production back on track within weeks only because Iran decided to graze, rather than demolish, the facility.

For the Saudis, the attack generated realization of two big problems. First, even after Mohammed wrested control from the competing family factions, the defense system remained in disarray. The Saudis had Patriot missiles to fire at the drones but no system for the Ministry of Defense to quickly request that they be deployed. And there was no way anyone would be held accountable—in a bureaucracy that sits below an absolute monarch, sophisticated systems are in place to shift and ultimately dissolve blame.

Someone working within the Defense Ministry at the time recalled seeing the process play out. Within hours of the attack, the official line was "this is not a Ministry of Defense issue," since the Interior Ministry was responsible for oil security. Interior officials anticipated that line and pointed out there wasn't anything they could have done because they lacked intelligence—and that was the fault of the General Intelligence Presidency, the awkwardly named agency responsible for gathering foreign information. In the end, the conclusion was that "it was nobody's fault," said the person inside the Defense Ministry.

The other big problem the attack exposed was the true nature of today's alliance between Saudi Arabia and the United States. For decades, American officials viewed the kingdom and its oil industry as vital to the proper functioning of the world economy. US diplomatic, military, and intelligence personnel developed deep ties with their Saudi counterparts, and the United States proved itself committed to defending Saudi Arabia and its oil fields, heading off threats from Saddam Hussein in the 1990s. One reason the Saudis could afford to have their disjointed defense structure was that the United States had taken the lead on keeping Saudi Arabia safe. Even after 9/11, the personal ties between longtime officials inside the US and Saudi governments maintained the alliance. King Abdullah visited President George W. Bush at his Texas ranch in 2005.

Things changed radically between the early 1990s and 2019. The spread of fracking turned the United States into the world's biggest oil producer by 2013. The American economy wasn't dependent on Saudi oil anymore. Now it could pump its own.

Then Barack Obama made the nuclear deal with Iran, alienating Saudi leaders. Mohammed had high hopes that Donald Trump, with his visit to the kingdom early in his presidency, would renew the kind of relationship Saudi Arabia had under previous presidents. But as Trump showed Mohammed in that embarrassing White House visit, when the president displayed a poster board showing arms sales to the kingdom, this new White House was purely transactional. The decades-long US-Saudi alliance didn't mean much to Trump and his deputies, and many of the old officials who kept that alliance going for both sides, men like Mohammed bin Nayef and former CIA director John Brennan, had been sent off to retirement, or worse.

Trump didn't even seem terribly concerned with the security implications of an Iran that was now engaging in overt acts of aggression against a US ally. In the days after the attack, many US officials braced for an armed response by the United States. For years, America's security establishment had believed that Iran didn't engage in direct hostilities because it knew the

United States would respond with force. Trump shocked them. In the days after the attack, he said there was "no rush" to respond, displaying what one longtime US intelligence official calls a "systemic gap" between the Saudis and the Americans. The Saudis wanted the old order, where America would serve as a regional protector, while the Americans now in the White House wanted Saudi business deals but had little interest in deploying American weaponry. The United States wasn't about to rush to the kingdom's defense.

"That was an attack on Saudi Arabia," Trump said. "That wasn't an attack on us." And if the United States did decide to take action against Iran, he added, Saudi Arabia would be involved. "And that includes payment." Trump did eventually send soldiers to the region, and the US killed Qassem Soleimani, a powerful Iranian general, in an airstrike months later.

———

More than sixty yachts, including some of the biggest in the world along with their billionaire owners, were lined up along Saudi Arabia's northwestern coast in October 2019 when Mohammed bin Salman's eleven-ship flotilla began its slow parade into position. The star of the group was *Serene*, the superyacht Mohammed bought in 2015 not long after beginning his rise to power, followed by a collection of boats that supported the bigger boats and had room for additional guests. The *Serene*'s captain had taken to calling himself "Commodore" and referring to the fleet as "my navy."

It was just a few weeks after the oil attack and just over a year after Jamal Khashoggi's murder and the global uproar that followed. Mohammed wanted to show that Saudi Arabia could still draw the world's richest and most powerful people. By that measure, "Red Sea Week," an invite-only event designed to entice investors to build hotels and infrastructure in the vast NEOM project, was a huge success. The *Serene* hosted a premium event for VIPs, including Fang Fenglei, a Chinese financier with strong ties to the communist rulers in his country, and Mukesh Ambani, the tycoon who ran India's biggest company. Tahnoon bin Zayed, the Abu Dhabi national security advisor, arrived in his own yacht and spent time with Mohammed on the *Serene*.

Rumayyan rented his own megayacht, *Ecstasea*, to host meetings, including with Carla DiBello and a business partner. Cocktails in hand, they played ping-pong.

The singer John Legend gave a private concert on Sindalah Island, a jigsaw-shaped piece of sand that Mohammed was planning to make into a centerpiece of NEOM. *Robb Report*, a luxury magazine, custom-built a small resort for the event. Michelin-starred chef Jason Atherton created a pop-up restaurant with a seven-course tasting menu inspired by the desert region. There was a bespoke spa, transparent kayaks, and a chance to race sports cars on empty desert roads along the coast. Ostensibly, Red Sea Week was to become a new event in the annual calendar akin to the Cannes Yachting Festival, but it had a bigger purpose for the crown prince.

For Mohammed, the *Serene* had become more than a mobile statehouse. Together with its support vessels, it was more of an armed, floating palace complex from which he could run the country, safe from would-be Islamic terrorists or coup plotters. It was a place to be himself as well.

The entire yacht was outfitted with the highest-quality video screens and music equipment, so that in a moment he could switch it from diplomatic gathering place to high-tech disco. There was one room even the crew weren't allowed to visit—a helicopter hangar converted into a cutting-edge nightclub fitted with poles for dancers.

The yacht was a safe space for Mohammed as he tried to pull

Saudi Arabia into the twenty-first century against the odds and the wishes of many cousins and thousands of clerics. And if the global public saw him as a budding autocrat, at least he could rely on the superrich to back him up.

In meeting after meeting, the discussion was about investment opportunities in Saudi Arabia. But each visiting financier couldn't help but ask if Saudi Arabia would like to invest some of its money in his or her new fund or project. Saudi Arabia's money, pooled so centrally and controlled so completely by the crown prince, remained a siren song for businessmen and politicians around the world. Few people on earth could slosh billions around so easily. The chance to catch some, even a few million, was too juicy to not take.

One afternoon, Masayoshi Son and Mohammed took a trip in a small boat to a pristine reef and went snorkeling for more than an hour. Pleasantries aside, Masayoshi had a secondary purpose. SoftBank was trying to raise a second $100 billion fund, and he was hoping his loyalty to Mohammed through his ups and downs would pay off. Would Mohammed like to be the cornerstone investor again? He had the gall to ask even as the first Vision Fund was reeling from big mistakes, like a massive bet on WeWork, an office-rental company masquerading as a tech start-up that would have been in serious difficulties were it not for SoftBank's doubling down on its initial bad bet, and the poor performance of many of the other investments in the fund.

There weren't many businessmen like Mohammed in the world, people with unbelievable access to money and the ability to decide in a second what to do with it. Masayoshi wanted him to look past the performance and think of the futuristic world just around the corner. Would he also double down?

That turned out to be what made him so unstoppable. It wasn't necessarily the Ritz crackdown and consolidation of power that gave Mohammed his ability to hold on even after the Khashoggi murder. It was how tangled up he'd become in the most powerful market economy the world has ever seen. His relationship with Trump was good, if transactional, but more important was the way Saudi Arabia's money was tied up in US infrastructure investments via Blackstone and technology companies via SoftBank's Vision Fund. Mohammed had been a nobody prince a few years back; now he was the *only* prince, as far as the rest of the world was concerned. He'd become a vital component of the global economy, controlling the price of oil with one hand and doling out billions to major companies, enabling them to beat their rivals, with the other.

In the end, Red Sea Week was more about Mohammed's ego than Saudi Arabia's development. It probably didn't help him temper his philosophy of international relations. He headed back to Riyadh emboldened.

Buoyed by what he felt was changing sentiment toward Saudi Arabia and a good reception by Donald Trump and other powerful leaders willing to maintain their relationships with him, Mohammed set in motion a plan to make 2020 his comeback year: 2015 had been his rise, 2016 the rollout of the vision for transformation, 2017 the beginning of change and consolidation of power, 2018 the global outreach and grand blowup after Khashoggi, and 2019 a year of regrouping and laying low.

To start to wipe the slate clean, Mohammed needed big achievements—or at least resolutions of issues following him around. He instructed his staff to make immediate plans to end the Qatar boycott, create peace in Yemen, and spare no expense in making Saudi Arabia's hosting of the G-20 meeting in October 2020 an event no one could forget. He assigned Fahad al-Toonsi, a Saudi minister in charge of all the "gigaprojects" like NEOM, to make the event his topmost priority.

But his dialed-down approach to international relations didn't last long. In December 2019, leaders of Turkey, Qatar, Iran, Malaysia, and Pakistan were scheduled to attend a summit of Islamic leaders in Kuala Lumpur. The publicly stated purpose was to discuss important issues afflicting Muslims around the world, but the underlying agenda was to rebalance the leadership of the Muslim world away from the axis of Saudi Arabia, the United Arab Emirates, and Egypt. After Mohammed's new, aggressive approach to leading the kingdom had fully developed, weaker countries felt Saudi Arabia had become a liability.

Angrily, Mohammed summoned Pakistani prime minister Imran Khan to Riyadh for a meeting. It was a far cry from the friendly trip he'd taken to Pakistan in February 2019, one of his first big international trips after the Khashoggi affair. Khan had rolled out the red carpet, grounded all planes, and ordered JF-17 Thunder fighter jets to escort Mohammed's fleet as it entered Pakistan's airspace. Some $20 billion worth of deals were inked as the crown prince was feted in the streets. Newspaper editors received directives from the government not to publish a single negative story or tweet during that visit, and they mostly complied. Pakistan needed money, and Saudi Arabia wanted Pakistan on its team.

Now, in Riyadh, it was clear that Mohammed considered the Kuala Lumpur summit an unacceptable move. Mohammed is said to have demanded coldly that Khan cancel the trip after Khan tried to explain the purpose in more diplomatic terms. He is reported to have threatened that Saudi Arabia and the UAE would cancel all Pakistani visas immediately if he did not and there would be four million Pakistanis, who send money home to their families every month, on the street. Imran headed home, calling Malaysian prime minister Mahatir Mohamad to inform him he was canceling his participation.

"He's a spoiled brat," Imran told an advisor afterward. "We can't afford to stand up to him."

Epilogue

DECISIVE STORM

As leaders around the world were just coming to understand the magnitude of the novel coronavirus and the economic devastation it would bring, Mohammed bin Salman was distracted by a niggling family drama and frustrated by the low price of oil. To achieve his grandest economic dreams, he needed much more money—hundreds of billions of dollars, not the mere $25.6 billion he earned from the Aramco IPO.

Standing in his office in a plain *thobe* speaking to advisors and ministers, he was frustrated with the pace of the 2030 transformation. Oil prices were hovering in the $60 range, well below the level he needed to build all the megaprojects at once while affording an expensive, never-ending conflict in Yemen and a populace still used to handouts. This problem had been gnawing at the kingdom since Salman took the throne, with a flood of oil from the US fracking boom depressing global prices.

And the problem was only getting worse. Saudi Arabia had been collaborating with Russia to limit production in order to keep the oil price from tanking, but that deal was fraying.

That was the backdrop for one of Mohammed's most profound decisions in five years as the day-to-day ruler of the Kingdom of Saudi Arabia. With discussions with Russia breaking down,

Mohammed decided to go nuclear. On a Friday evening in early March 2020, he ordered his older half brother, Minister of Energy Abdulaziz bin Salman, to boost supply and flood the markets. In the staid and formal world of oil negotiations, it was a bombshell.

By the open of the markets on the following Monday, prices had fallen by more than 20 percent and would continue to fall to the lowest level in decades. In the coming weeks, storage facilities became so full that in some regions oil buyers were being offered money by suppliers to take crude off their hands.

Mohammed was hoping that the price drop would put some of the companies responsible for the US shale boom out of business and put financial pressure on Russian president Vladimir Putin to reinstate a production cut. He also wanted Putin, along with Trump and other leaders, to understand that Saudi Arabia wouldn't be pushed around on oil prices. Mohammed would dictate oil policy as he saw fit for the good of Saudi Arabia. If other countries wanted the kingdom's help boosting prices, their leaders would have to come to Mohammed as an equal.

The problem was that Saudi Arabia was even more dependent on oil revenue than Russia. In an effort to boost the long-term price of oil, Mohammed was sabotaging the kingdom's source of funding for its ambitious transformation projects as well as day-to-day expenses.

At the same time, he was smoothing his path toward coronation. Within hours of Mohammed's decision to start an oil war, men in black masks stormed the homes of Mohammed bin Nayef, who had been restricted from leaving Saudi Arabia since the night he "resigned" as crown prince, and Ahmed bin Abdulaziz, Mohammed's uncle and one of the last surviving sons of Ibn Saud who was fully mobile and of sound faculties. It was an odd development for most palace watchers—neither man seemed like any kind of threat.

MBN was broken and grumbling, and Ahmed was a shiftless old codger who seemed to shrink from the occasion whenever family members wanted him to take a stand. He was one of those princes who preferred his rarefied London digs to Riyadh family dramas. His only importance was that he was a full brother of the king, and as the oldest surviving son of King Abdulaziz who wasn't on the throne, he was supposed to hold sway over the all-but-perfunctory Allegiance Council. But Ahmed hadn't even assumed that position.

The apparent impetus for the arrests, which later broadened to include other staff and associates of the men, seemed almost laughable. By 2019, MBN had a somewhat normal life compared to his house arrest in the months immediately following his withdrawal as crown prince. He was allowed to travel between his Saudi homes, including a ranch where he liked to vacation, and could attend family gatherings. His wife, suffering from cancer, was allowed to visit the United States that summer for treatment, bringing along one of their daughters. But MBN remained sullen, and his griping was making its way back to Mohammed, who decided it was a problem when Ahmed got involved.

Though he'd long been disengaged from family politics, Ahmed had surprised Mohammed and King Salman in September 2018 when he confronted protesters gathered outside his London mansion in opposition to the bombing of Yemen. Don't blame the Al Saud, Ahmed told the crowd; the bombing is the responsibility of just two men, the king and the crown prince.

Ahmed returned to Saudi Arabia not long after and made sure he got commitments from US and UK officials that they would intervene if the Royal Court acted against him. Once back in the kingdom, Ahmed too began griping. He took the portraits of King Salman and Prince Mohammed off his *majlis* wall—news of the insult quickly spread within the royal family—and his living room became a popular place for disgruntled members of the royal family to vent.

In late 2019, MBN was coming to Ahmed to complain, upset that the Royal Court had drained his bank accounts and slashed handouts to him and his family. After his wife's trip to the United States for treatments, MBN was told she couldn't travel outside the kingdom anymore until he paid the government billions of dollars that Mohammed accused him of stealing. It was an old accusation, one that Mohammed had leveled in 2017 claiming that MBN had misused Saudi government money earmarked for joint antiterrorism projects with the United States. MBN maintained that he spent government money properly and even contributed some of his own fortune for security efforts. Any other monies he received were blessed by the late king, as he and many others targeted for corruption would argue.

MBN said he had no secret stash of money, and on a visit in November 2019, he told Ahmed that his wife and daughters were being "starved" by the financial block placed on his family.

It may have been simple venting, and it was certainly hyperbole, but Mohammed's team caught the exchange. Later that month, MBN was called to attend a meeting at the National Guard—where the crown prince's childhood friend and close ally Abdullah bin Bandar was in charge—or face consequences. Feeling particularly ornery, he refused to go.

That precipitated the first crackdown. A few days afterward, Royal Court guards showed up at MBN's palace and escorted away his closest employees, including secretaries, IT staff, and his longtime personal guard. They even built a fence around his helicopter pad, possibly to prevent him from escaping, even though it had been used only to park cars in the preceding months.

The guards questioned the employees about any escape or coup plans. The staff were released, but people who answered to Mohammed bin Salman's Royal Court took over MBN's security.

Almost simultaneously with his declaration of an oil war, Mohammed had MBN and Ahmed detained. Musaad al-Aiban, the security official who helped plan President Trump's Riyadh trip, called members of the royal family to tell them Ahmed and MBN were suspected of treason, the *Wall Street Journal* reported.

Considering the tepid backstory, they clearly weren't a near and present danger. It was simply the right moment, amid a maelstrom of news and economic drama, to execute another crucial step in MBS's path to the kingship. With even these relatively weak threats extinguished, he had a clear view for going forward.

Faisal bin Abdullah, a son of the former king, wrote a letter to King Salman complaining of Ahmed's treatment. He too was arrested.

One clue that the family crackdown wasn't a staged plan was that MBS was planning a monthlong vacation to his château in France or the game park his family owned in South Africa just weeks before the oil war and family crackdown. Many of his top aides were planning to take some time off, too, after months of working brutal sixteen-hour days.

That Friday night was a quintessential MBS moment: a bold decision made, in the face of awesome and dangerous consequences, in the hopes that the bet would pay off. Every oil company in the world might curse his name and countries might go bankrupt for his action, but if it meant a better deal for Saudi Arabia, it was worth it. And the family crackdown wasn't necessary—it risked reinforcing his image as a strongman ruler who bossed around his uncles and cousins—but if it improved his odds by even a small margin, it was worth the risk. It was better to be seen as unnecessarily draconian than as tolerant of any criticism.

Mohammed had called the first phase of his Yemen war "Decisive Storm," or *Asifat al-Hazm* in Arabic. The phrase captured Mohammed himself. He wasn't always hasty, but he was definitely decisive. When a decision was made, he went in with guns blazing. And his changes often felt stormy, a pell-mell of decisions made in short succession seemingly without much consideration for how things might develop if they all happened at the same time. When the clouds parted, Saudi citizens couldn't help but feel a little dizzy. It had been five years of that kind of change.

Mohammed had started out thinking of 2020 as a year of restoring his place in the global power structure. Leaving behind the Yemen war, the Khashoggi scandal, and the bad press about jailing critics, he was planning for a G-20 meeting in Riyadh in the fall that would entrench Saudi Arabia as one of the world's influential and forward-looking powers, with a young leader who could rule for another half century. His aide Fahad al-Toonsi was placed in charge of the most important event on the year's agenda.

There was no merit system for hosting the summit. It was Saudi Arabia's turn because of the G-20 chair rotation. But it was a perfect opportunity to showcase the country in almost as big a fashion as when Donald Trump came on his first international trip as president.

The kingdom had already undergone major changes. Parts of Riyadh and other major cities felt increasingly like Dubai—men mixing with women wearing no head coverings in restaurants and shopping areas. Tourists were beginning to trickle in, inspired by Instagram celebrities paid by the Saudi government to come and spread the word about its offerings.

There was little doubt that Mohammed was the first royal to capitalize on the country's history, eschewing the Wahhabist-influenced notion that venerating antiquities bordered on idol worship. He refurbished the ancestral home of the Al Saud in Diriyah in Riyadh and making al-Ula in the north of the country into a world-class destination. They were genuinely interesting sites to behold, and the G-20 plans were being tuned to highlight them and show the new face of the kingdom.

In characteristically blunt terms, Mohammed told top aides to solve the country's biggest reputational problems, including the detention of women activists, the war in Yemen, and the boycott of Qatar.

Many observers thought of him as hot-headed and emotionally reactive. But these issues were, in large part, numbers on a chart to him. Surveys conducted by Western firms on behalf of Saudi Arabia highlighted them as obstacles to Saudi Arabia gaining its foothold in the world—just like the surveys he conducted at the outset that identified perceptions of religious extremism and the lack of women's rights among international audiences.

Meanwhile, the Public Investment Fund was meant to be on the hunt for big deals that could put Saudi Arabia back on the investing map. There were new funds to deploy for high-profile investments, like the planned acquisition of Newcastle's football team. Even after the Aramco IPO went from a potential financial event of the century to a less exciting regional event, bankers were starting to return in droves to Riyadh. There was talk of reviving an international listing, a means to raise more money but also to prove to innumerable critics that he was no financial novice.

One billionaire who met him during this time believed Mohammed to be genuinely in transition as a leader. In private conversations, MBS admitted to having been too thin-skinned in his first few years running the country and too worried about dissidents. He wasn't sorrowful, though. He was confident. But in the eyes of the rest of the world, the murder of Jamal Khashoggi wasn't going away. Mohammed had remained consistent since Saudi Arabia admitted he'd been killed, saying in meetings with officials and businessmen that he was responsible because he was in charge but that he had no prior knowledge of the incident.

Longtime Saudi observers and even some citizens in private moments doubted that such a detail-oriented workaholic could not have known about such a big operation—or that the employees of such a heavy-handed ruler would take such extreme action without his permission. But Mohammed insisted that with so many employees, he cannot always know what each is doing and that the killing was a mistake.

The affair would surge in importance at times, such as when the UN special rapporteur on extrajudicial killings published her findings in December 2019 and again when the US government declassified an intelligence report on the killing in early 2021, but a full-throated indictment never seemed to materialize. Any hard evidence, if it existed, probably lay in US intelligence vaults, and Washington didn't seem to see any advantage in pressing the matter further. The stain would undoubtedly persist until the day MBS's obituary was written, but it might grow fainter as the years went by—in the United States and Europe, at least—especially if he pulled off any big-picture moves such as shaking hands with an Israeli leader. That one might have to wait until he was king.

While Mohammed was planning a way forward, those left behind on his path to power continued to struggle. Saad al-Jabri, the former counterterrorism official who introduced a young Mohammed to his US contacts before being fired and accused of extremism, remained safely outside the country.

But it was hardly a comfortable exile. Mohammed was refusing to let two of Jabri's children, teenagers when he left the kingdom, leave Saudi Arabia. When his old US contacts asked about the man they knew as Dr. Saad, Saudi officials said he was a wanted man, in control of billions of dollars that MBN had taken, and his children wouldn't be allowed to leave the kingdom unless he returned the money.

American intelligence officials suspected that the children were being confined to keep Jabri from talking. The man had decades worth of government secrets that neither the Saudis nor the Americans wanted aired in public.

For nearly five years, the situation remained tense. Jabri stayed silent, while old friends in Washington and Canada tried to figure out if there was a way to extricate his children. An older son, a physician in the United States, told friends he wanted desperately to help but feared that any political action or involvement of the US government could anger Mohammed and imperil his younger siblings. So he worked behind the scenes to lobby journalists and US officials while his father remained silent.

The strategy failed. After Mohammed moved in March 2020 to boost oil production and crack down on dissent, detaining his uncle Ahmed as well as MBN, he had armed guards raid the home of the Jabri children who were already under a travel ban. They were put in jail and accused of financial crimes and trying to flee the country. Their home was ransacked and safes cracked in an apparent search for evidence to use against Jabri, leaving the family abroad to wonder what kind of progress Saudi Arabia had made since Mohammed came to power.

In the five years since Salman had become king, Saad al-Jabri had seen himself promoted to one of the highest positions possible for a nonroyal, entrusted with the kingdom's security and its relationship with its most important foreign ally, and just as quickly tarred as a terrorist, fired over Twitter, and driven into exile, his children held hostage while Mohammed trumpeted his reforms.

In the spring of 2020, the Jabri family would hire a Trump-connected lobbyist in a desperate effort to get the US government to pressure Mohammed to let the detained relatives leave Saudi Arabia. But the Trump administration had little, if anything, to gain from challenging the prince, and no obvious incentive to aid the Jabri family.

With all avenues exhausted, the Jabri family decided to go to war with Mohammed bin Salman, giving extensive interviews across the world about the arrest of the two young family members back in Riyadh. Then, in the summer of 2020, Saad al-Jabri sued Mohammed in Washington, DC, federal court, accusing him of inflicting emotional abuse and trying to have him killed.

Jabri's complaint opened with a quote from Shakespeare's *Richard III*. Its most potentially damning allegation may have been the assertion that in 2015, Mohammed asked Saad al-Jabri to use the Mabahith, a secret police unit and part of the Ministry of Interior, to abduct Prince Sultan bin Turki II. Not long after Jabri refused, he alleged, Mohammed created his own secret intelligence unit called the "Tiger Squad" that answered directly to him and Saad al Qahtani. It is "made up of approximately fifty intelligence, military, and forensic operatives recruited from different branches of the Saudi government with one unifying mission: loyalty to the personal whims" of Mohammed, according to Saad's complaint.

The Tiger Squad not only carried out the killing of Jamal Khashoggi, but sent a group to kill Jabri in Canada, too, the complaint alleged. The men were thwarted by Canadian border control who grew suspicious of the men when they claimed to not know each other.

The complaint seemed geared toward persuading the prince to abandon his dispute with the Jabri family, implying that the former spy chief could embarrass Mohammed. "Few places hold more sensitive, humiliating, and damning information about defendant bin Salman than the mind and memory of Dr. Saad— except perhaps the recordings Dr. Saad made in anticipation of his killing," Jabri's lawyers wrote.

Mohammed came up with a characteristically aggressive response. Rather than take the easy path of releasing Jabri's kids and letting the matter go, he had government-controlled companies sue Jabri in Canada alleging that he had misappropriated billions of dollars' worth of government funds. Jabri, they alleged, illegally diverted hundreds of millions of dollars from government-controlled companies to himself and his family.

A Canadian court put tens of millions of dollars of Jabri family holdings under a freeze; in subsequent filings, the Saudi government-backed companies asked US courts to freeze assets including the Jabri family's $25-million-plus worth of luxury apartments in Boston.

All Mohammed's plans for the year fell to the wayside in 2020 as bad news out of China rippled around the globe and a new president who sent chilly vibes to Saudi Arabia was elected in the United States.

The novel coronavirus required the world economy to halt for months, while billions of people sheltered in a series of lockdowns to stop the exponential spread of the virus and the collapse of medical systems.

Weeks after his oil war pushed prices under twenty dollars a barrel, close to a two-decade low, he agreed to rapidly cut back production following conversations with Jared Kushner, who also spoke with Russian counterparts about ending the disagreement.

Mohammed's oil-price war was killing US companies at a time when the global economy was shuddering. Throughout the dispute, the US government suggested it might sanction Russia for its role in the price slump. But it handled Saudi Arabia through diplomatic channels and direct contact between the White House and Mohammed. Though the price war may have cost Saudi Arabia billions of dollars, Mohammed could at least be assured people were taking him seriously. The move was reminding the world how much power Mohammed had over global markets.

As the world tried to get a handle on the virus, Saudi Arabia was also weighing up its options as the US presidential elections neared. Only a month before Americans were due to go to the polls, the UAE—and later joined by a coalition of Islamic countries—gave Kushner the greatest gift of his four years as advisor to the president by agreeing to normalize relations with Israel. Behind the scenes, the leaders of the UAE and Israel had developed strong intelligence and security ties over more than a decade, but this was a public coming-out ceremony that put Abu Dhabi in the hot seat as far as much of the Arab world was concerned.

Mohammed bin Salman was eager to embrace the Israelis, too. He was eager to reap the political and economic benefits of normalizing ties, hoping that NEOM itself would be a place where Israeli technology companies could move at least some of their operations and that people around the world would finally see how different he was than the leaders before him when it came to age-old Arab issues.

But he had two quandaries. For one, his father cared deeply about the Palestinian cause and felt any deal with the Israelis had to do right by the Palestinians first and foremost. The UAE deal with Israel put no pressure on Israel to empower Palestinians to have their own state. Secondly, what if Trump was defeated? Would the political boost persist or fade away under a new president?

Despite intense pressure from the Trump administration to help with foreign policy "wins," Mohammed and his advisors decided to wait. Trump had shown himself to be a guaranteed supporter of Saudi Arabia—a leader so supportive of Mohammed even after the Khashoggi killing that the prince didn't see any need to further earn Trump's support. And Mohammed understood that Trump was also a divisive figure in the US who might not be reelected. Mohammed needed to hedge his bets, especially because Joe Biden was signalling he'd be taking a hard tack with with the prince if he was elected.

The Saudi decision to wait proved wise. Biden won the election handily. As early concessions, Mohammed and the other Gulf states agreed to end the cold war with Qatar and released Loujain al-Hathloul, the jailed advocate for women driving who became an international cause celebre.

As the first few months ticked by, Mohammed and his advisors watched warily for Biden to give a broader signal about how he would deal with Saudi Arabia going forward. During the campaign, he'd said his plan was to make the Saudis "pay the price, and make them in fact the pariah that they are."

That might have made sense a generation earlier, when the US still held unchecked sway in the Middle East and most of all in the kingdom itself. By 2021, MBS had concentrated power in a way no previous monarch had even imagined and built powerful economic ties around the world through his sovereign investments. There was no one waiting in the wings. The US, especially not under a left-centrist like Biden, wasn't going to try to foment regime change.

The Biden move ended up being a rap on the wrist. He declassified a report containing conclusions about the Khashoggi murder that had already been well circulated for years in the form of leaks to newspapers—nothing new. And in a slight to Mohammed, he made clear he'd only engage personally with his counterpart, the aging King Salman. Longtime Saudi hands grinned at the hollowness of the gesture. One of Mohammed's many titles was being the head of the king's Royal Court. Not even a shred of paper crosses the king's desk without Mohammed's knowledge and agreement.

It didn't make things particularly easy for Mohammed, who needed something big to demarcate his early years in power with what he wanted to convey: maturity, strength, ambition. But the Biden moves didn't slow him down, either.

As Saudis retreated into their homes for lockdowns like people across the globe, they were likely to find on Twitter and social media campaigns lauding their gracious king and his courageous son. Ads on the website of the *Wall Street Journal* and other publications trumpeted the latest NEOM project, a city more than one hundred miles long that would be called "The Line" and feature underground transport using renewable energy.

In places like the Philippines, Hungary, and China, criticism of dictatorial leaders was shunted aside to make way for emergency measures. Surveillance powers increased without protest, and governments became more powerful than ever, bailing out companies and handing out money to millions of unemployed people. This was no time for subtly nudging citizens through behavioral analysis—the most effective policy was ordering people indoors without giving them any choice in the matter.

It was a time of ascendance for strong leaders, even authoritarian ones. For much of 2020 and early 2021, Mohammed traveled with a group of close advisors to his family's palace at NEOM, staying there and on the Serene for long stretches. International visitors would sometimes have to wait in quarantine for two weeks to meet with the crown prince.

After years of sending Saudi money out of the country via the Vision Fund and other big-ticket investments, he announced a plan to focus inward. Over the next decade, the Saudi government and private-sector companies it majority owned would spend more than $3 trillion on refurbishing the economy, he announced in March 2021.

"So there is spending in ten years more than the history for the entire Kingdom of Saudi Arabia, since three hundred years before the discovery of oil and after. That's huge. That's huge," he said in a televised interview. "This is a new Kingdom of Saudi Arabia where spending is more than what has been spent the past three hundred years."

Through the long nights, he and his team talked about the years ahead. Forget the critics, they said. Mohammed had many years to prove his vision. He wasn't even king yet. His legacy might come in ten, twenty, even thirty years.

ACKNOWLEDGMENTS

We are most indebted to our sources, many of whom remain anonymous to protect themselves against the risk of retaliation. Without their agreement to tell what they know, despite the risks, we would not have a book to write.

We would never have had the chance to delve so deeply into this topic if not for the urging and encouragement of editors at the *Wall Street Journal*, especially Elena Cherney, who spearheaded the newspaper's early, agenda-setting coverage of the economic transition efforts and IPO of Aramco in the face of substantial headwinds. Mike Allen edited, and championed, those early stories. Other editors who played a pivotal role in our work—and other reporting—on Saudi Arabia are Charles Forelle, Alex Frangos, Ken Brown, Matthew Rose, Steve Yoder, Tammy Audi, Peter Wonacott, and Chris Stewart. We are thankful to Matt Murray for his strong stewardship of the newspaper as a whole and special attention to the Middle East. Bruce Orwall provided encouragement in moments of self-doubt.

We are also lucky to have talented and deeply sourced colleagues at the *Journal*. Summer Said, based in Dubai, is one of the most fearless and knowledgeable people in the Middle East about Saudi Arabia's changes, its royal family, and the oil market.

She has been generous and patient throughout this process. We have also been fortunate to work closely with Maureen Farrell, Keach Hagey, Kelly Crow, Josh Robinson, Warren Strobel, and Rory Jones.

Many experts have helped us learn more about the Al Saud dynasty, including family tree researcher Michael Field, Gulf States News research director Eleanor Gillespie, and longtime journalist and Saudi resident Robert Lacey. We were privileged to work with two phenomenal researchers, Lucy Woods in London and Kareem Shaheen in Toronto.

Stephen Kalin, a fierce competitor while at Reuters and new colleague at the *Journal*, provided feedback on the manuscript, as did good friends including Gabe Friedman, Steve Lefkowitz, Rob Guth, and Jenny Gross.

Thank you to our agent, Steve Troha, at Folio Literary Management. Paul Whitlatch encouraged us to pursue this topic and helped conceptualize this book, while Brant Rumble at Hachette Book Group thoughtfully edited it. We also thank the whole team at Hachette, including publisher Mary Ann Naples and associate publisher Michelle Aielli. Thank you to Jen Kelland for her deft copy editing, and Carolyn Levin and Kirsty Howarth for their legal guidance.

Lastly, we wouldn't have been able to spend so much time traipsing around the world reporting or spending hour upon hour editing this book without help and guidance from our families, especially Farah Halime and Chelsea Dodgen.

INDEX